THE WORLD'S BEST
TROUT FLIES

The World's Best Trout Flies

Edited by

JOHN ROBERTS

Colour illustrations by
Aideen Canning

TIGER BOOKS INTERNATIONAL
LONDON

Previous books by the same author:
The Grayling Angler (1982) Witherby
The New Illustrated Dictionary of Trout Flies (1986) Allen & Unwin,
(1988) Unwin Hyman, (1991) Harper Collins
To Rise a Trout (1988) The Crowood Press, (1989) Stoeger USA
A Guide to River Trout Flies (1989) The Crowood Press
Trout on a Nymph (1991) The Crowood Press

This edition published in 1995 by
Tiger Books International PLC, Twickenham

ISBN 1-85501-730-X

First published in Great Britain in 1994 by Boxtree Limited

1 3 5 7 9 10 8 6 4 2

Designed by Behram Kapadia
Typeset by SX Composing Ltd, Rayleigh, Essex

Printed in Italy by New Interlitho, Spa

A CIP catalogue entry for this book is available from the British Library.

Contents

Acknowledgments   7

Introduction   9

The Contributors   14

Theo Bakelaar, HOLLAND   15

Al Beatty, USA   20

Paul Canning, UK   24

Bob Carnill, UK   29

Brian Chan, CANADA   33

Oliver Edwards, UK   38

Tony Entwistle, NEW ZEALAND   45

Mogens Espersen, DENMARK   51

Marjan Fratnik and Bozidar Voljc, SLOVENIA   56

René Harrop, USA   61

Torrill-Kolbu, NORWAY   68

Jurek Kowalski, POLAND   74

Wayne Luallen, USA   78

Paul Marriner, CANADA   84

Darrel Martin, USA   89

Václav Mazura, CZECH REPUBLIC   94

Marcelo Morales, ARGENTINA   98

Roman Moser, AUSTRIA   103

Lars-Åke Olsson, SWEDEN   109

Francesco Palu, ITALY   116

Masao Sakaguchi, JAPAN   120

Ernest Schwiebert, USA   125

Adam Sikora, POLAND   130

Robert Sloane, AUSTRALIA   134

Jennifer Smith, USA   141

Juha Vainio, FINLAND   146

Hans van Klinken, HOLLAND   151

Hans Weilenmann, HOLLAND   157

Dave Whitlock, USA   162

Ruth J. Zinck, CANADA   169

Hair-Wing Dry Flies *by Al Beatty*   175

ACKNOWLEDGEMENTS

The text of this book is only half the story; the other half is the flies themselves and their illustration. I am greatly indebted to Aideen Canning who has painstakingly, and in such fine and vivid detail, reproduced each of the flies tied by the contributors. In illustrating the flies in this way, and in the selection of the different angles to view a fly, I believe that far more detail is passed on than through even the very best photograph. Aideen has produced true masterpieces of art to portray the one hundred and eighty works of the fly tyer's art and craft collected from across the world.

My thanks go to all the following who have helped or advised to a greater or lesser extent with the book in ways too numerous to mention: Franco Alinei, Al Beatty, Paul Canning, Peter Carty, Geoff Clarkson, Stanislow Cios, Al Cohen, Marjan Fratnik, René Harrop, Mike Mee, Hans van Klinken, Paul Marriner, Lars-Åke Olsson, Edgar Pitzenbauer, Jennifer Smith and Peter Spurney. Particular thanks are due to Al Beatty for the additional section on tying hair-wing dry flies, and to Runar Warhuus for the translation of Torill Kolbu's contribution.

I am grateful to Tony Entwistle, Marcelo Morales, Roman Moser, Rob Sloane, Hans van Klinken, Dave and Emily Whitlock for providing additional photographs.

JOHN ROBERTS

INTRODUCTION

Even before I seriously considered preparing a book on some of the world's most successful trout flies I realized that such a task was far beyond the scope of any individual. If any credibility is to be granted to such a collection it would have to be compiled with the assistance of experienced, expert trout fly fishers on rivers and stillwaters from the major fly-fishing areas of the world. If they were expert tyers as well as anglers, so much the better. If they had wider fishing experience than their own country too, better still. After seeking advice internationally from friends, authors, editors and expert tyers and anglers I made a list of thirty potential contributors who were thus qualified and representative of the main trout-fishing regions. Additionally many of these men and women have success and skill in fly fishing or fly tying proven at a high level through the very competitive world of tying competitions or the World Fly Fishing Championships. I felt very confident that these extremely accomplished contributors with almost seven hundred intensive fishing years between them would have the necessary qualifications for offering a wise and widely tested choice of flies.

Each angler was asked for the six flies that were either their most successful or offered some distinctive feature that brought success under particular circumstances. Each of the selected patterns has remained faithful to that requirement. Some patterns, outstanding for their success over a wide range of circumstances or for their ability to be able to offer what a fish needs to see in a variety of hatch situations, could remain on the leader every day of the season such is their overwhelming attraction to trout or grayling. Others are deadly for a specific hatch or may represent a natural fly during only a second or two of its life cycle.

The one hundred and eighty flies described encompass some standard world wide dressings but I offer no explanation or apology for there being no listing for the Muddler Minnow, Montana Nymph or Greenwell's Glory or any other potential 'standard'. Thirty highly experienced fly fishers have made their choice . . .

There is surprisingly little duplication. The Wright's Royal, Royal Wulff, Usual, Squirrel Sedge and Woolly Bugger were each sent by two contributors. In most instances where this occurred one contributor supplied a substitute.

By the selection of the contributors I knew that I would receive a mix of internationally known standard flies, regional dressings and individually developed patterns. It is some of the flies in the latter category that are the most interesting.

All the flies received were tied to an incredibly high standard. Some, received from award-winning tyers, authors and instructors were minutely examined with a magnifying glass and they left me, a no-better-than-average tyer, awe-struck at their detail, scale, precision and neatness. Perhaps I enjoyed handling most those that screamed at me that here was a fly that trout would love. The tactile sensation of handling those flies was amazing. They called out to be pulled through, floated on or drifted in a trout water. I knew that these were outstanding patterns even though I had never used them. Sometimes it was the fly design, in others the use of materials or in combination with a fishing technique that left me desperate to experiment with the flies myself. My sincere hope is that each contributor's comments and Aideen Canning's superb illustrations whet the reader's enthusiasm too.

I have been fascinated by each of the thirty selections and have found in each one flies of great interest and significance. Ernest Schwiebert's selection is based around a single proven tying style; many are considerably more diverse. Perhaps Jennifer Smith's selection is the most balanced with a terrestrial, an attractor dry, a general dun imitation, a specific dun imitation, a nondescript subsurface fly and a lure – six flies to cover most eventualities throughout a season. She

The significant feature of a great fly pattern is that it will work anywhere in the world. This rainbow fell to a Gold Ribbed Hare's Ear fished deep on the River Test. The captor is Mike Mee.

OPPOSITE
A beautiful autumn grayling which fell to the editor's small Hare's Ear Gold Head on the River Wylye.

10

also highlights two important aspects. The first is that in the Wright's Royal she feels she is using several flies in one. Juha Vainio, Darrel Martin and Lars-Åke Olsson also express a similar desire. Surely such versatility is the key to a successful and lasting pattern. Secondly, in offering a No-Hackle dun Jennifer suggests it is the perfect dun imitation. She may be right but the pattern's frailty means that for other than highly selective fish, anglers should look for something more durable.

Marcelo Morales also offers a very balanced selection with an outstandingly beautiful lure, a caddis, an attractor dry, a nymph and two emergers. He also gives us a taste of fishing in Argentina, a country few of us get the chance to experience for ourselves.

There are some flies that are not for fly-tying beginners. Luallen, Edwards, Whitlock, Sakaguchi and others have produced some relatively complicated dressings. It is my view that a difficult fly to tie has to be exceptional to survive as a pattern in regular use. Too many are lost in fish and vegetation to justify the effort in tying or the expense in buying them. For each of these contributors the success due to their extra effort has proved worthwhile. At the other extreme, some of the easiest patterns to tie come from the Polish contributors, Adam Sikora and Jurek Kowalski. They specialize in deep nymph techniques on a very short line; indeed sometimes there is no fly line beyond the rod tip. They fish simple, yet highly effective, patterns.

Cul de canard feathers feature in the choice of seven contributors. René Harrop has been a publicist in the USA for the material and has developed a series of six flies from nymph to spinner. He claims that the use of these feathers has improved his catch rate dramatically. Perhaps no one has done more than Marjan Fratnik who initiated the renewed interest in these feathers in Europe about a decade ago. The feathers themselves have been used for over a century but now the world has caught on to the secret Europe kept hidden even from itself. Perhaps the most unusual use of the cul de canard feather is in the stillwater pattern offered by Paul Canning.

The other European development and outstanding success is the use of gold or brass beads or balls at the heads of nymphs and lures. Goldheads

now seem to be in use the world over and Theo Bakelaar, Francesco Palu and Torrill Kolbu have offered such dressings. Darrel Martin has a very attractive silver bead adaptation of the Pheasant Tail nymph. I have noticed a reluctance by some fly fishers to use these nymphs. Certainly sometimes they can be just too successful. Is it some ethical question that causes some to think twice about their use and confine them to a last resort?

Two contributors offer new materials. Roman Moser, who has always been at the forefront of tackle and pattern design, ties a fry imitation with Plushille, a highly effective yet very easy and satisfying material to work with. Francesco Paul has developed a very hairy body material worthy of much wider notice. His unusual flies include two emergers and three nymphs for fishing very deep. With these five patterns he has chosen flies for the main trout and grayling feeding zones. The most unusual material of all comes from Adam Sikora who uses a nymph back of the skin of a smoked mackerel.

Emerging natural flies can often be a main trout target during a hatch and consequently are important to all fly fishers. Mogens Espersen reawakens interest in the Flymph and includes three other flies for the critical inch in or below the surface film. Paul Marriner is among the many other contributors who offer caddis or mayfly emerger patterns.

Perhaps the best emerger pattern to be devised in recent years is Hans van Klinken's Klinkhamer Special. I have used it for six years and caught thousands of trout and grayling. In another book, I wrote that I thought it was the best river fly to be developed over the last decade. I'll happily reiterate it. No other fly comes near it in a riffle. I've fished it with outstanding success under the noses of sceptical hosts and sent samples to correspondents across the world, many of whom have replied with high praise. I have fished with Hans in Britain and in Europe. He is prepared to be unconventional, to do the unorthodox to catch fish. This is represented in his pattern development which he freely acknowledges may take the best of another idea to which he adds his own essential ingredients. Very similar in design to the Klinkhamer Special is Torrill Kolbu's Crocheted Caddis Emerger with a unique crocheted body. The fine detail of the crocheting which features in a number of her dressings is representative of the neatness and extremely high standard of her tying. The crocheting techniques mean that her flies are extremely durable. Sadly, I lose most of my flies before their durability is ever tested.

As scientists, Brian Chan and Václav Mazura base their selection and fly imitations on sound logic. They play is safe. If it is found in trout diets they will fish a copy. Isn't this the nub of what fly fishing is all about? Dave Whitlock's philosophy seems fairly similar but has lent towards offering trout the biggest mouthful they can cope with. The resulting patterns have found success across the world.

Robert Sloane opts for functional flies, simple but effective. His outstanding fly, in my view, is the Rabbit Fur Fly which is highly mobile and a real fish catcher. It simply looks alive. The same is true of Ruth Zinck's nymph, the Zinck Mink and Dave Whitlock's Red Fox Squirrel Nymph. In a totally different way the nymphs of Maso Sakaguchi, Tony Entwistle and Oliver Edwards also appear alive. They look as though they could crawl across the palm of my hand. They are tied in a realistic or semi-realistic style. Such dressings demand a fairly high level of tying skill and a little more time.

Oliver Edwards supplies the six flies with the greatest contrast in their styles. Partly at my suggestion, in the knowledge that Oliver would readily concur, he has offered three North Country spider patterns, the soft hackles of modern terminology, and three of his own nymph patterns. In these six he has selected some extremely killing patterns. The three spiders are typical of northern England and are the evolutionary antecedents of many modern flies. For all their simplicity they are often tied incorrectly, and Oliver sets the record straight. In contrast to the simple tying of the spiders, Oliver offers three more complicated nymphs. Your patience and perseverance with these will be well rewarded.

Dry flies are well represented in the selection. Al Beatty chooses five North American standard patterns and also contributes a chapter on the tying methods for hair-wing dry flies. His methods and tips as a commercial tyer are invaluable. Both Lars-Åke Olsson and Hans Weilenmann offer thorax-hackled flies as being as good a dun imitation as can be found. Wayne Luallen's Sparkle Parachute is his answer to the problem; it closely mirrors my own choice. Wayne's six flies are meticulously tied. I read somewhere that he uses left-handed and right-handed peacock herl to get the herl to lay correctly in a Royal Wulff. To less thoughtful tyers it may sound like using a left-handed screwdriver. He, like many other tyers for this book, has produced tiny works of art, and yet it is art for everyday use.

Of the stillwater insects, perhaps midges feature most highly on trout menus. Trout preoccupied with these pupae can be notoriously difficult to catch. Bob Carnill provides his dressing which has become a British standard pattern for the pupa. Brian Chan, Darrel Martin and Paul Canning also provide midge pupa patterns and Brian and Dave Whitlock include excellent leech dressings that have an enticingly mobile action through the water.

Finally, if anyone is interested in a thirty-first selection I offer my own. I'm afraid I shall break my rules and offer seven patterns; I simply cannot choose which of these to omit. The Klinkhamer Special, for reasons already mentioned; a parachute Black Gnat (size 12-20) as a general terrestrial imitation; a parachute Olive Dun with an upright poly wing (size 14-22), to cover many of my hatch encounters; a Gold Ribbed Hare's Ear, weighted and unweighted (size 10-22), to copy caddis larvae on the bottom and pupae at the surface; a cul de canard Emerging Caddis Pupa (size 14-20); a Hare's Ear Gold Head with a partridge hackle because it catches fish when nothing else can; and lastly, a Partridge and Orange (size 14-16), because it works in all sorts of situations from the beginning of my trout season until the end of the grayling season eleven months later.

A Note About Hooks
Almost every contributor specified the make and model of hook they preferred for each dressing. A brief description of each hook is given, eg XL: extra long; XS: extra short; wide gape, curved shank, D/E (down eye), etc in the event that the preferred hook is unavailable and a substitute is required. Where the hook has been mentioned more than once in the dressings from a contributor, the description is offered on the first occasion only. Only rarely has it been impossible to trace a description, when a hook has not been are available in the UK.

A Note About Colour Illustrations
The flies on the colour plates are illustrated to approximately twice life-size. The exceptions to this scale are:

Morales – No. 1 (life-size), No. 2 (×1.5 life-size)

Schwiebert – (life-size)

Whitlock – (all ×1.5 life-size)

THEO BAKELAAR

HOLLAND

Theo Bakelaar is better known as 'Mr Goldbead' ever since he tied at the Dutch Fly Fair in 1990 with his face and had sprayed with gold paint. His notoriety has extended far and wide and the mailman has delivered letters addressed simply to 'Dutch Goldbead'! He has demonstrated his tying techniques with gold beads in Norway, Sweden, Belgium, Germany and the United States – often dressing in gold from head to toe. He has twice represented The Netherlands at the World Fly Fishing Championships and has also successfully fished his Goldbead flies in Scandinavia, the United Kingdom and Montana. Like many other Dutch anglers he enjoys high-quality fly fishing for pike, zander (walleye) and other coarse (whitefish) species in his native rivers and lakes.

Theo finds fly tying the best form of relaxation and therapy after his daily routine as a physical education instructor in a Dutch state prison. He is forty-six years old.

Bead heads are not new in fly fishing. They have been around for eighty or ninety years and were originally glass or metal. Except for isolated pockets of central Europe the fly-fishing world remained in ignorance of these until less than ten years ago. Now the popularity of Goldbeads or Goldheads has spread throughout Europe and they are enjoying success in the United States, Japan and wherever people fly fish. Fly fishers are beginning to believe in the Goldbeads, and because they believe they catch more fish. Only some very simple patterns were around six or seven years ago and so I began to develop a more comprehensive range. My patterns were spread far and wide to friends across the world and have been fished in many different waters for a range of fish species. Trout, grayling, sea-trout, salmon, steelhead, large-mouth bass, various coarse fish (whitefish), even catfish are all Goldbead victims.

When I am tying at a seminar or fly-tying show I'm frequently asked about the purpose of the gold bead. I reply that although no fish has confirmed it for me, yet I believe the shiny golden ball works in four different ways: weight, air bubble, jig system and colour.

Weight: There is enough weight in these heavy metal beads to get a nymph down deep very quickly. As the weight is on the outside of the dressing, unlike most weighted patterns, there may be some significance in the sound of the bead bouncing along the stones of a rocky bottom. Additionally there is the attractive 'plopping' sound as the nymph lands in the water. It certainly draws attention to itself and very often the nymph will be taken as it continues to sink.

Air bubble: Under water the gold bead looks very much like the air bubble attached to a pupa or under the pupal skin. If this is true then maybe a silver bead would look more realistic but my own experience is that silver is less effective. Perhaps the bubble effect would be more natural if the gold bead is tied in the centre of the shank. I've tried this with less success than having the bead at the head, probably because it loses the effect of the jig system.

Jig system: Left to sink and drift freely, the nymph sinks head first; but when it is being lifted the nymph turns head up. With many species a jig is a deadly weapon. It is easy to imagine the Goldbead nymph as it moves over the bottom or through the water. Giving the nymph that extra action with the rod tip is deadly on both rivers and stillwaters, particularly over a sandy or flat bottom. Short jumps over the bottom against a slope in a deep lake or a big river pool are effective.

Colour: The shiny golden colour, glittering deep below the surface draws attention to the nymph.

Even the novice fly tyer can manage the Goldbead Pheasant Tail without too many problems and it is the first nymph pattern I teach people to tie. It is an imitation of the small mayfly nymphs just like the original Pheasant Tail nymph of Frank Sawyer but it sinks much faster and may be fished deeper.

A few years ago at a fly-tying seminar in Norway I had a young tyer who tied only the Goldbead Pheasant Tails. A year later he returned to the workshop with an enormous fly box full of these nymphs in different colours. With great satisfaction he told me how he had fished this one pattern throughout the summer. He had used it with a normal Pheasant Tail nymph, interchanging them as droppers and point flies. It was the Goldbead that caught all the fish . . .

I always begin my fishing with this nymph, no matter where, on a floating or sinking line as appropriate. By changing the size of the hook and the colour of the thorax you can represent different species.

The colour of the peacock herl within the Goldbead Peacock Runner has created a lot of problems for trout and grayling. Traditionally it has been used on a great many successful dry flies and nymphs. I've held this nymph on a leader close to a rocky riverbed and it looks very realistic, like a small stonefly nymph. Sometimes I give further turns of lead wire under the body to ensure the fly gets down very fast. This style of fly has no upper or underside and presents no problems as it tumbles through the currents.

My Swedish friend, Lars-Åke Olsson asked me for some Peacock Runners when we were tying together in Norway. He wanted to try them in Swedish Lapland. Ten weeks later he wrote of its excellent success and how it had been included in the Lennart Bergquist catalogue for the Scandinavian fly fishermen. It is well worth a try anywhere in the world.

The Goldbead Hare's Ear Shaggy is a simple fly which has all the necessary qualities to catch fish.

Just looking at the fly you feel that here is a fly in which you may have great confidence. It is very important to believe in the fly you are using; such faith brings its own success. This nymph has the right colours and it moves well and because of its hackle and tail has 'life' in the water.

The original dressing for the Double Legs included a luminous butt which after being subjected to daylight or a bright light source would glow in the dark. This provided an aspect to the fly which was highly visible when fished deep or at dusk, or when night fishing. I still use it when winter fishing or in low light conditions. For normal use I now tie just a fluorescent butt. The double partridge hackle gives the fly considerable mobility and I've no doubt that the life-suggesting movement it gives adds to its attraction. Even when fished in a dead-drift the current works to enliven the hackle fibres. On Scandinavian rivers a dark version works better with a darker body fur and two brown partridges for legs.

My Big Bull Goldbead Stonefly really is a big fly and an incredible weapon. It has often been used as a last resort when all else has failed and many times over it has been the big trout that have taken it. Although the Big Bull is a large fly I've seen much larger real stonefly nymphs crawling between the rocks in Montana. Most other countries have big stonefly species too. We Dutchmen like to use bigger flies; perhaps we believe it's true that bigger flies catch bigger fish. I fish them on a full sinking line in very fast and deep water where trout hit them very hard indeed. If there are no large stoneflies in your waters I suggest that they should be tied on sizes 8 or 10.

My final fly is a Goldbead Zonker called Miss Beautiful. The Matuka or Zonker style is improved by having two strips of rabbit fur, one on the upper side as usual and the other on the lower side. Because there is so much long-fibred fur the fly has lots of mobility within the dressing and it appears very much alive in the water. Its action is highly attractive and because of the gold bead it rises and falls as it is retrieved, just like a jig.

This Zonker variation has gone all over the world. The results have been amazing. In Alaska the pink and white variation worked well on salmon; black ones on the Umpqua River in Oregon for steelhead, and other variations for Dutch zander. It has also had excellent results on large-mouth bass. Probably its most unusual catch was from the United States where Ray Tanner hooked a record catfish of seventy-eight pounds. I fished the pattern myself for the first time when on my fly-fishing club's annual visit to Bewl Bridge Reservoir in England. My boat partner and I fished them on a sinking line with a retrieve of very short pulls. Every two or three casts we each had a fish, or an offer of a fish, and our limit was very quickly caught.

Goldbead Pheasant Tail

HOOK: Tiemco TMC 3761 (1XL, 2X heavy, 2 D/E) size 10 – 16

THREAD: Brown

BEAD: Gold bead; 3mm for size 10 and 12, 2mm for size 14 and 16

TAIL: 6 or 7 cock pheasant tail fibres

ABDOMEN: Cock pheasant tail fibres

RIB: Fine gold wire

THORAX: Black-brown hare's ear, rabbit or squirrel dubbing

Goldbead Peacock Runner

HOOK: Tiemco TMC 3761 size 10

THREAD: Brown

BEAD: 4mm gold bead

TAIL: 2 widely spaced goose biots

BODY: 5 or 6 peacock herls twisted together with the thread

LEGS: 2 goose biots

THORAX: 6 peacock herls twisted together with the thread

Goldbead Hare's Ear Shaggy

HOOK: Tiemco 3761 size 10 – 12

THREAD: Brown

BEAD: gold bead, 4mm for size 10, 3mm for size 12

TAIL: Bunch of rabbit-fox hair

BODY: Hare's ear fur, also woven between the hackle and the bead

RIB: Fine gold round tinsel

LEGS: Mottled hen hackle

Double Legs

HOOK: Tiemco TMC 3761, size 10

THREAD: Brown

HEAD: 4mm gold bead

BUTT: Fluorescent Kreinik metallic braid

LEGS: Grey partridge in 2 or 3 turns

BODY: Brown squirrel or rabbit fur

HACKLE: Several turns of grey partridge

Big Bull Goldbead Stonefly

After the body has been wound or dubbed and ribbed, tie in a length of Flexibody for the wingcase. Dub the first thoracic segment and tie in a goose biot leg at each side; tie in the wingcase over the first segment. Repeat for the smaller size hooks; repeat twice for large hooks.

HOOK: Tiemco TMC 5263 (3XL, 2X heavy, D/E) size 2

THREAD: Brown

TAIL: 2 widely spaced goose biots, each either side of a small butt of thread

HEAD: 5mm gold bead

BODY: Brown Flexibody (illustrated) or brown fur dubbing

RIB: Gold wire

THORAX: Kelson brown dubbing or natural brown fur in 3 segments

LEGS: 3 pairs of goose biots, each pair in front of a thorax segment

WINGCASE: Brown Flexibody in 3 segments

ANTENNAE: Wild boar fibres

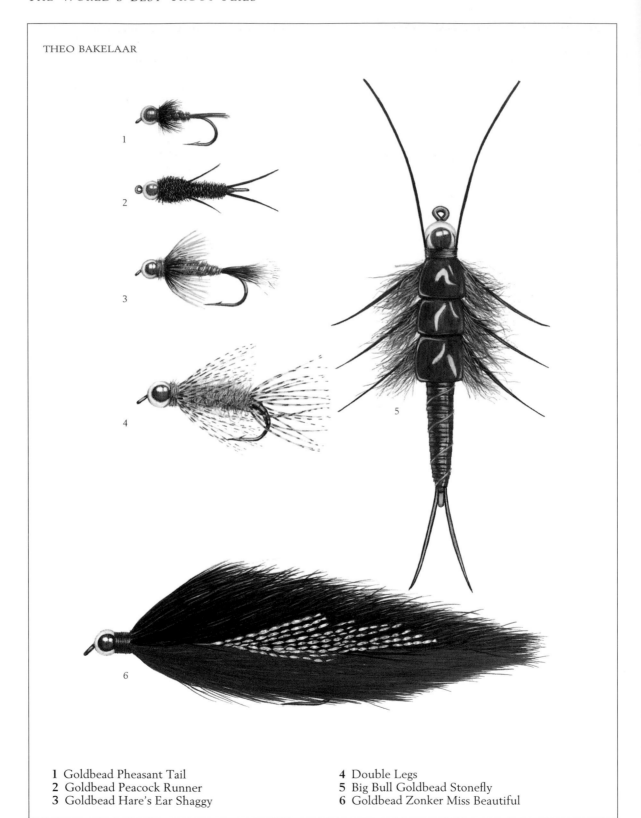

THEO BAKELAAR

1 Goldbead Pheasant Tail
2 Goldbead Peacock Runner
3 Goldbead Hare's Ear Shaggy

4 Double Legs
5 Big Bull Goldbead Stonefly
6 Goldbead Zonker Miss Beautiful

Goldbead Zonker Miss Beautiful

Most commercially available zonker strips are not long enough for this pattern so it is better to cut your own.

HOOK: Tiemco TMC 5263 (3XL, 2X heavy, D/E) size 2 – 8

THREAD: Black or to match one of the zonker colours

HEAD: Gold bead, 5mm on size 2 – 4, 4mm on size 6 – 8

UNDERBODY: Knitting wool wound the length of the shank, colour-matching one of the zonker strips

STRIPS: 2 zonker strips of dyed rabbit skin in a suitable colour combination. Width of the strips should be 5 or 6mm. These should be secured by coating the wool underbody with textile or carpet glue (usually coloured white). The strips are then secured against the upper, lower and sides of the underbody. Optionally include some lengths of Lureflash, Krystal or Twinkleflash tied to show between the zonker strips

AL BEATTY

USA

Al Beatty has been a commercial fly tyer and avid fly fisher for thirty-six of his fifty years. His main forte is the hair-wing dry fly. He has taught and demonstrated fly tying in Holland, Sweden, Canada, Mexico and his home country, the United States. He is a regular contributor to The FlyFisher *magazine and has three fly-tying video tapes on the US market. Al lives in Bozeman, Montana, where he divides his fly-fishing time between Washington steelhead waters and Montana trout streams. His favourite streams are the Big Horn River in eastern Montana and the Wenatchee River in Washington. He is presently the President of the International Federation of Fly Fishers. He is easily recognized on the stream; he's the bald-headed fellow wearing glasses who falls in the water a lot, casts terribly, and thoroughly enjoys all aspects of fly fishing.*

I have selected the flies described here for two reasons – their excellent fish-catching ability and the special fly-tying lesson they each illustrate. They are also the flies I use for my own river-trout fishing. The flies are arranged in the order they appear so the lessons learned from a previous fly receive additional application with the next pattern. A full method of tying these and other hair-wing flies will be found on page 175.

I can not begin to tell you the number of times the Grey Wulff has saved the day for me while on the stream. In different sizes it effectively represents many of the mayfly species we have in the western United States from the large Grey Drakes to the very small Tricos. Like all hair patterns, it floats well and is extremely durable. On more than one occasion a single fly has accounted for more than twenty fish. More flies are lost to trees on a back cast than wear out fishing.

Why the Royal Wulff is so darned effective, I can only guess. I think my theories would have no more validity than anyone else's. Just take my word for it, the fly is deadly. Let me share with you a story about its effectiveness.

I was fishing the Rail Road Ranch section of the Henry's Fork River in south-eastern Idaho in June 1988. This stretch of river was far enough away from my home that I did not get to fish it more than a couple of times a year. I was not familiar with the hatches and stopped at a local fly shop to learn what was happening on the river. The shop owner advised me of the hatches coming off throughout the day. So off to the river I went, confident of the day's strategy.

What followed were four very frustrating hours as I changed fly after fly trying to imitate the three different hatches that seemed to be coming off at the same time. I was looking through my fly boxes for the one-hundredth time when I spied a size 16 Royal Wulff. 'Why not?' I thought. 'Nothing else is working.'

I tried it on the leader and on the first cast a fish swirled at the fly and refused it. I've learned if this happens I can usually go down one hook size in the pattern and try again. I couldn't readily find a size 18 so I settled for a size 20 Royal Wulff instead. The following hours were the best fishing on that river I'd ever had up to that day. Today when I fish the Henry's Fork, the first fly I tie on, and usually the last, is a size 18 or 20 Royal Wulff.

The Royal Trude, like its cousin the Royal Wulff, is just another fly that works for no apparent reason. It certainly doesn't look like any of the bugs I have encountered in nature. I particularly like it in sizes 10 – 14.

I spend a lot of my spare time guiding friends on the various rivers in western Montana. If there are no evident hatches when we put the drift boat in the water, I'll usually start the day with a Royal Trude as a searching pattern for one of the fly fishers and a yellow-bodied Humpy or an Elk Hair Caddis for the other. Often the Royal Trude produces the first fish of the day.

During a stonefly hatch it is particularly effective in a size 10 or 12. Fish the fly through a regular dead drift. Let it swing downstream, dance across the current, and skitter for a few seconds straight downstream before you make another cast. The skittering action can provoke an explosive strike, so a heavier tippet may be advisable.

I tie the Elk Hair Caddis as the originator, Al Troth, intended with clipped hair rather than hackle at the head. This fly is very versatile, covering a wide range of fishing situations and is incredibly easy to tie. I carry it in my fly box in sizes from 16 to 24 and in a range of colours including tan, olive, grey, yellow and chartreuse.

In the large sizes I fish it as a stonefly imitation and in the smaller sizes it can be used as either a caddis or stonefly. Where the fly is really great, though, is in the very small sizes when fished as a midge pattern. If I could have only three dry-fly patterns in my box, I assure you one of them would be the Elk Hair Caddis in a wide range of sizes and colours.

The Humpy was originally developed with the rough western United States waters in mind. It floats well through just about any type of turbulence and is as versatile as the Elk Hair Caddis when it comes to fish-catchability. This fly would also be included if I could have only three dry-fly patterns.

I could tell many stories of fishing success with a Humpy but that's not the intention. My purpose is to eliminate the myth that this fly is difficult to tie by describing the critical points and measurements in the tying process.

The tail is tied to the shank just in front of the one-half point but still behind the one-third point on the shank. After tying on the tail leave the thread hanging just in front of the hook point. This should be near the middle of the shank. The wings and overbody are formed from the same clump of hair. This gives many tyers a real problem but there is a simple solution. To get a properly proportioned overbody and wings, the clump of hair *must* be equal to twice the length of the hook shank. If the tail has already been measured to equal the shank and, of course, the hook shank equals itself, then by measuring from the tip of the tail to the eye of the hook, you have a measurement that is twice the length of the hook shank.

With this measurement in mind, hold the clump of wing hair above the hook that already has the tail attached, align the tip of the tail and the tip of the hair-wing fibres so they are even. Trim the clump of wing hair even with the eye. The clump of the hair should now be equal to twice the length of the shank.

Tie this clump of hair on the hook with the thread left hanging in the middle of the shank. Bind the clump there with very tight wraps. As you wrap to the bend and back, use snug, but not tight, holding wraps. You need to wrap over this area several times, covering all exposed hair fibres, because the coloured thread forms the body.

Advance the thread to the one-third point on the shank, pull the hair over the top of the body, and tie off the hair at this point to form the wings and the overbody. It's much easier to form a nice tight overbody if you push forward, pressing from the bend, on the hair fibres. You can pull on the ends of the fibres forever and never get an overbody tight, but pushing from back to front works every time. The fly is finished like any hair wing from this point.

I originally developed my Muddle May in 1987 as a mayfly dun imitation. My goal was to accomplish three things: provide a slender profile on the water, maintain excellent flotation, and eliminate the use of a hackle. It is successful in all respects and has proven to be a superb fish catcher as well. It has replaced the mayfly dun patterns in my fly box. Maybe it will in your box as well.

Some tyers find this pattern a bit difficult to tie. A spun muddle head on a size 20 hook? Impossible. Not really! I will explain one simple technique that makes it very easy.

On this pattern I tie the tail longer than a normal hair-wing fly: about one and a half times the length of the shank. I also put half as many fibres as you would normally; remember, my goal is to keep this pattern's profile as slender as possible. The hackle fibres are tied on the hook at the quarter point just as if you were tying a set of hair wings. These hair fibres will be stood up eventually to form a collar across the top half of the fly. First, however, the wonder wings are tied on the body directly behind the hair collar. Pull the wings up straight and wrap a few turns of thread in front of them but still behind the collar; this will hold the wings upright. Dub on a body of a colour to match the insect making sure you stop at the hair collar. Stand the collar up using the 'through-the-clump' method described on page 21. The thread should be left hanging in the middle of the small space left in front of the collar.

The head is formed from one or two clumps of spun deer hair. Use two clumps on the larger sizes (12s or 14s) and one clump on the smaller flies. The clump of hair should be about the size of a pencil diameter, possibly less on very small flies. The trick to this operation is to trim the hair tips off before spinning them. Trimming the hairs first keeps them from becoming mixed with the collar and avoids difficulty in trimming the head later. To prevent the hair slipping over the eye, begin the spinning action by pulling down *and* back on the tying thread with the same motion. When completed, tie off the thread. Then trim the head to shape with a distinct taper to the eye.

Grey Wulff

I tie and fish this in size 10 – 14 but in the waters I fish size 16 – 18 provide the most consistent results.

HOOK: Partridge E1A (D/E, slightly long shank, 4X fine wire) or L3A (D/E, wide gape) size 10 – 24

THREAD: Grey

TAIL: Deer body hair

WINGS: Deer body hair, tied in an upright 'V'

BODY: Muskrat belly fur

HACKLE: Blue dun or grizzly

Royal Wulff

HOOK: Partridge E1A or L3A size 8 – 20

THREAD: Black

TAIL: Deer body hair

WINGS: White calf body or tail hair, tied in an upright 'V'

BODY: Peacock herl with a broad band of red floss in the centre

HACKLE: Brown (natural red) cock

Royal Trude

HOOKS: Partridge E1A or L3A size 8 – 16

THREAD: Black

TAIL: Deer body hair

WINGS: White calf tail, tied Trude-style

BODY: Peacock herl with a broad band of red floss in the centre

HACKLE: Brown (natural red) cock

Elk Hair Caddis

HOOK: Partridge E1A or L3A size 6 – 24

THREAD: To match the body colour

BODY: Tying thread, colour to match the insect

HACKLE: Palmered cock, to match the insect, with the upper fibres trimmed

WING: Trude-style, elk or deer body hair

HEAD: Clipped ends of the hair

Humpy

HOOK: Partridge E1A or L3A size 10 – 22

THREAD: To make the required body colour

TAIL: Deer, elk or moose

BODY: Coloured tying thread

OVERBODY: Elk or deer body hair

WINGS: Elk or deer body hair

HACKLE: Mixed grizzly and brown (natural red) cock

Muddle May

HOOK: Partridge E1A or L3A size 12 – 24

THREAD: To match the body colour

TAIL: Moose body hair or Micro-Fibets

BODY: Dubbed fur of plain tying thread

WINGS: Wonder wings to match the natural

HACKLE: Deer hair to match the insect

HEAD: Spun deer hair to match the insect

AL BEATTY

1 Grey Wulff
2 Royal Wulff
3 Royal Trude
4 Elk Hair Caddis
5 Humpy
6 Muddle May

PAUL CANNING

Paul has fished for thirty-five years, twenty-five of those as a fly fisher and tyer. He has extensive experience of the major English trout reservoirs, where much of his fishing is done from drifting boats. He has also spent many years bank fishing on larger and smaller lakes. He has fished on numerous waters, rivers and streams throughout the UK as well as fly fishing in France, Germany, Italy, Belgium, Norway, New Zealand and USA.

He has fished in two England World Championship teams and two Commonwealth teams, becoming Commonwealth Champion in 1990 and runner-up in 1991. He has fished for England in six UK Home Internationals including being team captain in 1992. He is the only competitor to have won all the individual medals. He has also won numerous team and individual prizes in the European Grand Slam.

Paul is a regular contributor to Trout and Salmon *magazine and he lectures, tutors and demonstrates fly fishing.*

He is a graduate engineer and also has an MA in Product Design. His work includes the design and development of fly-fishing tackle. He lives in East Sussex, a few minutes from Bewl Bridge Reservoir, one of the major English trout lakes. There whenever possible he fishes with dry flies or nymphs. His favourite fly fishing is during difficult rises triggered by small midge pupae and nymphs.

The Haystack is a dry adult midge pattern I developed for stillwaters. It fishes as a low-riding fly, designed to fish in or just on the film. In a flat calm, Haystacks are frequently taken savagely and confidently. Many fish try to swallow the fly, and throat hookings are common. It is cast easily with minimal air drag. The hairy 'wing' causes it to parachute down and alight gently, maximizing a good float. A wet or slimed Haystack is easily revived with a quick wash and dry followed by a light application of floatant on the longer fibres.

Trout may be able to see hatching midge from below as a result of a number of triggers. One that may be crucial to this and many other surface flies is the silvery halo surrounding them where the water surface is bent down. Light is locally re-fracted differently in this little area. It is possible fish may learn to associate this halo effect with emerging insects. Perhaps trout cruising deep can read light signals in a way we yet know little about. Trout may utilize such light signals for long-range spotting and then other clues as they come closer to inspect the fly. It could be silhouette, the half-in/half-out appearance, the ill-defined shape and the silver halo surrounding the fly that are key factors to the Haystack's undoubted effectiveness.

Cruising lake trout will often refuse a high-riding pattern but readily accept this one when adults are dragging themselves out of their shucks at the surface. If fish are betraying their presence by a rise form, the fly should invariably be placed ahead of their predicted path.

The size of the fly should be matched to the natural's size; this could be between 6 and 20mm body length. The Haystack can be cast singly to cruising fish or in a team of two or three as a searching tactic.

The Perky is the most extraordinary and most successful lake dry fly I have ever seen or used. Devised by English expert lake dry-fly fisherman Clive Perkins, it deserves to be acknowledged as one of the major fly-tying milestones in stillwater dry-fly fishing. The Perky is a master blend of features that perhaps come closer than we have ever done before to a hatching midge pattern.

The fly is ingenious for many reasons. The long-shank lightweight hook cocks the fly into an upright position. There it sits as a perfect imitation of a hatching midge. The wing is highly visible. From below the CDC wing must give an enhanced illusion of a hatching insect. Trout know they don't have much time before the natural midge hatches off and so takes to this sort of fly are very positive.

It is fished singly or in a team of three. Cast out and leave static or work it back to create a wake, pausing at intervals to allow the fly to cock upright. Watch the fly at all times. Strike at any swirl which means a fish is sucking in the subsurface portion. Tease the fly away if you fail to move a fish and re-cast well ahead. This sort of fishing is immensely exciting and totally addictive. Fish can come from nowhere at any moment. In addition to watching your fly constantly, scan the water for signs of moving fish.

It is a sad, but untruthful myth that caenis-feeding trout are virtually impossible to catch. The truth is they are catchable if anglers persisted with small flies in the right way at the critical time of the hatch. The hatch should be enjoyed rather than bemoaned.

Over many seasons I've proved that my Caenis Nymph does work on caenis feeders. During the hatch it is in the initial stages that trout feed on the subsurface nymph and as trout bulge close to the surface chasing the tiny wriggling nymphs this pattern scores. When the spinners fall it is less effective than a small spent dry fly.

As you see a series of swirling rises and are able to follow the path of an individual fish, cast the nymph into its path. A Caenis Nymph drawn past them will often result in a trout chasing your fly.

When one does follow, try either stopping the retrieve completely or speeding up. Don't strike but draw your fly away to see if it has taken. If it has not, pull into a backcast and re-present.

To aid presentation I tie the fly in two weights. The heavier goes on the point and the lighter fly on the dropper. Maximum precision is required during a hatch as flies just an inch below the feeding band will be ignored as will flies presented too far to the side of a trout's path.

My Hackle Stalk Buzzer is an ultra-simple yet highly effective midge pupa or buzzer pattern. It was designed to drop fast yet maintain the illusion of a midge pupa via profile and tone contrast. I like to use it when stalking in clear water. Big fish, cruising at depth, may have seen other flies and can be very suspicious. Certainly ones with too much lead can do this. This will fool them when other flies might not.

In the plethora of tying materials we enjoy today, it is easy to lose sight of a simple truism: slim, simple flies catch a lot of trout. Apart from the fact that it is highly effective, the great attraction of the Hackle Stalk Buzzer is that it relies on a simple and often wasted material for shape, colour and contrast.

My good friend Bob Barden devised the Pearly Hare's Ear which has become one of my all-time favourite lake nymphs as a midge pupa imitation. Perhaps you may think it is Gold Ribbed Hare's Ear variant without the gold rib. This is not quite true. Often a natural pupa is no fatter than the hook we start with! It is no coincidence that spider patterns are highly effective in midge hatches. This fly is a good example of a minimalist fly that has the illusion of life about it. This pattern will endure.

I have experimented with different highlights in this fly – so-called 'hit' spots. These include such things as orange wing buds, bright heads, fluorescent bands, and tufts at the tail. Yes they do work but I am losing interest in such fish teasers. At its basic level, this fly is the epitome of deception and, for me, to dress it up is moving away from what fly fishing is supposed to be. I prefer to deceive than to tease fish into taking my fly. Keep it simple and the use of this fly will repay you handsomely. I recommend a relatively heavy hook as trout seem particularly vulnerable to taking this fly on the lift.

Loch-style boat fishing on Malham Tarn, a limestone water in North Yorkshire.

In early summer on the big Irish loughs no other hatch seems to get trout so excited as the mayfly. Then the big dour browns become vulnerable. I have fished the Mosely May amongst heavy hatches and had brown trout take it in preference to naturals floating inches away from it. Some mayfly tyings have that extra something, the power to lure fish up when others are ignored. The Mosely May seems to be one of those special patterns. This is an Irish dry fly (of unknown origin) that deserves to be better known – even in Ireland!

The tradition is to fish from a boat, drifting broadside to the wave. A team of wet flies is cast a short distance in front using a floating or slow-sinking line. The flies are worked just under the wave or eased to the surface so that they make a slight disturbance. A good wave is preferred but if the conditions are calm and the mayfly are 'up', big wily trout may be on the cruise regardless of conditions and this fly will deceive them.

I suspect the Mosely's allure has to do with its excellent profile combined with the colour blending of the wing. If this is true, then it is an important fly because it offers a simple yet unusual tying method easily adapted to other upwinged flies. The result is a large, air-resistant fly. You have to build leaders and cast accordingly. I will fish three together as widely spaced as possible. I fish the dry version static and wait for a take.

PAUL CANNING

1 Haystack
2 Perky
3 Caenis Nymph

4 Hackle Stalk Buzzer
5 Pearly Hare's Ear
6 Mosely May

Haystack

After tying in and supergluing the butt and allowing it to dry, restart the thread at the eye and leave a 4-inch (20mm) length trailing back. Tie in the free end along the shank to the butt. Generously dub the tying thread with fur, spread evenly and push to the shank. Using the free end of thread spin it round the dubbed thread under tension. Wind the resulting hairy rope in touching turns up the shank, encouraging as many fibres as possible to stick out sideways. At the head separate the two strands and tie in. Ensure it is bulky and not too thin. Brush the fibres upward at about 45 degrees with Velcro.

HOOK: Kamasan B980 size 16 – 20, Kamasan B830 size 14, Kamasan B400 size 10 -12

THREAD: Black 6/0 Uni-Thread

BUTT: Pearly mylar over the tying thread, superglued for colour change and durability

BODY: Hare body guard fur with no underfur mixed in. This has longer spikier hair than from the mask. Dark shades or those with dark tips are preferred to the blonde or ginger furs

Perky

The thread or hackle stalk body patterns enable the fly to cock more readily.

HOOK: Kamasan B400 size 10 – 12, B830 size 14 (lightweight, longshank)

THREAD: Black

BODY: Fine dubbing, herl, tying thread or stripped hackle stalk, superglued for strength

TOP WING: One, two or three cul de canard feathers, depending on the wave, tied over the eye

Caenis Nymph

HOOK: Drennan Traditional Wet size 14 (heavier fly) or Kamasan B980 size 14 (lighter fly)

THREAD: Black

TAIL: Cock grizzle or badger hackle fibres

ABDOMEN: White ostrich herl

THORAX: Brown/golden olive strich herl

RIB: Fine oval silver (French tinsel for maximum shine)

Hackle Stalk Buzzer

As a guide to the hackle stalk length you will need four to five times the shank length. Soak the stalk in water before winding to reduce the likelihood of breakage. Dyed dark capes provide the stalk with the most contrast.

HOOK: Kamasan B980 (S/E, 2X short shank) size 14 – 20

THREAD: Black

HEAD: Lead wire (0.037mm diameter) formed into a small ball, painted black with head cement or enamel, two coats

BODY: Stripped hackle stalk, good light/dark contrast is best. Superglue for durability

Pearly Hare's Ear

Beware of using too light a hook, of using too much dubbing, of not tapering the body, of using too narrow a rib, and tying it too long.

HOOK: Kamasan B175 size 1014

THREAD: Black

BODY: Hare's fur in all shades in a slight carrot-shape

RIB: Wide pearl lurex generously wound and tight

Mosely May

Tie in the hackles with the base ends stripped. Soft, low-grade capes are excellent. Tie in the first behind the eye. Lay it good side up parallel to the shank, tip to the eye. Repeat with hackles two and three. Tie in the tail. Dub the body in a tapered shape and finish one-third down the shank. Palmer the first hackle along front third of the shank. Avoid touching turns. Palmer the second and third hackles. Wind the thread forwards and half-hitch at the head; do not cut off. Turn the fly over. Use a dubbing needle to divide the underneath fibres. Splay the hackles sideways with figure-of-eight turns of thread on what will be the underside of the fly. Five or six cross lays should enable the bunches to be pulled to the sides. The result should be a 180-degree hackle. The wet pattern omits this and has a full 360-degree hackle.

HOOK: Kamasan B400 or B830 size 10

THREAD: Black

TAIL: Badger fur dyed olive or cock pheasant tail fibres, equal to the shank length

HACKLES: One each of yellow, medium olive and medium blue dun cock saddle hackle, fibres equal to the shank length

BODY: Natural hare's mask fur or equivalent dyed medium olive

BOB CARNILL

UK

With fifty years of fishing, and thirty of those fly fishing, Bob Carnill is an expert stillwater angler who also loves to fish on rivers and streams. Bob has created a string of highly successful patterns which have proved their worth by contributing to the remarkable rod average of 6.1 trout per outing taken over a twenty-one-year period. Anyone who fishes the hard-fished public reservoirs of the English Midlands knows how amazing this statistic is.

As well as being an ambulanceman, Bob has a second career giving presentations to clubs and branches of The Fly Dressers' Guild, as well as tying at numerous game fairs. He has made four fly-tying and fly-fishing videos and has co-authored with Kenneth Robson a book on lure fishing, Dressed to Kill, as well as contributing to other books.

Since 1977, Bob has written a major monthly column for Trout Fisherman, *the UK's principal stillwater magazine. He has been responsible for setting and judging the prestigious Benson & Hedges fly-dressing competition.*

I think flexibility plays a very important role in successful fly fishing; you must be prepared to change flies and tactics in tune with the progression of the season, the time of day, the weather, and (most importantly) the mood of the trout. On stillwaters the unremitting lure fisherman will have his day, but overall he won't be as consistent as the observant angler with an open mind who is prepared to experiment on a wide scale. In addition, you must *want* to catch trout, as opposed to having a day out with the fly rod.

During the mid to late 1960s I was asked by my good friend, the late Jim Sharpe of Nottingham, to create a close copy of the chironomid pupa that would tempt the more discerning, preoccupied trout. Jim was not a tyer himself, but being a director of Tom Watson's Fishing Tackle, Nottingham, and well versed in all aspects of flies and their component parts, he could speak with authority on the creation of new patterns. Pulling out a slim oak display cabinet drawer, Jim took one of each chironomid pupa they sold and laid them out for my inspection. 'All of these will

catch trout on their day, Bob; but on other days, none of them will!'

What he wanted me to do was to create something that was a much closer copy of the real thing; something that would tip the scales in our favour when trout are being particularly choosy. He thought that the bodies of the contemporary pupae were either too solid looking or too flashy. He wanted to see a softer, more subtle effect for the abdomen and a translucent segmented sheen. Jim suggested using polythene, or something similar, and urged me to include my own thoughts and observations to improve upon the standard tyings.

My answer was the Poly-Rib Buzzer. I gave the new pattern a slim abdomen of soft herl, ribbed through with clear polythene to simulate the translucent sheen of the natural. In addition I added tiny shaped wing buds, using swan biot quills, a material which, as far as I am aware, was not generally recognized at the time. The head-breathers were improved by creating a large orb-like plume either side of the head.

Jim was so impressed with the fly, he used it exclusively for all his buzzer fishing until his untimely death, eight years later. Although I now have a number of excellent buzzer patterns available, the Poly-Rib will always be my favourite.

When the adult midges return to the water my Adult Buzzer series is extremely effective. I developed seven patterns, one for each month of the English trout season from March to September. They are all 'wet' flies, intended to represent the dead or dying, drowned or drowning adult.

The Blae & Black Adult Buzzer is a delicate little fly, the kind of thing that most trout would take quite instinctively as it could be mistaken for any number of aquatic or terrestrial flies. It is during a midge hatch or especially during a fall of egg-laying females that it really comes into its own.

It was originally tied for Ullswater in the English Lake District where substantial hatches will be found from mid March to mid May. On the rawest of days and evenings, the native trout would rise quite freely to the spent females, even when frosty air began to put ice in the rod rings.

On my home waters of the Midlands it plays an important 'top-of-the-water' role in the early season. A very successful method is to fish from a boat at anchor on the windward shore when trout are dimple-rising to the naturals in sheltered water. Usually a team of three is drifted round on the light ripple before retrieving with a very slow figure of eight once the line has come to rest down wind. Takes come on the drift or on the retrieve.

Ullswater was one of my prime test-beds for patterns in the 1960s. My Cased Caddis quickly became my number-one point fly, but the Williams fished on the first dropper completed the most deadly duo I ever fished on Ullswater in the early spring. On the first occasion they were fished together they accounted for forty-seven trout in my day-and-a-half's fishing. The Williams began life as a William's Favourite which underwent a series of metamorphoses: first losing its tail, then including a lead underbody before bulking out the body with seal's fur as opposed to black silk. The final touch substituted black hen for the cock hackle, tied much more densely. It was no longer a William's Favourite but certainly a Williams of sorts.

I initially dressed the Black Gnat as a wet imitation but it also fishes in the film like a natural blown onto the water. However, for successful surface-film work it is important that it is treated with one of the better floatants, Gink or natural cul-de-canard oil being preferred. When waterproofing the fly, pay attention to the underside of the wings as well as the usual areas.

Whenever black gnats are on a stillwater fishery and trout are taking them, I will fish three to a leader, presenting them just under the surface at eye-ball level with a targeted trout. If fish are working the wind lanes, sport can be fast and furious. Some of my best results have come from a boat anchored to one side of a wind lane where trout have been seen on patrol. With trout regularly passing through, the flies can be presented and worked in a slow figure-of-eight retrieve.

My fifth selection, the DRF Yellow & Black Spider, has also been successful for wild river brown trout and sea-trout at dusk and dawn. However, it is mainly used to counter one of the most frustrating facets of stillwater trout fishing – a mirror calm on a summer's evening and trout rising constantly to an invisible food form and refusing everything the fly fisher offers them. My own observation is that the culprit is a minute water beetle or crustacean that rises to the surface as light begins to fade. Identification is very difficult as this tiny creature is not much bigger than a full stop and looks remarkably like one in both size and colour.

Whenever I have fallen foul of the mysterious black creature, the DRF Yellow & Black Spider has always come to my rescue. Cast into the path of a cruising trout and retrieved extremely slowly, it has provided me with memorable catches while those around have blanked. Why a size 14 fly, so much bigger than the real thing, should be taken so confidently by difficult trout is one of the mysteries that makes fly fishing, and trout, so special.

Thirty years ago I stumbled on the fact that summer-fed trout that were fat and wise and feeding in the shallows on a combination of larval corixa and coarse fish fry were easily fooled by a tiny buff-beige spider drifted round in the light ripple. Over the years I have proved that the buff-beige spider was highly imitative of the tiny translucent corixae larvae. I have forgotten why I experimented with a wing but the results were spectacular and proved the Cameo Lady to be the best answer I've come across for dealing with lure-

BOB CARNILL

1 Poly-Rib Buzzer Pupa
2 Blae & Black Adult Buzzer
3 Williams
4 Black Gnat
5 DRF Yellow & Black Spider
6 Cameo Lady (Larval Corixa)

conditioned fry-feeding trout *and* late summer/autumn trout feeding heavily on adult corixa. It looks nothing like either fry or corixa but that is hardly the point. Fished two or three to a cast, in the vicinity of weed beds and fry/corixa-feeding trout, it can be unbelievably effective.

Poly-Rib Buzzer Pupa

HOOK: Size 10 – 14 standard shank or 12 – 16 curved sedge hook

THREAD: To match the colour of the pupa being tied

TAIL-BREATHERS: 3 – 5 strands of fluorescent Electron White nylon floss, or Datam Glo-Brite floss (No 16)

RIB: Narrow, pre-stretched heavy duty polythene

BODY: Dyed herl; turkey, goose, swan, etc in various colours – black, claret, olive, brown, etc, tied as a slim abdomen

THORAX-COVER: A web of the same fibres as the body material

WING-BUDS: 2 goose or swan biot quills; natural or orange-dyed

THORAX: Dubbed dyed mole's fur to match the overall colour. Go slightly darker if anything

HEAD-BREATHERS: Fluorescent white wool; 100% soft nylon is the best. Tie in on a horizontal plane just behind the hook etc using a figure-of-eight lashing, then trim to size and fluff out

Blae & Black Adult Buzzer

HOOK: Size 14 – 16 curved sedge hook

THREAD: Fine waxed black

UNDERBODY: Slightly tapered using the tying thread and taken at least halfway round the bend of the hook

BODY: A well-marked natural peacock eye quill, stripped and wound in neat, touching turns

WINGS: 2 matching white cock hackle points dyed pale iron-blue dun. Wings should be tied on a flat, horizontal plane and slightly splayed or semi-spent

THORAX-COVER: Web of black fibres; dyed swan, goose, turkey, etc

THORAX: Black-eyed mole's fur, dubbed. Do not make too bulky

HACKLE (LEGS): Sparse black hen. Strip away the leading fibres before winding. This produces a spray effect as well as cutting down on bulk

Williams

HOOK: Size 10 – 12 standard shank

THREAD: Waxed black

UNDERBODY: Fine lead wire

BODY: Black seal's fur or a substitute

RIB: Fine to medium oval silver tinsel

HACKLE: Black hen, rather full

Black Gnat

The wing features should have a metallic green sheen, with a well-marked pale tip. These are found high on the wings, parts of the breast and the back. Those on the head may be too small or narrow but are worth investigating.

HOOK: Size 14 – 16 standard shank

THREAD: Fine waxed black

ABDOMEN: Either black tying thread built to shape and ribbed very fine silver wire, or 3 strands of black dyed swan or substitute, spun into a thin rope and wound on. No rib on the latter

WINGS: 2 identical feathers taken from an old cock starling

HACKLE: Same as for the wings. Two full turns in front of the wings

DRF Yellow & Black Spider

HOOK: Size 14 – 16 standard shank

THREAD: Waxed black

UNDERBODY: Silver lurex

BODY: DRF (fluorescent) phosphor-yellow nylon floss

HACKLE: Black hen

Cameo Lady (Larval Corixa)

The more specific corixa imitation omits the wing from this dressing.

HOOK: Size 12 – 16 standard shank

THREAD: Waxed straw-coloured

TAIL: Small bunch of fibres taken from a creamy or stone-coloured hen. If this is not available, cream-coloured is the nearest substitute

BODY: Pale buff-beige soft underfur with just a little pink mixed in

HACKLE: Hen hackle as used for the tail

WING: Paired slips taken from the palest mallard flight feather; dress slim and low over the fly

BRIAN CHAN

CANADA

For the last nineteen years Brian Chan has lived in Kamloops, British Columbia, where there are hundreds of small productive rainbow trout lakes within a two-hour drive. Professionally, he is a fisheries biologist with the Provincial Ministry of Environment, Lands and Parks. He is responsible for the management of small lake resources within the Thompson/Nicola region where there are approximately 1,000 trout lakes.

Understandably, Brian has a preference for stillwater fly fishing. His favourite method is with a floating line in a chironomid hatch. This will have stood him in no stead at all for his saltwater trips for bonefish and tarpon in Belize, Cuba, Cayman Islands and Christmas Island.

He is actively involved in the British Columbia Federation of Fly Fishers and contributed to The Gilly, *the first detailed book of fly fishing in BC. His highly acclaimed book,* Flyfishing Strategies for Stillwaters *has sold extremely well. He writes for Canadian fishing magazines and is a frequent speaker at Federation of Fly Fishers' conclaves in both Canada and the USA. In 1993 he represented his country in the Commonwealth Fly Fishing Championships in his home province.*

There are literally thousands of small productive lakes in the interior regions of British Columbia. These lakes are blessed with nutrient-rich water, long growing seasons and abundant aquatic invertebrate populations. Wild and stocked populations of rainbow and brook trout (char) are able to grow to very large sizes. Fish in excess of eleven pounds are not uncommon on some lakes managed for quality angling. The fishery resources in Canada are public resources and available to most anglers.

Most fly fishing on stillwaters is from anchored boats or canoes. Bank fishing is not feasible because of soft lake bottoms, extensive shallow water zones and forested shorelines. The majority of trout feeding is done on the shoal or littoral zone of the lake. This is defined as the portion of the lake where sunlight can penetrate and allow photosynthesis to occur. This is usually up to about twenty-three feet in depth. Insect hatches occur at about the same time each year, so anglers wait in anticipation of their favourite hatch.

Freshwater shrimp are the most abundant food source. A staple diet of shrimp is reflected in the deep orange flesh colour of these trout and char. The most prolific populations of *Gammarus* are found in the calcium-rich lakes such as those in the Kamloops region. Shrimp are available throughout the year and inhabit the rich vegetation that covers the shallower depths of the lake. *Gammarus* are extremely prolific, breeding up to eight times each year. Under ideal growing conditions, *Gammarus* can reach over an inch in length. Their colour varies with the water and habitat. The most common colours include olive green, yellow-green and a brownish green.

Shrimp patterns must be fished close to the bottom of shallow water. Intermediate and slow-sinking fly lines are popular with local anglers. A floating line and weighted patterns can be an effective method when fishing water less than ten feet deep. Shrimp are not fast swimmers and their movement is best imitated with a slow hand-twist retrieve interspersed with quick short pulls.

Chironomids or midges are a primary food source for most lake trout. In the highly productive waters of British Columbia there are literally thousands of species of varying sizes and colours. I developed the Red Butt Chironomid to represent the emerging pupa that have red haemoglobin-like fluid in the posterior end of the abdomen. This type of midge pupa was frequently being found in trout stomach contents. Although the larvae are often referred to as bloodworms, the red colouring is actually a haemoglobin-like respiratory fluid that allows the larva to live in very low-oxygen environments.

A good midge hatch will result in thousands, if not millions, of pupae rising to the surface to emerge as adults. Trout and especially very large trout love to eat emerging chironomids.

Our preferred fishing technique is from anchored boats or float tubes using floating lines and sixteen-to-twenty-foot leaders. The fly is cast out, allowed to sink to an appropriate depth and then retrieved with a dead-slow hand twist. Trout often just inhale the fly, thus requiring considerable concentration on the part of anglers to detect the strike.

My favourite sedge pattern is the Mikulak Sedge developed in the mid 1970s by Art Mikulak of Calgary, Alberta. It imitates the adults of the large travelling caddis (*Limnophilus* sp.) that are present on many small lakes in the interior of BC. This pattern has three features that make it very successful. The body is made of seal's fur which has excellent light-gathering qualities. Elk hair is used for the wing case. The large-diameter hair follicles make elk hair one of the best deer family hairs for tying floating flies. The hackle design adds great stability to the fly and ensures an upright presentation cast after cast.

Trout will actively chase these large adults as they scamper or lumber across the surface in an attempt to get airborne. Intensive hatches of caddis will often be matched with slashing rises. The typical technique is to cast ahead of a feeding fish and immediately after the fly lands on the water begin a quick retrieve of two- to four-inch long pulls. Pause briefly after five to seven pulls and then resume the retrieve. The resulting strikes will certainly be explosive.

Butler's Bug was created by Glen Butler, an innovative fly tyer from Vancouver. It is tied to represent the nymphal stage of the Darner family of dragonflies. These nymphs can reach up to two and a half inches in length and are an inviting trout meal. Nymphal colour ranges from shades of green to tan to black. Individual nymphs will adapt their colour to their habitat. They spend their lives amongst bottom vegetation and submerged woody debris. They are active predators, searching out shrimps, damselfly and mayfly nymphs and any other organism smaller than themselves. They use a form of jet propulsion to propel themselves through the water. Water is expelled with great force through vents located at the tip of the abdomen. This gives the nymphs great speed needed for hunting food or escaping predators.

The imitation must be fished close to the lake bed and sinking lines are essential. A good dragonfly retrieve is several quick two- to four-inch pulls followed by a pause of several seconds and then repeated.

One of the largest aquatic insects is the damselfly. The adults are easily distinguished from dragonflies by their slender bodies and their wing position when at rest. Damselflies fold their wings along the back of the abdomen while dragonfly wings are held out horizontally like an aeroplane wing.

The nymphs are an important food source particularly as the mature ones begin their emergence and swim to shore. They swim in the top three feet of water and upon reaching some emergent vegetation they crawl out of the water to complete the change from nymph to adult. The swimming action is a slow sinusoidal twisting of the body. Damselfly nymphs come in a variety of colours dependent on species and habitat. The commonest colours are olive green, yellowy green and a reddish brown. Immature nymphs are found hiding among bottom vegetation.

The nymph emergence swims can be best fished with either a floating or intermediate fly line. The nymphs are swimming close to the surface and you will see them as they head for shallow water. Try a retrieve consisting of several slow hand-twists followed by a brief pause, then repeated. At other times trout will feed on migrating nymphs right in the bulrush patches. Trout will knock over the bulrush stems along with the damselfly nymphs and then swim back to pick up

BRIAN CHAN

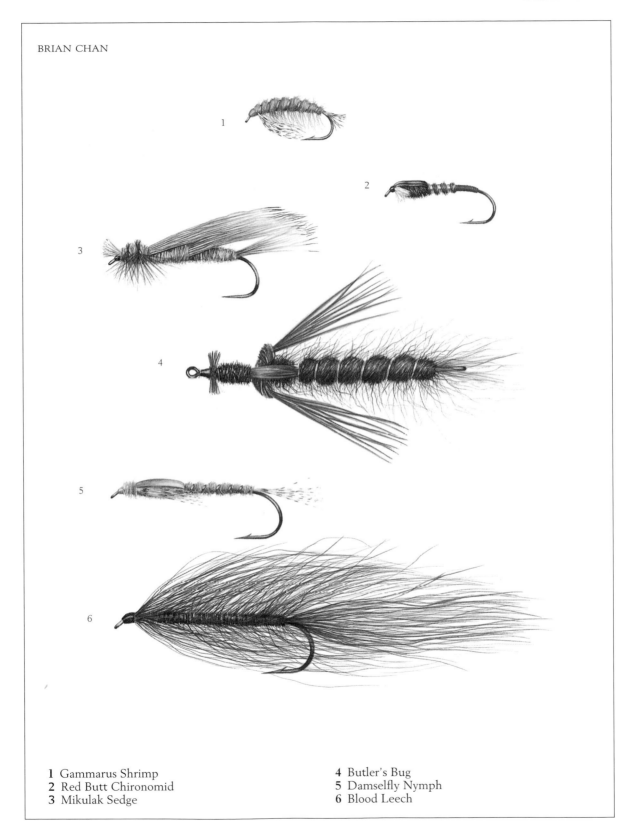

1 Gammarus Shrimp
2 Red Butt Chironomid
3 Mikulak Sedge

4 Butler's Bug
5 Damselfly Nymph
6 Blood Leech

the struggling nymphs. A floating nymph pattern can offer some very exciting surface action.

This damselfly nymph pattern utilizes seal's fur as the body material. The light-gathering qualities of seal's fur gives the fly a very lifelike appearance. Blending various colours of seal's fur allows the tyer to match the specific nymphal colours encountered on individual lakes. The soft hackle fibres used for the legs and tail also add to the lifelike appearance of the fly.

Leeches are found in almost all stillwaters and they are an important food item because they are available all year round. They are found living close to the lake bed around rocks, woody debris or vegetation. They can attain around half an inch in length when swimming fully extended. The most common colours include black, shades of brown, mottled maroon and black, and mottled black and green. They swim in a slow up-and-down undulating motion.

The Blood Leech was developed by Jack Shaw of Kamloops. One of the keys to its success is the mohair wool used to tie the pattern. When tied to the dressing below, this fly has movement within the dressing to simulate the natural undulating through the water.

Gammarus Shrimp

The body colour will vary by lake and river type.

HOOK: Tiemco TMC 2457 (D/E, 2X wide gape, 2X short, 2X heavy) size 8–4

TAIL: Several fibres from a rump feather of Hungarian Partridge

BODY: Kaufmann's olive gammarus scud dubbing over an optional lead-weighted underbody. Pick out some fibres as legs on the underside

RIB: Fine gold wire

THROAT: Several fibres from a rump feather of Hungarian Partridge

Red Butt Chironomid

HOOK: Tiemco TMC 3761 (D/E, 2X heavy) size 10 – 14

BUTT: Red floss

ABDOMEN: Several strands of cock ring pheasant tail

RIB: Fine gold tinsel

THORAX: Peacock herl

SHELL BACK: Synthetic brown raffia

GILLS: White ostrich herl

Mikulak Sedge

The tying of this sedge takes a little explanation. After tying in the tails, wrap the dubbing forward to just short of the mid point of the shank. Tie off and add 20 – 24 fibres of stacked elk hair for the first wing. This wing should extend to the tips of the tail fibres. Continue the body dubbing to half-way along the rest of the shank. Add the second wing of stacked elk hair. Tie in and trim so the butts extend over the hook eye. The wing should extend almost to the tips of the first wing. Tie in the hackle by the base. Continue the dubbing to just behind the eye. Wind the hackle forward and tie in. Trim the upper and lower hackle fibres.

HOOK: Tiemco TMC 5212 (D/E, 2XL, fine wire) size 6 – 10

THREAD: Olive green

TAIL: 12 – 16 pieces of stacked elk hair. Length should be approximately one-third of the shank length

BODY: A tightly twisted strand of drab olive green seal's fur in a dubbing loop

WINGS: Elk hair, preferably with light-coloured tips

HACKLE: Dark brown (natural red) cock hackle

Butler's Bug

This is a very effective pattern because of its overall impressionistic shape plus some special tying features. The underbody of the fly is deer hair which adds buoyancy to the fly and helps keep it fishing just off the lake bottom. The single pair of legs also add to the movement of the fly as it is retrieved through the water. As with many fly patterns tied with a dubbed body, the more the fly is fished, the more lifelike its shape becomes.

HOOK: Tiemco TMC 300 (D/E, 6XL, heavy wire) size 4 – 8

TAIL: 20 – 25 strands of deer hair tips

UNDERBODY: Deer hair strands lashed along the length of the shank; the tips are used for the tail

ABDOMEN: Dubbed seal's fur or substitute in a suitable natural colour, slightly broader at the rear and tapering to the thorax

RIB: Gold or copper wire

THORAX: Dubbed seal's fur as for the abdomen

SHELL BACK: Cock ring neck pheasant tail

LEGS: 10 – 12 fibres of ring cock pheasant tail. Tie one overhand knot approx 1 inch (25mm) from the fibre tips. The bend in the legs should be approx 2 inches (5mm) from the outside of the thorax. Tie in the legs so that they sit pointing slightly downward

HEAD: Peacock herl

EYES: 5 – 10 fibres of ring neck pheasant tail lashed at right angles to the shank then overwrapped with peacock herl

Damselfly Nymph

The abdomen should be tied with a gradual taper. Use a dubbing loop to ensure the dubbing is tightly spun and trim the body to shape.

HOOK: Tiemco TMC 5212 size 8 – 12

THREAD: Pale green

TAIL: 6 – 8 fibres of Hungarian Partridge rump feather

BODY: Dubbed seal's fur of an appropriate colour

RIB: Fine gold-coloured wire

LEGS: 4 – 6 fibres of Hungarian Partridge rump feathers on each side of the thorax area

SHELL BACK: Olive green synthetic raffia

HEAD: Dubbed seal's fur

Blood Leech

The colour of this fly is an important factor in its success. The colours of maroon and magenta stay visible deeper in the water column than other colours. When combined with the natural wavy motion of mohair you can see why this fly is worth tying. After tying, dip in hot water for several seconds to straighten out the mohair fibres. These are then combed back to form a flowing body around the entire hook. Trim the mohair so that it does not extend more than one hook shank length beyond the bend. A piece of Velcro is the ideal tool for combing out hair.

HOOK: Tiemco TMC 300 size 4 – 10

THREAD: Black

TAIL: Maroon mohair fibres twice the length of the hook shank

BODY: Maroon mohair wool wound forward along the shank and, as it is wound, pick out the mohair strands to form a covering around the entire shank

OLIVER EDWARDS

UNITED KINGDOM

Oliver has been fly fishing for almost forty years during which time he ran fly-tying classes for almost twenty years. In 1980 and 1981 he won the International Fly Tyer of the Year Competition and was subsequently invited to join the judging panel the following year. He is a regular tying demonstrator for Partridge of Redditch and, as well as tying throughout Britain, he has demonstrated in Sweden, Norway, Denmark and Belgium and is a regular demonstrator at the Dutch Fly Fair. In 1991 he tied at the Federation of Fly Fishers' conclave at West Yellowstone, Montana. He is a qualified casting instructor and contributes to UK game-fishing journals.

Oliver's local rivers are the Yorkshire Dales rivers but he regularly fishes elsewhere in Britain and has fished in Norway, France, Italy and the USA. He is the only angler to win the Yorkshire Grayling Championship four times. He was second in the inaugural National Rivers Championship in 1990 and was an England team member on the Rivers International on the River Wharfe in 1993. He was the England reserve team member for the World Championships in Italy in 1992.

His favourite fish (after salmon!) is the grayling, and his preferred style is fast-water nymphing, fishing his patterns in a dead drift.

As a Yorkshireman contributing to a book by a fellow fly-fishing Yorkshireman and a good friend, my choice of flies would hardly be representative of my fishing, the editor's, our county and indeed of the whole of the northern counties of England were I not to include a selection of the famous wet flies of our northern dales – the North Country Spider.

Of many patterns I have to choose from, three are outstanding fish catchers by virtually unanimous decision. These are the Waterhen Bloa, Snipe and Purple, and Partridge and Orange.

Just who first devised the North Country Spider is, of course, lost in antiquity. However, for those fly fishermen wishing to find more dressings of these simple yet subtle little flies, two books still circulate in specialist booksellers' catalogues. These are *Yorkshire Trout Flies* by T.E.Pritt, 1885 (which subsequently underwent a title change to *North Country Flies* in 1886) and

Brook and River Trouting by H.H.Edmonds and N.N.Lee, 1916. These two books have helped in no small way to keep the North Country Spider alive (and catching), particularly the latter which, thankfully, was reprinted as late as 1980 in facsimile.

The dressing recipes I give here are from both books, and, as you will note, they changed little during the thirty years between the two publication dates. I'm pleased to report also that little, if anything, thankfully, has changed since!

The Waterhen Bloa is probably unequalled as a fish catcher when large dark olives (*Baetis rhodani*) are hatching. The large dark olive is a two-brood fly, the main emergence period being spring and autumn, although sightings do occur in every month of the year. Quite regularly the fly hatches on the foulest of days, with a raw biting wind interspersed with squally showers – an observation recorded by Pritt. I've often mar-

Oliver Edwards fishing the River Wharfe with a weighted nymph in fast water. He watches the end of his fly line for signs of a take.

velled at the fact that the species manages to re-produce when emergence takes place on such downright inhospitable days. The result of a hatch on such days is that many large darks just sit there riding the surface, while many others struggle and fail to pull free clearly of their nymphal shuck – the so-called cripples and stillborns in modern fly-fishing parlance. The net result is that an early spring hatch of large dark olives can be a

real feast for our trout and grayling. At such times, the Waterhen Bloa can be quite lethal since a well-wetted correctly dressed pattern is uncan-nily like a half-drowned or crippled large dark olive.

This fly is a great favourite of mine and I tie it on both size 14 and 16 hooks and strive to fish it as dead drift as possible. I usually position it at the top dropper. It is doubtful whether spider pat-terns are worth fishing any deeper than the top four or five inches even when in the point posi-tion.

I am on record in print as saying that if I had to choose just one, and only one, North Country

Spider for all my river fishing, the Partridge and Orange, also known as the Orange Partridge, would be the one. I am also on record as saying that this pattern – over a season – will outfish every other fly in *Brook and River Trouting* by a long way. I haven't changed my mind.

However, to this day, I'm unsure just what trout and grayling take it for. From my own observations over many years on our Yorkshire streams, the only insects (including their aquatic stages) which have chestnut brown bodies are spent spinners, the sexually mature adults of the Ephemeroptera. I feel I would be stretching a point if I made the suggestion that the Partridge and Orange could be a spinner pattern – or could it! Edmonds and Lee seem equally at odds; they suggest the insect orders Perlidae (stoneflies) and Ephemeridae (mayflies). The one insect which does have some resemblance to the Partridge and Orange, albeit vaguely, is the nymph of the blue-winged olive (*Ephemerella ignita*). The dark brown well-barred legs and tails of this nymph are reasonably well copied by the dark speckled hackle barbs of a partridge back hackle.

Whatever fish take this pattern for, one thing is very certain, it is a most deadly pattern. I fish it at any time of the year and, from my own experience, it is just as effective for grayling as it is for trout. I nearly always fish it at the middle dropper.

Please note that the silk shade 6a, given in the Edmonds and Lee dressing, refers to Pearsalls 'Gossamer' brand of pure silk (as with all Edmonds and Lee dressings). However, be careful when purchasing No 6a today, as this is not the 6a that is indicated on the shade chart in *Brook and River Trouting*. This modern 6a is a wishy-washy pale orange, not the good strong chestnut orange of old.

The Snipe and Purple completes what many would consider to be the famous three; they are often fished together on the same leader.

This tiny scrap of nothing is a must for many North Country fly fishers, to such an extent that, without it on the leader, they would feel downright disadvantaged! It is generally considered to be first-class medicine when the iron blue (*Baetis niger*) is hatching. Edmonds and Lee suggest that its season is March to the middle of April and again in September, which more or less coincides with the iron blue's emergence period. However, I'm quite happy to use it at any time since it also performs well when any small to very small terrestrials are about. To copy the diminutive iron blue, I personally tie these on hooks smaller than Edmonds and Lee suggest, usually an 18 but sometimes even a 20. I virtually always fish it at the point position.

The Rhyacophila Larva is one of my own personal success stories. It occurred to me several years ago that a great fish-catching pattern was there just waiting to be devised, since I kept finding these one-inch long juicy green grubs in the stomachs of trout and grayling, often in good numbers. Searching the stream bed of the rivers I fish reinforced my feeling, because on the underside of almost every rock and stone which I turned over in fast riffles, I would find their pupal shelters, and every pupa has, of course, at one time been a larva! Some of our rainfed rivers harbour tens of thousands of these voracious green grubs per hundred yards of riffle. I reasoned that they had to be irresistible food for trout and grayling. I was right and I got the pattern almost right first time too. In fact I was so elated with my little green grub that I included it in a fly-tying series I was writing for one of our game-fishing magazines. Since then, I've changed the tying very little. In fact, I've really only changed the material from Fly-Rite Extra Fine Poly to Kaufmann's 4-ply Antron yarn. I also now tint the dorsal surface with an olive waterproof felt pen as well as darkening the first three segments with a black felt pen.

The pattern in its current form is absolute dynamite for grayling in autumn and winter, fished quartering upstream on a high-density leader and allowed to drift downstream with the current, just tapping the bottom. It is also a deadly summer pattern for trout, as well as grayling, and on a recent outing on one very well-known and hard-fished ticket water of the River Wharfe, it accounted for a spotted beauty of eighteen inches.

My earliest attempts at copying the very distinctive Heptagenid nymphs were only moderately successful. Feeling that the nymph's unique large head with its half-saucer shape and steeply tapering body were the key triggers, I pressed on with my quest. The three long forked tails and the gilled tapering abdomen were easy but the correctly shaped head eluded me for quite some time. Nevertheless, even these early experimental tyings caught fish. I called those early patterns Ecyonurid nymphs. However, it is obvious once you become familiar with the other two genera of the flat stone clingers that one pattern, with the correct silhouette trigger, will suffice for all the UK genera of stone clingers, eg *Ecdyonurus*, *Heptagenia* and *Rhithrogena*. All the fly dresser needs to do is simply vary the hook size, typically from say 18 to 14 (standard shank) or 16 and 18 if using a longer-shanked 'nymph' hook.

The pattern as it stands now is as developed as I wish to take it. It is extremely effective in the doldrum months of June, July and August, with a very large one doing the business in May when the large brook dun nymphs (*Ecdyonurus torrentis*) become active. The stretch I fish on the Wharfe has huge populations of the yellow may dun (*Heptagenia sulphurea*) and this artificial on a size 16 dry-fly hook (Partridge E1A) is quite lethal. I fish it absolutely dead drift in streamy water – either popply or crinkly – and, on hot sticky late afternoons when not a fish stirs, I've many times had upwards of a dozen fish when the dry-fly rods have struggled for one or two fish.

Artificial stonefly nymph patterns have never really become popular in the northern counties. I can only surmise that the reason for this lack of interest was that, in the past, when most of the dales rivers held healthy populations of large stoneflies, it was easier for anglers to catch and mount a live nymph on a hook than bother to tie one of these large awkward patterns.

However, all is not totally lost in the northern dales on the stonefly front and, if our populations of the largest *Perla*, *Perlodes* and *Dinocras* stoneflies are down, we still have quite healthy populations of the medium and small species. Of these, the nymph of the yellow Sally (*Isoperla grammatica*) is one of the most attractive with its pale yellow underside and legs and cryptically marked yellow-olive and very dark browny-olive dorsal side. Furthermore, the nymph is attractive to trout and is taken whenever it makes the fatal mistake of exposing itself.

This is one of my latest patterns and follows closely the method of construction perfected by some of the American fly-tying artists. I tie it in two forms – impressionistic and semi-realistic. The one illustrated is the semi-realistic tie which has already given a good account of itself with browns up to sixteen inches.

Waterhen Bloa (Edmonds & Lee No 2)

Pritt's dressing is dubbed with water-rat fur and omits to mention a head. His wing hackle feather is not so specific. One of the key features of this fly is the extremely sparsely dubbed body so that the silk is clearly visible through the fur. On all North Country Spider patterns the body should be tied short, typically ending in line with a point midway between the point and barb. Sometimes they are tied as short as in line with the hook point.

HOOK: Partridge L3A (D/E, medium weight, wide gape) 16 and 14 (originally size 1 or 2)

WING: Hackled with a smokey grey feather from the under coverts of a waterhen's wing (the darker side of the feather towards the head of the fly)

BODY: Yellow silk, No 4 dubbed with mole's fur

HEAD: Yellow silk

Partridge and Orange or Orange Partridge (Edmonds & Lee No 6)

Pritt's dressing omits the rib and does not mention the head. For body length see Waterhen Bloa.

HOOK: Partridge L3A size 16 (originally size 1)

WINGS: Hackled with a brown mottled (not barred) feather from a partridge neck or back

BODY: Orange silk No 6a, or orange silk No 6a ribbed with about four turns of gold wire or tinsel

HEAD: Orange silk

Snipe and Purple or Dark Snipe (Edmonds & Lee No 5)

Pritt's dressing is 'hackled with a feather from the outside of a snipe's wing' and omits to mention the head. For body length see Waterhen Bloa.

HOOK: Partridge L3A size 16 (originally size 1)

The River Wharfe in Yorkshire, typical of the Dales rivers where the North Country spider patterns evolved. Oliver Edwards dead-drifting a nymph through a productive pool.

WINGS: Hackled with the dark feather from the marginal coverts of a snipe's wing

BODY: Purple silk, No 8

HEAD: Purple silk

Rhyacophila Larva

HOOK: Partridge K4A (D/E, heavy wire, curved shank) 10 – 12

THREAD: Fine and very strong typically Kevlar or any Kevlar blend, colour yellow

WEIGHT: Narrow strip of wine bottle lead in one or two layers

ABDOMEN AND THORAX: 4-ply knitting yarn, 100% synthetic fibre, or synthetic and natural blend. Preferably with the addition of Antron, or other highly reflective 'sparkle' fibre. Colour bright mid green. Take out 1 ply, use 3 ply only

RIB: 3 – 5lb b.s. clear or dyed green mono, or a single strand of green Flashabou, a double strand of Datam Glo-Brite fluorescent floss, yellow shade 10

LEGS: Partridge grey hackle barbs dyed yellow-olive

UPPER ABDOMEN TINT: Medium olive waterproof felt pen. First three segments dotted with black waterproof felt pen.

HEAD: Yellow thread or tint yellow if using white thread sealed with Dave's Flexament

Heptagenid Nymph

HOOK: Partridge H1A (medium wire, 2X long shank) 16 – 18, or Partridge E1A (D/E, 4X fine, long shank) 14 – 18

THREAD: Danville's Spider Web

1 Waterhen Bloa
2 Partridge and Orange
3 Snipe and Purple

4 Rhyacophila Larva
5 Heptagenid Nymph
6 Yellow Sally Stonefly Nymph

WEIGHT: Narrow strip of wine bottle lead foil or fine copper wire

CEMENT: Dave's Flexament

TAILS: Pale moose mane hairs dyed yellow-olive, or any pale, stout, quick-tapering animal hair, dyed yellow-olive. **Note**: tail hairs should have good definition.

ABDOMEN: Thick polythene 0.008 inch (0.2mm) dyed yellow-olive, or yellow-olive Flexibody

UNDER ABDOMEN TINT (optional): Brown waterproof felt pen on the dorsal side; fluorescent yellow highlighter pen on the ventral side

ABDOMEN GILLS: Ostrich herl dyed yellow-olive

THORAX AND HEAD CAPSULE: Fine synthetic dubbing, golden yellow eg Davy Wotton Finesse Masterclass Blend Mc 6

HEAD CAPSULE COVER: Brown Raffene strip

LEGS: Guinea fowl undercover or flank hackle dyed yellow-olive, coated with flexible head cement and re-coated after heat-kinking to shape

WING BUDS: Dark, brick red, red grouse hackle coated with flexible head cement or clear flexible adhesive

Yellow Sally Stonefly Nymph

All the yellows are a pale 'soft' primrose yellow or could also have a hint of olive. Lemon yellows should be avoided.

HOOK: Partridge H1A (D/E, medium weight, 2X long shank) or K14ST (curved shank emerger) 14 – 16

THREAD: Danville's Spider Web

WEIGHT: Strip of wine bottle lead foil

CEMENT: Dave's Flexament

TAILS: 2 yellow-dyed light grey moose hairs or any other stout quick-tapering animal hair dyed pale greyish yellow or a fine stripped hackle quill dyed yellow (after stripping)

ABDOMEN (VENTRAL) AND THORAX: Fine synthetic dubbing, very pale yellow or very pale yellowish olive

ABDOMEN (DORSAL): Partridge speckled tail quill feather dyed yellowish olive, lacquered with flexible head cement and stroked out to make a fairly narrow strip

RIB: Fine gold (brass) wire, 7 or 8 turns (abdomen only, binding the ventral abdomen to the dorsal abdomen)

WING BUDS, PRONOTUM AND HEAD: Folded continuation of the dorsal abdomen material

LEGS: Grey partridge hackle dyed pale yellow coated with flexible head cement and re-coated after heat-kinking

ANTENNAE: Any finely tapering pale animal guard hair dyed pale yellow

Note: Very detailed tying instructions for these last three patterns can be found in Oliver Edwards's book *Oliver Edwards's Flytyer's Masterclass* being published in 1994 by Merlin Unwin Books.

TONY ENTWISTLE

NEW ZEALAND

Tony Entwistle is widely acknowledged as one of the best guides in the business and was President of the New Zealand Professional Fishing Guides Association from 1988 – 1990. He has been fishing for thirty-four of his forty-one years and in 1980 turned his back on teaching to become a professional fishing and hunting guide. He owns one of New Zealand's most established and successful trout-fishing guiding businesses, incorporating a team of top guides and a specialist fishing and hunting store.

Tony was a member of his country's team to the World Fly Fishing Championships when they were held in England, Tasmania, Finland, Wales and Italy and was on the organizing committee for New Zealand. Nearer to home, Tony has very wide experience of New Zealand's South Island where he concentrates on the big, wild brown trout of the clear waters around Nelson, Marlborough and the West Coast. His best brown weighed 10½ pounds (released).

He has written for various New Zealand fishing magazines and is a regular speaker on trout fishing and a tutor of fly casting.

These six nymphs had their birthplace and evolution in the wild, fast waters of the northern rivers of New Zealand's famed South Island. The area is a trout fisherman's paradise, with an incredible variety of freestone streams and rivers, spring creeks and lakes. In these waters the brown trout is king, averaging three to four pounds, with many bigger. Trophies in excess of ten pounds exist and are caught every year.   Fishing for such large trout in fast water requires specialist flies, especially when fishing to the more selective feeding brown trout.

The key to regular successful fishing for brown trout in the larger freestone streams is the diligent use of weighted nymphs. Twenty years ago, nymphing was not widely practised on these waters, the limiting factors being knowledge of good techniques and a suitable variety of patterns. To be successful in turbulent water a nymph needs to give the impression of life. Dubbed fur bodies are an effective way of achieving this. Fur from the Australian brush-tailed opossum, hare,

rabbit and seal are excellent. Synthetic materials like Krystal Flash and Antron can also be incorporated to good effect.

The standard New Zealand fast-water nymph is the Hare and Copper, a rougher-dressed and simpler-tying version of the old Hare's Ear. However, the productivity of the good old Hare and Copper can be easily exceeded by the wise use of a wider variety of nymphs. The collection of nymphs detailed here has evolved during the last thirteen years of guiding overseas' anglers, as we have attempted to represent more adequately the most important food sources, and find flies that are consistently more successful.

The Buller River probably provides the finest fast-water nymphing for good-sized brown trout anywhere in the world, if the angler has the skill to manage the wild water.

In nature there is no specific invertebrate that is the Buller Caddis. This nymph pattern of my devising has features from different bugs common in the Buller River.

*Tony Entwistle with a magnificent six-pound brown
trout caught on a Green Stonefly Nymph from one of the
wilderness rivers of North-West Nelson.*

TONY ENTWISTLE

1

2

3

4

5

6

1 Buller Caddis
2 Nelson Brown
3 Nesameletus
4 Pete's Coloburiscus
5 Green Stonefly Nymph
6 Red Gill

The principal influence in the Buller Caddis comes from the grey-green net-building caddis, *Aoteapsyche colonica*, common in the river's many bouldery rapids. Another major influence comes from the hellgrammite or 'Creeper' as it is known in New Zealand, *Archichauliodes diversus*. Finished with a small wingcase of peacock herl including a highlight of peacock Krystal Flash, and the distinctive black tuft tail, the Buller Caddis has proved to be a consistent fish catcher in turbulent waters. It also has particular appeal to very large trout and is often my first-choice nymph to cast to trophy trout.

The Nelson Brown is based on noted American angler Gary Borger's Red Brown Nymph. My modification uses fur from the Australian brush-tailed opossum. It is a versatile and widely productive general mayfly nymph pattern, useful throughout the season. With its bulging wingcase it fishes particularly well under an active hatch of larger mayfly species. As a modestly weighted nymph it fishes best in tandem with another weighted nymph when fishing blind and is an excellent first-choice fly when prospecting new water.

Nesameletus ornatus is a free-swimming mayfly found in the clear, fast waters of many of our forested back-country streams. Its neat torpedo shape and short tail are distinctive and are keys to be imitated in this darting mayfly.

The tail is best tied from tips of the bronze chest feathers from a ring neck pheasant. These are more durable than the tippets from the neck of a golden pheasant. The little dark tips of the tails are a major key to its success.

The rest of the fly is simple, with elements of the traditional Hare and Copper Nymph. I also gave it the addition of a simple brown fur thorax and it is important to make sure that a fine taper, without too much bulk, is achieved when forming the overall shape of the fly.

Trout can be frustratingly selective when feeding on the natural, and where many people rely on the Hare and Copper, they would do better with this pattern. Nesameletus is also a good pattern to fish in tandem with another nymph, like the Nelson Brown.

Pete's Coloburiscus was created by one of our guides, Peter Carty. It is tied to simulate the nymph of the spiny gilled mayfly, *Coloburiscus humeralis*, which is prevalent in all fast waters from October to early January. The adult of this species is represented by two famous New Zealand dry flies, the Twilight Beauty and Kakahi Queen.

The peak of the *Coloburiscus* activity is from mid-November to mid-December. While this mayfly is a prolific daytime hatcher, the trout expend most of their effort intercepting the nymphs midwater as they rise from the bottom to hatch. This can be frustrating for the dry-fly purist, surrounded by large numbers of hatching duns and only the occasional rising fish.

This pattern has now developed a significant following throughout New Zealand as anglers learn of the fish-catching power of this nymph. It is also a great general-purpose nymph.

The nymphal form of the large green stonefly, *Stenoperla prasina*, is one of the more dramatic aquatic forms in New Zealand streams. Another of the principal denizens of the fast-water environment, this is the country's largest stonefly (although not particularly large in the world of stoneflies).

Because of its distinctive green colour and appeal to trout, especially during the first part of the season, this has long been a favourite subject for New Zealand fly tyers to imitate.

This pattern is another of Peter Carty's ties and is, without a doubt, the most effective green stonefly pattern I have used. Fished singly in the roughest and toughest water, this fly accounts for a large number of big trout during the first half of the season.

'What the * * * * is that supposed to represent?' This is the usual reaction when anglers first see this fly. The Red Gill doesn't pretend to imitate any specific insect. It is, however, one of those wonderful quirks of fate that falls from the fly-tying vice from time to time, and a fly I hate to be without in my fly box.

As a guide on call you don't always have the luxury of being able to choose the weather or river conditions to fish in. Normally our rivers are the clearest water you will ever see (making the legendary gin-clear waters of some famous chalk streams look like milk in comparison). But for our area to have such a wide variety of rivers and streams takes rain, and plenty of it. As any angler who has fished in New Zealand can tell you, heavy rain can be expected at almost any time!

When heavy rain brings the rivers up in spate they generally colour quickly. Fortunately they clear again just as quickly but for the day or two when they are coloured, a guide needs something special in the fly box to continue fishing successfully. These are the conditions for which I designed the Red Gill, and it excels in them. It is a high-visibility fly to be used in cloudy and dirty water and on very dull days, when most anglers would give up any hope of catching a fish. The fluorescent green body, the red wool gills and sparkle yarn wingcases with Krystal Flash highlight, are all used to accentuate the visibility of what is unashamedly an attractor fly.

Buller Caddis

HOOK: Tiemco TMC 2302 (D/E, 2XL, slightly humped shank) size 8 – 12

THREAD: Black monocord

TAIL: Black opossum or squirrel tail cut short, cut at an angle to accentuate the hook bend

RIB: Dark copper wire wound with two turns through the thorax

UNDERBODY: Five or six lengths of lead wire laid lengthways extending slightly around the bend. Lay to the side and on top of the shank only

ABDOMEN: Blue-grey opossum fur

THORAX: Brown opossum fur, well picked out

WINGCASE: Five peacock herls (which can be improved by including three strands of peacock Krystal Flash)

Nelson Brown

HOOK: Kamasan B830 size 12 – 12

THREAD: Black monocord

UNDERBODY: Five or six pieces of lead wire layered at the thorax only, on the top and sides of the shank only

TAIL: Red-brown hackle fibres with one or two turns of thread under to flare

RIB: Fine, dark copper wire, with two turns through the thorax

ABDOMEN: Red-brown opossum or dyed hare belly fur, tied slim

THORAX: Darker brown opossum fur, tied bulky and well picked out

WINGCASE: Peacock herls (which can be improved by including 4 – 5 strands of peacock Krystal Flash)

Nesameletus

After coating the shank with head cement, wind on the lead wire and cover with tying thread. The finished nymph should be a slim torpedo shape.

HOOK: Kamasan B830 size 12 – 14

THREAD: Black monocord

UNDERBODY: Wound lead wire

TAIL: Black-tipped whisks from a bronze chest feather of a ring neck pheasant

RIB: Dark copper wire

ABDOMEN: Chopped and well-blended hare's fur

THORAX: Brown opossum fur

Pete's Coloburiscus

Wind the shank with thread and coat with head cement. Wind the lead wire and cover with thread.

HOOK: Kamasan B830 or Tiemco TMC 5262 (D/E, 2XL, 2X heavy) size 10 – 14

THREAD: Black monocord

TAIL: Dark brown hackle fibres

RIB: Fine dark brown copper wire wound opposite way to the ostrich herls

UNDERBODY: Wound lead wire in the middle two-thirds of the shank and flattened with pliers

ABDOMEN: Dark brown ostrich herl, trimmed top and bottom

THORAX: Dyed brown hare's fur, well picked out

WINGCASE: Brown latex, about $3/16$ inch (4–5mm) wide

HEAD: Black thread

Green Stonefly Nymph

Wind the shank with thread, then wind the small dubbing ball and tie in the tails. Coat the hook with head cement and wind on the lead wire. Tie in the Swannundaze, wind thread to the eye and back to the bend. Flatten the lead wire. Dub the body material and wind half-way down. Rib with Swannundaze, tie off and trim. Dub a small amount of thorax material and wind two turns on the hook. Cut ¼ inch strip of latex. Fold in half lengthways and cut at 45 degrees to form wingpad. Tie in latex so the 'V' just covers the dubbed thorax. Repeat with another two turns of dubbing and another 'V'. Tie in latex for wingcase. Tie in soft hackle by the tip. Dub thorax. Pull legs feather over thorax and tie down. Pull latex over legs and tie down. Tie biots on each side of the head pointing forward, tie off and cement head.

HOOK: Tiemco TMC 2302, size 8 – 10

THREAD: Green monocord

UNDERBODY: Lead wire flattened with pliers

TAIL: Yellow biots, widely spaced with a small dubbing ball between

RIB: Pale transparent olive Swannundaze (#8)

BODY: Pale green dubbing

WINGCASE AND WINGPADS: Olive-green latex

THORAX: Olive-green dubbing

ANTENNAE: Green biots

LEGS: Green-dyed soft hackle

Red Gill

Apply head cement to the shank and wrap with lead wire over the middle three-quarters.

HOOK: Kamasan B175 size 10

THREAD: Fluorescent green single-strand floss

UNDERBODY: Wound lead wire

TAIL: Light ginger hackle fibres

RIB: Dark copper wire

ABDOMEN: Green floss

GILLS: A short length of bright red wool protruding by about $\frac{1}{16}$ inch each side of the rear of the wingcases

THORAX: Blend of yellow fur mixed with clear Antron, well picked out

WINGCASE: Light grey Antron with 3 strands of pearl Krystal Flash for a highlight

MOGENS ESPERSEN

DENMARK

Mogens Espersen, born in 1942, is a foreign news reporter with Danish Broadcasting. He fishes whenever foreign rulers, despots or warlords permit, which is not as often as he would like. He is the originator of several fly patterns and is a specialist on salt-water fly fishing for sea trout.

Mogens has written several books on fly fishing, fly tying, and other angling subjects, his most recent in 1993 being a book on a history of fly tying. He is a regular contributor of articles and illustrations to Danish and Scandinavian angling journals. He teaches fly tying and fishes mainly in Nordic waters for trout and salmon.

N ever trust trout. Some days they will inhale anything a fly tyer happens to wrap around a hook shank or even a bare one. If, after such a day you think you are almost able to walk on the stream, be assured that trout on your next outing will reject even the most juicy, beautiful and edible flies ever invented by ingenious fly tyers.

From time to time, trout behave as if they know more about flies than any other living being. It is the blank days, and not the red-letter ones which are few and far between, that lead to contemplation and experiments at the vice from which flies, and dreams, are hatched. Trout are experts in nothing but survival and are thus hard to fool. With luck nobody will ever stumble upon that guaranteed combination of silk, fur and feather; it would be as hellish as in the famous Skues tale.

Flies capable of deceiving trout reasonably often may be devised but the spotted judges will see that it does not happen too frequently. This means that a tribe of soft killers are the workhorses of my fly box for trout and grayling. I fish them with great confidence as they have been with me for more years than I care to admit. They have caught their fair share as they have often been on my leader. Confidence is important in fly fishing.

Denmark is a great country for fly fishers, as most of the year-long season you must choose between equally tempting possibilities. You might try for browns or grayling in the streams; deceive rainbows in lakes; venture for sea trout in rivers; fish in chestwaders along any Danish beach for sea trout migrating and feeding in saltwater; or you might try to lure salmon which are now back after many years of conservation.

I tend to keep my flies simple, as trout and grayling do not, after all, change their tastes over the years; only fly fishermen and fly tyers do. Of course, my flies develop over the years, but I like, anyway, to consider them not too fixed, but rather steps dictated by trial and error. I like to think they hatched from my vice, but I am quite sure I have stolen ideas and materials from elsewhere. The six flies I have chosen underline perhaps what might be described as a soft Danish way with trout. After all, I like to spend more time fly fishing than fly tying.

Against this conservative background, it is not surprising that my first choice at the stream is a traditional fly in not very elaborate disguise. The Gold Ribbed Hare's Ear was an early favourite of mine, as it was easy to tie, looked edible, and certainly attracted trout. I am not one to improve on a very good pattern, as improvement in this case obviously would be for the worse but like most fishermen I have my own GRHE variant. Mine is the Partridge Flymph, very much within the tradition and hardly an innovation, neither elaborately dressed nor bursting with ingenuity.

I discovered that it hatched many years ago when I traced fly-fishing history from Scotsman, W.C. Stewart and spiders, and Yorkshire flies, via Skues and his nymphs, to Americans James Leisenring and Vernon S. Hidy. I found the connections obvious, as they followed the same line of thought – choosing flies with a soft, seductive hackle. Leisenring and Hidy coined the term 'flymph', a cross between a fly and nymph, designed to allude life and to fish the critical inches below the surface film. Many today would term the flymph an emerger – an insect, a future dun or sedge, being neither nymph (pupa) or mature – and thus fast food for trout and grayling.

Hidy did tie a March Brown Flymph, which was, in fact, a GRHE with a partridge hackle. The Partridge Flymph is to me a rare example of a fly devised jointly at the vice from books and the experiences of fly fishermen – and eaten by trout. Mixed wool from the base of a hare's ear, a soft partridge feather, and a hint of gold is the proven combination, only I wanted a longish very soft tail to add 'life' to the thing. Soft fibres from a summer duck substitute – dark teal or brown mallard tinted yellow-brownish proved to be good.

The Partridge Flymph confirms what I mean about stealing ideas. Plagiarism should be acceptable among fly fishermen, provided it is freely acknowledged.

The fly is definitely from the GRHE tribe. The main feature is perhaps the pulsating hackle, the soft mobile tail and the ragged body. I often wind the hackle semi-palmered the Stewart way to add 'kick'.

It should be fished upstream, as all Flymphs should be, when trout are bulging. Dead drift is the usual way but an occasional twitch sometimes helps to deceive doubting trout. I tie it on light or heavier hooks to fish different depths from the top of the water to a few inches below.

I am not a strong believer in exact imitation; I stick to Skues' observation that most successful flies are probably caricatures. I am not able to compete with nature, which is clear from my Calf's Tail Emerger. I do not know what it is, except to say that it has some of the features of a hatching dun. The white wing is seldom found in nature, but I need a fly easily visible to me. Although being a dun, it even works when sedges are on the water, which is fine as sedges are more prominent in many Danish rivers than duns. The clipped deer hair thorax is there to provide floatability, otherwise it is a member of the GRHE family.

My Hatching Elk is a trouble shooter for problem fish feeding on emergers. It floats flush in the film catching browns in streams and rainbows in lakes. I like to think of it as a caricature of a wide range of hatching duns. In a way this fly is my fly-tying philosophy wound around a hook: natural materials, soft and edible looking. I think – but I do not know if trout agree – that soft materials give the angler an extra split-second to tighten, as trout seem to keep the fly a little longer in their mouths. I think stiff materials are more often rejected, but even if I reached the impressive age of Skues, I would not know for sure.

I tied the Hatchin' Something because a rather large soft morsel landing softly sometimes produces trout. That is why I gave it a parachute hackle. Polypropylene yarn is great to wind a parachute hackle around as it is both flexible yet firm. The colours vary a great deal in my fly boxes. The creature might eventually hatch into a dun or sedge. It is a general fly for the cream of the season when trout and grayling rise freely.

En bette Swot ('a tiny black one' in a local dialect) has from time to time proved as stimulating to trout as the drink which gave it its name is to fly fishermen. The poison, known as the national dram of Jutland, is black coffee with a liberal dash of akvavit (a very strong Scandanavian drink, distilled from grain or potatoes) added. It's good for celebrating trout, and even better for keeping you warm and confident when trout are brainwashed by tiny black insects.

The fly was certainly stolen. I would never be without Oliver Kite's Imperial and the thorax style he stressed, as it leads to a fly floating high with its hackle tips fingering the water. En bette Swot was tied originally for Norwegian browns in a tumbling river where swallows and trout were competing for duns after a heavy rainstorm. The trout needed the stimulation of an unsinkable fly floating high.

The Jysk Chillimps is an old standby and as Danish as bacon, salted butter and minority governments. It is a wet pattern invented some fifty years ago by Danish fly fisher Valdemar P. Haugaard. It resulted from an enviable chance of free fishing in a Jutland stream, and is a summary of what Haugaard found in trout autopsies – a cross, as he said, between a shrimp and a sedge larva. It was tied from materials at hand: a green-ish-blue pile from Haugaard's overcoat, medium brown cock hackles and whisks from a lady's hat. The fly works best fished downstream to make the palmered hackle pulsate, or it can be used for deep nymphing with a few turns of lead around the forward part of the shank.

Partridge Flymph

The hackle may be wound with the tip tied in first, with the good side facing the eye, and then wound backwards towards the body. The thread can be secured behind the hackle to ensure it has a 'kick' or wound through to the eye. The hackle can also be wound Stewart-style by tying in the feather by the tip and spinning it round the thread prior to winding backwards. It may not look as tidy but a very 'living' hackle is produced.

HOOK: Partridge GRS2A (for a heavier fly) or Mustad 94833 or Partridge L2A (lighter) size 14 – 16

THREAD: Light orange

TAIL: Summer duck substitute

BODY: Mixed hairs from the base of a hare's ear or lighter from a hare's mask spun in a dubbing loop

RIB: Finest oval gold

HACKLE: Soft, well-marked partridge, with fibres two to three times longer than the hook gape

Calf's Tail Emerger

Wind on the body fibres to cover the wing roots which have been secured by the tying thread and a dab of varnish. The tips of the wing should protrude over the eye. Secure the body in front of the wing then fold the wing back to tie in a small bundle of deer hair in muddler-style, and repeat the deer hair. Carefully trim the thorax, avoiding the wing fibres.

HOOK: Tiemco TMC 100 (D/E, 1XF, wide gape) size 12 – 14

THREAD: Medium brown (do not cover the front third of the shank)

TAIL: Light badger saddle fibres, tied well into the bend and well spread

BODY: Mixed fur from the hare's mask, spun in a dubbing loop and tied into the bend and tapered

WING: White calf's tail

THORAX: Deer hair spun and clipped muddler-style, to cover the front third of the shank

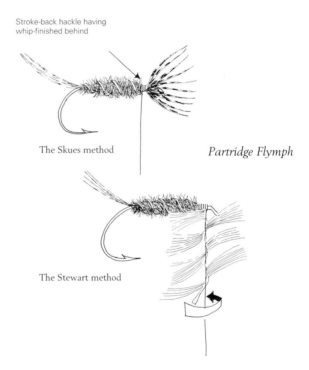

Stroke-back hackle having whip-finished behind

The Skues method

Partridge Flymph

The Stewart method

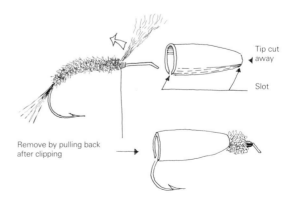

Calf's Tail Emerger

Tip cut away

Slot

Remove by pulling back after clipping

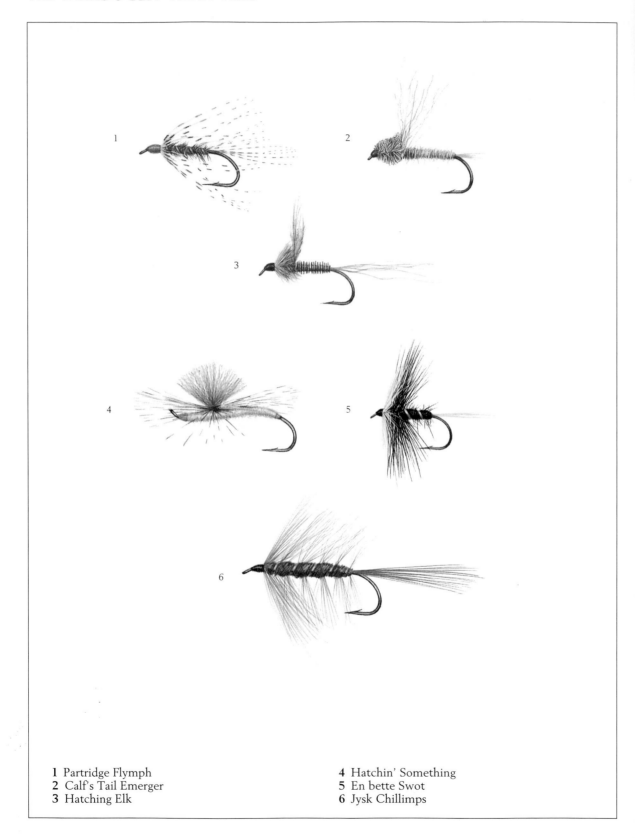

1 Partridge Flymph
2 Calf's Tail Emerger
3 Hatching Elk
4 Hatchin' Something
5 En bette Swot
6 Jysk Chillimps

En bette Swot

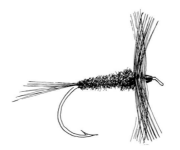

Hatching Elk

Make a dubbing loop in front of the body and wind the thread forward to tie in the partridge fibres with the points over the eye. Wind the thorax, at the same time pulling back the wing fibres into position.

HOOK: Mustad 94833 size 12 – 14

THREAD: Brown

TAIL: 4 – 5 elk hairs, fairly long

BODY: 2 grey heron herls, tied in together

THORAX: Mixed furs from a hare's forehead spun in a dubbing loop

WING: Downy fibres from the body feather of a partridge (those you would normally discard)

Hatchin' Something

The hackle is easier to wind if a base of tying thread is wound round the base of the wing as a support.

HOOK: Partridge GRS7MMB (U/E, curved nymph hook) size 14 – 18

THREAD: Light orange or yellow

BODY: Fly-Rite or other poly-fur to match the natural

WING: Polypropylene yarn folded and re-folded, colour to match the natural's wing or for visibility

HACKLE: Grizzle cock would in parachute style round the base of the wing

En bette Swot

HOOK: Partridge L3A (D/E, wide gape) size 12 – 26

THREAD: Black

BODY: Black seal's fur or substitute with a pronounced thorax

HACKLE: Black cock with a cream cock wound in front. The concave sides of the hackles should face each other and should occupy about a third of the shank

Jysk Chillimps

HOOK: Partridge SH3 (slightly long shank) size 10 – 14

THREAD: Black

TAIL: Scarlet soft hackle fibres, tied rather long

BODY: Greenish blue darning wool, tapering slightly to the rear

RIB: Fine oval gold, wound through the palmered hackle

HACKLES: Medium natural red for the body hackle, with a slightly bigger hackle at the front.

Note: Mogens Espersen originally included a Squirrel Sedge which was an almost exact duplicate of the pattern of the same name submitted by Lars-Åke Olsson. Mogens kindly agreed to include a substitute.

Hatchin' Something

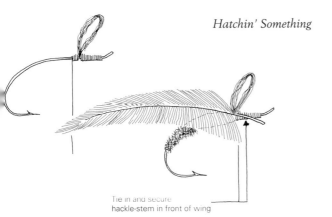

Tie in and secure
hackle-stem in front of wing

MARJAN FRATNIK AND
BOZIDAR VOLJC

SLOVENIA

Marjan Fratnik is a retired business executive who, although Slovenian-born and fishes extensively in his home country, now resides in Switzerland and Italy. He can remember his first trout on a fly, caught on a Red Spinner, at the age of sixteen, on 16 June 1935. He is a contributor to Italian, Slovenian and German fly-fishing magazines. Marjan is one of the sources for the revival of interest in cul de canard feathers now proving popular across the world. They have been used by Marjan since the early 1980s.

Dr Bozidar Voljc is a Professor of Medicine and the Minister of Health in the Republic of Slovenia. He has co-authored a number of fly-fishing books and is a contributor to German, Italian and Slovenian journals.

Marjan Fratnik

Slovenia is a small country but a real fly-fishing Eldorado with probably the largest number of fly fishermen per head of population in the world and a fly-fishing tradition that goes back to the end of the eighteenth century. Alpine streams, spring-fed creeks and chalk streams provide prime fly-fishing waters which rank alongside the best in Europe. Rivers like the Soca, flowing from Alpine limestone are a cerulean blue lined with white gravel and flow through scenic mountain valleys. The Soca contains brown trout, rainbows, marbled trout and grayling. Even in August the water temperature does not exceed 55°F (13°C). Amongst Slovenia's other chalk streams the jewel is the Unec which is rated as probably the best in Europe. In addition to its magnificent setting its cool waters are home to good brown trout and excellent grayling which feed avidly on the incredible populations of mayflies, sedges and stoneflies.

Another top-class chalk stream not far from the Unec is the Obrh (pronounce it as you can because the correct way is impossible), shorter and narrower than the Unec and home only to brown trout but they are of considerable size. One of the interesting features of the river is the massive population of *Siphlonurus* flies. On some days it is impossible to fish because the river surface is so covered with drifting flies there is nowhere to land an artificial. In years past the local farmers would collect the dead flies and use them as fertilizer on the fields.

The Slovenian rivers are clean and unpolluted, flowing through valleys of meadows and woodland against a spectacular mountain background. They provide some of the most beautiful, wild rivers in Europe with predictable and prolific fly hatches. It is no wonder that they are beginning to attract fly fishers not just from the rest of Europe but from as far afield as North America and Japan. Many of these visitors come from the grayling fishing and not for the trout. This is the big challenge for both domestic and foreign fly fishers. On all Slovenian rivers, especially in autumn, the grayling are extremely selective, freaky and suspicious and will come up to look at the fly repeatedly only to go back and renew their interest all over again or disappear.

My F Fly series using the cul de canard feathers were inspired by the Swiss author Jules Rindlisbacher. In 1977 I read his book in which he wrote 'If after trying most flies you have a blank day there is only one thing which may help: the Entenpurzel fly'. I had no idea what the author was talking about nor could any dictionary offer a translation of the word for these unusual feathers. I ordered flies from Rindlisbacher but it wasn't until a year later that I discovered that the unusual materials were cul de canard feathers from around a duck's preen gland and had been used in the French and Swiss Jura region for over a hundred years. The flies were excellent fish catchers but expensive as they were unusable after each catch. After trial and error I developed in 1983 the F Fly without a body or hackle and just one feather for hooks 18 – 20, two feathers for size 14 – 16 and three for size 12. The only change I have made to my original version has been a very sparsely dubbed grey body. As far I'm concerned the change doesn't make any difference to the fish. The fly which did not resemble a normal fly, was given to friends to test on Continental and British waters and was viewed with great suspicion. After a very short time it was widely used and acclaimed as one of the best trout and grayling patterns. It is easy to tie, floats like a cork and is very visible.

In 1985 I started experimenting with the F Sedge, which again is simplicity itself and maximizes the benefits of cul de canard. I adopted it two years later after it was tested on the Continent and in England. Nothing has changed with respect to the original version and it is a good fly at any time of the day.

In my fifty-eight years of fly fishing I have always tried to figure out why trout take a certain fly, nymph or streamer which looks nothing like anything found in or on the water. Having found some almost impossible things in trout and grayling stomachs – cigarette filters, pieces of charcoal, a yellow pencil point, a small mouse and a sixteen-centimetre long and four-centimetre wide wood stick – I convinced myself that these fish will sometimes take anything food-like but also other definitely non-food items. Therefore I decided to tie a monster fly which should not resemble anything living in or near the water. Against all schools of fly-tying tradition I tied the final version of the Netopir Fly. No tail, no body, no hackles, but large and made simply of black thread and five to eight CDC feathers, depending on the quality. It is fished like any other dry fly. After each catch wash it and dry it with a few false casts. It floats like nothing else, it rides the waves and is visible as far as you can cast it. I wouldn't like to guess what fish take it for, but I know only that especially in the late afternoon and in the evenings they grab it constantly and without hesitation.

Bozidar Voljc

About twenty years ago I became deeply involved in the entomology of interest to fly fishermen and of all the aquatic flies, the *Trichoptera*, sedges have been my main fascination. My attention to the sedges stemmed from the late May and early June evenings when thousands of all types of insects would swarm over my rivers and when matching the hatch was extremely difficult, if not completely impossible. Therefore I started to observe the sedges more intensely and started a love affair with them that has remained undiminished although my attitude has matured and I've calmed down.

I am still of the opinion that palmered flies are the best imitation of the adult sedges. The roof-shaped wings were such a prominent feature I decided that my artificials could not do without them. In my experiments and testing with natural and synthetic materials I discovered that natural materials were better because they were lighter and more naturally coloured to match the wings of various sedges. Among the natural materials the best were the feathers of various birds. The problem was that glued feathers did not resist the casting strain and the teeth of trout. The glues available at the time were unsuitable. I was looking for an appropriate support for the feathers and found that non-elastic ladies tights were the best solution. I spread the stocking mesh tight on a frame and glued the underside of the feather to the mesh so that the shiny upper side was visible. The feathers were then singly cut out, trimmed to shape and tied over the palmered body. As the final touch a hackle was wound behind the eye.

The sedges were tested with friends for a whole year before I wrote about them for the German magazine *Der Fliegenfischer* in 1975. I soon found out that duck and other waterfowl feathers were the best due to their strong structure and fat content but partridge, pheasant and hen feathers were also excellent for the imitation of different sedge species. With the mesh wings it was possible to tie large flies which were more resistant to the wear of casting and trout's teeth. Eventually I succeeded in finding suitable feathers for all the Slovenian sedges, from the spring grannom to the late autumn caperer. The Slovenica Sedge range was shown to the world for the first time in Taff Price's books, *Fly Patterns* and *The Angler's Sedge*. They have become better known in English as the Voljc Sedges.

These sedges should be fished like other sedge patterns, either as specific imitations during a hatch or as egg-laying females. Often, if fish are rising but are refusing the floating sedge, a pull underwater will induce a savage take. They are also excellent search flies for use without a hatch in progress.

After the sedges I created the stonefly series called Carniolica. It was based on the reversed glue-treated feathers as used by the French in their Altiery pattern. I believe that these feathers so prepared are the near perfect imitation of the *Plecoptera* species, from the needle fly to the large stonefly.

Flies in the stonefly series are fished like any other dry fly but are most effective when the egg-laying females are returning to the river surface. The Yellow Sally, a common species in many European countries, is illustrated. Other species are copied by appropriately coloured materials.

The edible dormouse is constantly present in many Slovenian traditions and literature. In the autumn they are trapped and eaten on traditional dormouse picnic evenings. It is a culinary tradition dating back to the Romans. The skins provide one of the warmest furs available and the tails are an excellent source of materials for the bodies of nymphs and dry flies. I noticed that because of the extremely high fat content the tips of the dormouse tail hairs are very shiny. Since it is almost impossible to eliminate the fat the points remain shiny even under water after long usage and abusage. Furthermore because the tail hair is rather coarse the small spiky hairs make a shaggy body and provide some mobility to the fly.

The F Fly

Although this fly may be tied without any body materials it is also possible to colour-match the body of a natural dun with a fine dubbing.

HOOK: Standard 12 – 20

THREAD: Black or grey 8/0

BODY: Tying thread or very sparse muskrat underfur

HACKLE AND WING: The hackle and wing are combined – one small cul de canard (duck preen gland) feather for hook size 18 – 20; two small feathers for size 16; three for size 12 – trimmed to shape

The F Sedge

HOOK: 12 – 14 standard or slightly long shank

THREAD: Brown

BODY: Very fine beige dubbing tied very slim

HACKLE: Palmered brown (natural red) cock

WING: Two cul de canard feathers, tied slightly longer than the hook

The Netopir Dry Fly

HOOK: Size 12 – 14

THREAD: Black

HACKLES: Between 5 and 8 cul de canard feathers, depending on their quality and density, tied in tightly one after the other and wound to the eye without being overlapped.

Voljc Sedge – Cinnamon Sedge

Other sedge patterns can be imitated with different coloured materials.

HOOK: Size 12 – 16

THREAD: Black

BODY: Palmered dark ginger cock with the upper fibres trimmed away

WING: Hen mallard body feather, glued to a non-elastic stocking mesh then trimmed to shape and tied in a tight 'V', extending beyond the body

HACKLE: Dark ginger cock

MARJAN FRATNIK AND BOZIDAR VOLJC

1 The F Fly
2 The F Sedge
3 The Netopir Dry Fly

4 Cinnamon Voljc Sedge
5 Carniolica Yellow Sally
6 Dormouse Nymph

Carniolica Series – Yellow Sally

HOOK: Size 12 – 16

THREAD: Yellow

BODY: Palmered yellow-dyed cock

WING: Yellow-dyed reverse-feather treated with PVC glue

HEAD: Yellow-dyed cock

Dormouse Nymph

HOOK: Size 10 – 14

THREAD: Black

TAIL: Dormouse tail fibres

UNDERBODY (optional): Fine lead or copper wire

ABDOMEN AND THORAX: Dubbed dormouse tail fur, more thickly wound at the thorax

WINGCASE (optional): Any dark grey feather

RENÉ HARROP

USA

As a native Indian René Harrop's history as a hunter and fisherman goes back many centuries. It is with an Indian's perspective that he has approached fly fishing and fly tying. Indian people possess a reverence for all living creatures and even though he does not pursue them for food, trout and the organisms upon which they feed have been essential for his family's survival. He and his wife Bonnie have been professional fly tyers for twenty-five years and are now joined by their daughter Leslie and son Shayne.

René's forty-seven years have been spent in the part of Idaho that adjoins Yellowstone National Park. Idaho, Montana and Wyoming contain enough trout waters to occupy several lifetimes and he seldom travels elsewhere. For a trout fisherman it is the perfect home.

He is a self-taught fly tyer but acknowledges and respects the work of great tyers including Puyans, Whitlock, Schweibert, Gartside, Talleur and numerous others. For many years René has written and illustrated fishing and fly-tying articles and has contributed to more than a dozen books.

As a lifetime resident of the trout-rich region of Yellowstone National Park, it has been my good fortune to have some of the world's greatest fly fishing right in my own back yard. As a supplier of premium trout flies it has also been my challenge to stay abreast of the changes in what the trout and my customers will accept.

Fly fishing has become a fashionable American activity in recent years and the number of practitioners has increased by tens of thousands. Few productive trout waters have eluded discovery and the days of quiet solitude are but fond memories for the fly fisher of today. Fortunately, through thoughtful management, there is still good fishing to be had but the best waters are likely to be crowded during the peak of the season. The practice of catch and release has prevented the depletion of trout populations and in most instances there are enough fish to go around. The legendary streams of Montana, Idaho and Wyoming still deserve their reputation and status as trout producers but anyone who visits this mystical region is destined for disappointment if they

expect the fishing to be fast and easy.

The effect of heavy and unrelenting angler pursuit has produced an elevated ability in the trout population in general to elude capture. Many anglers who come away with the impression that the fishing in Yellowstone Country is bad are wrong. The trout are there but they are also very difficult to fool. Angling pressure is partly to blame but it falls short of explaining completely the selective feeding behaviour that has allowed trout to identify effectively the difference between an artificial fly and the real thing. Logic and science tell us that any creature responds to experience and that repeated contact with the enemy produces conditioned behaviour that contributes to that creature's chances of survival. Catch and release saves a trout and that is good; it also produces a memory of frightening experience that causes a released trout to become progressively more difficult to catch. For the angler, and particularly for the novice, catch and release is a two-edged sword. Healthy and sizeable trout populations assure the continuation of our sport but excessively elusive trout can be a frustration

The Yellowstone River in Yellowstone Park. Mike Lawson playing a cutthroat trout.

especially for the individual whose enjoyment of fishing is proportionate to the number and size of the fish he hooks and lands.

The majority of the world's trout fishers do not live in close proximity to productive water. The average fly fisher also enters the game when he or she is an adult with defined and often unrealistic expectations that act as a barrier to the accomplishment of success. Many take an inappropriate approach to fishing with fly rod by comparing it to tennis, golf or skiing. Fly fishing, like shooting, is not an athletic endeavour and the opponent is not human. Physical skills and specialized equipment are indeed important but success depends upon numerous factors that extend beyond mechanical abilities. The most accomplished fly caster I have ever known is not a very effective fisherman even though he can drop a fly in a teacup at sixty feet and can double haul a cast that is longer than a city block. Like a host of others this angler underplays the importance of onstream awareness and a comprehensive understanding of a trout's environment and behaviour. Technology has produced incalculable improvements in fly-fishing tackle that make the act of fishing more comfortable and efficient. The best rod, reel, line or accessory will not by themselves, however, make you a better angler. Success today involves far more than merely tossing out a fly that is somewhat close to a living insect and waiting for the fish to take. Much of a trout's life is spent trying to elude the army of anglers that has become part of its daily existence and it has become very good at doing just that.

Serious fly-tying anglers have an indisputable bias towards the value and importance of a well-designed and well-tied fly. They are skilled observers of trout and also of the living organisms upon which they feed. Changes occur constantly and any fly fisher's success is dependent upon his or her ability to be alert to those changes and to adapt to them as well. It is important to remember that trout, like any other wild animal, relies upon all of its senses to detect danger. Historically we have relied upon visual deception as the primary criterion for trout-fly efficiency. Logically, however, we must also deceive the other senses such as smell, touch and hearing if we hope to convince a large, wary trout that what we are offering is real.

As one who has spurned synthetic fly-tying materials I was particularly impressed with the arrival in the US of a European fly-tying discovery that is natural and also uniquely effective in dealing with the challenge of insect duplication. Preen feathers from waterfowl, or cul de canard as they have become commonly known worldwide, have greatly influenced my personal fly tying and improved my catch rate dramatically during the three years I have been using them. I can truthfully say that in what approaches fifty years of fly fishing and tying flies few, if any, natural materials I have tried can equal cul de canard in producing the life-giving effect that has become so important on hard-fished waters.

The fishing I prefer is the hatch matching that is found on spring creeks, tailwaters and meadow streams. Big trout are especially appealing to me, not because they are big but because they are more experienced and represent a greater challenge. A large trout in hard-fished water has more than likely been caught and released on numerous occasions. Some are so elusive as to be all but impossible to fool. They seem selective not only to the distinct life stages of aquatic insects but to the interim or transitional phases as well. The natural buoyancy, scent and texture of cul de canard can scarcely be equalled in bringing a full range of life-giving qualities to an artificial fly.

It may seem strange or extreme to accept six different patterns as literal descriptions of a single insect but in the world where I fish the patterns are valid. They are inspired by reality and reflect the actual complexity of a single hatch. Each fly has proven itself not just once or twice but many times over a number of years. These flies and their reasons for being can be attributed to the ongoing evolution of our sport brought on primarily by its ever-increasing popularity. Fly fishing and fly tying today is not necessarily better or worse than it was, it is just different.

Tying note: Harrop fine natural dubbing is an extremely fine exotic fleece that is of the highest quality. Uniquely, it is processed with preen oil from the duck's preen glands to ensure maximum water-repellency. A fine natural dubbing is a suitable substitute. Harrop fine natural dubbing is not heavily processed with preen oil to make it float. I would suggest that neutral buoyancy is obtained which makes the dubbing much more versatile. I use this dubbing for nymph and emerger styles, many of which are not intended to float on the surface.

The small amount of preen oil does contribute some flotation value but it is minimal. We add the oil to eliminate dryness in the fibre which en-hances the 'workability' or ease with which it can be used to make tight, smooth-tapered flies. We prefer to describe the dubbing as a multi-purpose product.

Cul de Canard Transitional Nymph

The beginning of the transition, or change from nymph to dun, first appears when the enclosed winged insect breaks through the wingcase of the nymph. This style features a basic nymphal configuration but the bulging wingcase indicates the colour of the emerging dun – in this case a blue-winged olive. Emergence usually occurs close to or in the surface film. A greased leader or small strike indicator can be used for a shallow subsurface presentation. A partially submerged position is especially effective. Dress only the thorax portion with preen oil floatant which will cause the front of the fly to be suspended in the film and the back portion to sink.

HOOK: TMC 200 curved shank, medium weight

THREAD: 6/0 waxed

TAIL: 3 – 4 mottled turkey hackle fibres

RIB: Fine wire

ABDOMEN: Coarse dubbing to match the colour of the natural nymph

WINGCASE: 2 cul de canard feathers tied in by the tips and folded loosely over the thorax. Wingcase should duplicate the colour of the dun

THORAX: As for abdomen

LEGS: 6 – 8 turkey hackle fibres equally divided on each side of the thorax

Cul de Canard Captive Dun

This fly depicts an emerging dun that has freed about 50% of itself from the nymphal shuck. The rear portion is intended to sink and the front portion to float. If floatant is needed, apply only to the front part of the fly and use only preen oil fly dressing. Fish it like a dry fly.

HOOK: TMC 100 wide-gape dry fly

THREAD: 6/0 waxed

TAIL: Tuft of marabou to match the nymph colour, tied over 3 – 4 turkey hackle fibres

ABDOMEN: Marabou fibres to match the nymph colour, twisted together and wrapped like herl

TRAPPED WING: 2 cul de canard feathers tied in by the tips and folded loosely over the thorax. Colour should match the wing of the dun

THORAX: Harrop fine natural dubbing to match the colour of the dun

LEGS: 10 – 12 cul de canard feathers divided equally on each side of the thorax

Cul de Canard Transitional Dun

The wings of this pattern are upright but it still shows an attached nymphal shuck. It represents a helpless insect that cannot escape and is popular because it is easy to see on the water.

HOOK: TMC 100 wide-gape dry fly

THREAD: 6/0 waxed

TAIL: Tuft of coarse dubbing to match the nymph colour, tied over 3 – 4 turkey hackle fibres

ABDOMEN: Harrop fine natural dubbing to match the natural's colour

LEGS: Butts of cul de canard wings tied back along the sides of the fly and clipped even with the back of the abdomen

Cul de Canard Floating Nymph/ Emerger

Environmental extremes such as cold, heat, wind or rainy weather can hamper the ability of a mayfly dun to reach adequate development to escape. A downwing posture can signify vulnerability, and evokes an eager response from hungry trout. This is a versatile fly that should be presented with a natural dead drift.

HOOK: TMC 100 wide-gape dry fly

THREAD: 6/0 waxed

TAIL: 3 – 4 turkey hackle fibres

RIB: Fine wire

RENÉ HARROP

1 Cul de Canard Transitional Nymph
2 Cul de Canard Captive Dun
3 Cul de Canard Transitional Dun
4 Cul de Canard Floating Nymph/Emerger
5 Cul de Canard Tailwater Dun
6 Cul de Canard Biot Spinner

ABDOMEN: Harrop fine natural dubbing to colour-match the natural

WINGS: 2 cul de canard feathers arranged to flare away from each other and mounted in the normal wing location. Colour should match the natural's wing

LEGS: 8 – 10 turkey hackle fibres tied in at the throat

THORAX: As for the abdomen

Cul de Canard Tailwater Dun

A realistic imitation of the fully developed dun, tied without a hackle, is often the most effective way to imitate this familiar stage. This soft and buoyant style is extremely useful when trout key on the upright-winged stage of the mayfly.

HOOK: TMC 100 wide-gape dry fly

THREAD: 6/0 waxed

TAIL: 6 – 10 still cock hackle fibres divided equally on each side of a small ball of dubbing

BODY: Harrop fine natural dubbing to colour-match the natural

WING: 2 cul de canard feathers arranged to flare away from each other and mounted in the normal wing position

LEGS: Butts of cul de canard wings tied back along the sides of the fly and clipped even with the rear of the abdomen

Cul de Canard Biot Spinner

The spinner stage of a mayfly occurs after the final moult. It is the time when the insects mate and return to the water to lay their eggs and die. The outstretched wings lying flush on the water identify this stage. Spinners are important because they cannot escape and trout feed ravenously on the helpless insects.

HOOK: TMC 100 wide-gape dry fly

THREAD: 6/0 waxed

TAILS: 4 – 8 stiff cock hackles, flared with a turn of thread under the base of the tail

ABDOMEN: Biot to match the colour of the natural. Use goose biot for small flies and turkey biot for larger imitations

WINGS: 2 cul de canard feathers tied spent in the normal wing location

THORAX: Harrop fine natural dubbing to match the colour of the insect

TORILL KOLBU

NORWAY

Torill Kolbu was born in 1963 in a farmhouse fifty yards from the best pool on the River Engeråa, once the finest river an angler could imagine, home to two-pound grayling and ten-pound wild browns. In this hamlet three hours drive north-east of Oslo Torill grew up in a fly-fishing family, with Erling Sand, the legendary Norwegian tyer just down the road. She lived close to nature in her formative years.

A fly fisher and fly tyer could not get a better start in life. Having fished since the age of five, Torill has that important inbred familiarity with the river and all river life to make her a cunning predator and ferocious hunter by the stream. Extensive fishing experience, perseverance, and a probing and creative mind stand behind the world's best flies; Torill has this sort of experience and instinct. Knowing that she has only been tying since 1986 it is evident that she is only at the beginning of her career.

Her breakthrough came in 1990 when she took a first and second place in the Norwegian Fly Fishing Days' fly-tying competition. In 1991 she won a Bronze Medal in the World Championship Atlantic Salmon Fly-Tying in Quebec. In 1992 she took the Silver twice, and in 1993 won the first four prizes in the hairwing creation category. Torill now ties professionally and since 1992 has been contracted to Mustad for whom she does product development and trains factory fly tyers. She is on the jury of the world's largest fly-tying competition, the Mustad Scandinavian Open, and to prove she is no mean fly fisher she is also in the Norwegian World Championship fly fishing team. Although a running-water specialist, Torill finished fourteenth in the 1993 championship fished entirely on Canadian stillwaters.

Before the Crocheted Caddis Pupa was born in 1990, I had been wondering how to achieve a more insect-like abdomen – broader, flatter and with different colours on top and bottom. One evening, after I had gone to bed, I had an idea. I got up, took out a crochet hook and raced down to my fly-tying room. It worked! The first woven fly body I ever saw was my own. Since then I have developed the technique in various directions.

I tie the Crocheted Caddis Pupa in many colour schemes: olive, orange-brown and cream. The only difference in the first two is the colour of the Antron. In my cream variant I include a thin pearlescent strand of Lureflash or similar when weaving the rear body. This fly has a white badger hackle, tied collar-style, to represent the legs, and the same thorax dubbed with grey Antron mix.

I have used this fly a lot and caught very many fish with it. While I was tying it for the Norwegian Fly Fishing Days in 1990, a gentleman told me he did not believe it would work. I convinced him to buy a sample to try. He called next day to order more. On the first fly he bought he caught thirty-three good-sized grayling in one evening.

I fish the pupa upstream to rising fish in Jim Leisenring style. I let the fly sink and lift the rod tip just in front of the rise so that the pupa rises to the surface. The fly is also good for prospecting, using various techniques.

My Crocheted Caddis Emerger is designed to float with the abdomen hanging down under the surface film. Only the thorax, hackle and wing should be treated to float.

I agree with Gary LaFontaine, who fished my native River Engeråa with me in 1991: sedges in various stages of their life cycle are very important staple food items for fish. Where I fish, sedges are more important than mayflies most times. I have had great success with this fly. It has many grayling, trout and whitefish on its conscience.

For my Fantastic Caddis I use a special wing material I call Fantastic Wing. I experimented with lots of different materials before I found one with the right characteristics. It looks very realistic and has good aerodynamics because it lets the air pass through. There is no propellering through the air and spiralling leader with this one.

It should be fished like any other sedge imitation, dead drift or with a retrieve to create a wake. Many friends testify how well it works.

Gold head nymphs are becoming more and more popular here in Norway. There are many similar patterns and the Crocheted Gold Head Brown Stonefly Nymph is my variation on the theme. I fish it deep, right along the very bottom.

Fox hair and fur are simply marvellous fly-tying materials, and I use them in many patterns. I use fox hair for a tail on my Damselfly Nymph. When they are given movement by retrieving or lifting the rod tip, the soft tail will effectively imitate the undulating abdomen of the swimming nymph.

The transparency and reflective qualities of Antron are very effective on the rear body of my Midge Emerger. It even worked during a trico hatch on the South Platte in the Rocky Mountains, where I was fishing with John Betts. John had tied and given me a whole box of his beautiful size 26 zing-wing trico dries and other tinies to fish with. They worked like a charm but with an 8X tippet it was all too easy to break off, so I lost my best flies. At the end of the hatch I tied on a size 22 Midge Emerger and it worked! John is a fine friend but I simply did not have the heart to tell him at the time – now he knows.

The Crocheting Technique

Patents are pending for some of the crocheting techniques. This makes it illegal for anybody else to sell flies tied with these techniques. However, I am more than happy to let fly fishers who tie their own flies use them.

Crocheting has two great advantages compared to traditional weaving: it allows all the material to be inserted between each knot since the weaving is done without tying off thread; and it is faster, once you get the hang of it.

This is the sequence for crocheting the Caddis Pupa and the numbers refer to line-drawings on page 72. Other patterns follow the same method.

1. Fasten the lead wire, wind it over the first one-third of the shank and fix it with superglue.
2. Fasten two strands of Antron yarn of different colours at the bend.
3. Dub the rear three-quarters of the fly with Antron Mix.
4. The hook, as seen from above. The two yarn pieces are separated. Do not tie off your tying thread.
5. The weaving starts by making one simple overhand knot on top of the shank.
6. Tighten up.
7. Place the darker Antron over and across the hook and, using a crochet hook, hook and pull the second piece of Antron over the first, underneath the hook shank and through the loop formed by the first.
8. Tighten up.
9. Place the lighter-coloured Antron underneath and across the shank, again using a crochet hook, hook and pull the darker Antron underneath the lighter-coloured, over and across the fly body and through the loop formed by the lighter-coloured Antron.
10. Tighten up. Steps 7 – 10 are then repeated until the dubbed abdomen has been completely covered. Tie in the two pieces of Antron with the thread and cut away the surplus.
11. The body as seen from above.

Crocheted Caddis Pupa

HOOK: Mustad 80250 or 80200 KEBR

UNDERBODY: Lead wire

BODY: 2 pieces of Antron yarn in the desired colours on top of a dubbed underbody

LEGS: Brown partridge hackle fibres

WINGCASE: 2 sections of mallard wing feathers, rear-facing

ANTENNAE: 2 bronze mallard fibres, rear-facing

THORAX: Dark grey dubbing

Crocheted Caddis Emerger

HOOK: Mustad 80250 size 10 – 16

UNDERBODY: Naturally coloured dubbing

ABDOMEN: 2 pieces of Antron yarn in the desired colours, crocheted

WING: A small upright bunch fibres with the rear-pointing butts protruding the upper rear thorax dubbing

HACKLE: Good-quality cock, would round the base of the wing

THORAX: Dark grey dubbing

Three fine Scandinavian grayling, each over two pounds.

Fantastic Caddis

In order to achieve a symmetrical shape of the Fantastic Wing, it should be folded before trimming. The bottom hackle fibres are cut level with the lower edge of the roof so that the fly will sit steadily on outrigger hackle tips on the surface film.

HOOK: Mustad 81833 KEBR or 79702 BR size 10 – 18

ANTENNAE: Stripped cock hackle stalks

ABDOMEN: Fox fur dubbing

UNDERWING: Deer hair, laid flat

WING: Fantastic Wing, cut to shape

THORAX: Fox fur dubbing

HACKLE: 1 – 2 Metz cock hackles

TORILL KOLBU

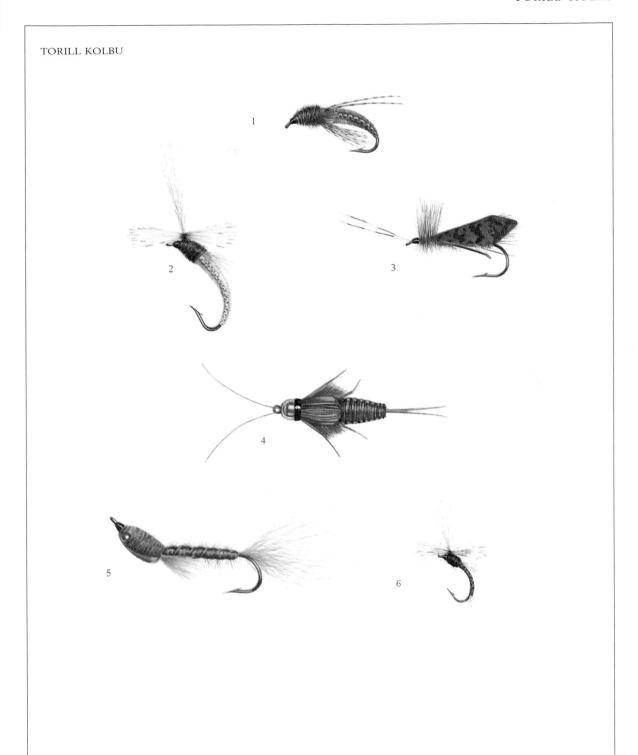

1 Crocheted Caddis Pupa
2 Crocheted Caddis Emerger
3 Fantastic Caddis

4 Crocheted Gold Head Brown Stonefly Nymph
5 Damselfly Nymph
6 Midge Emerger

Crotcheted Caddis Pupa

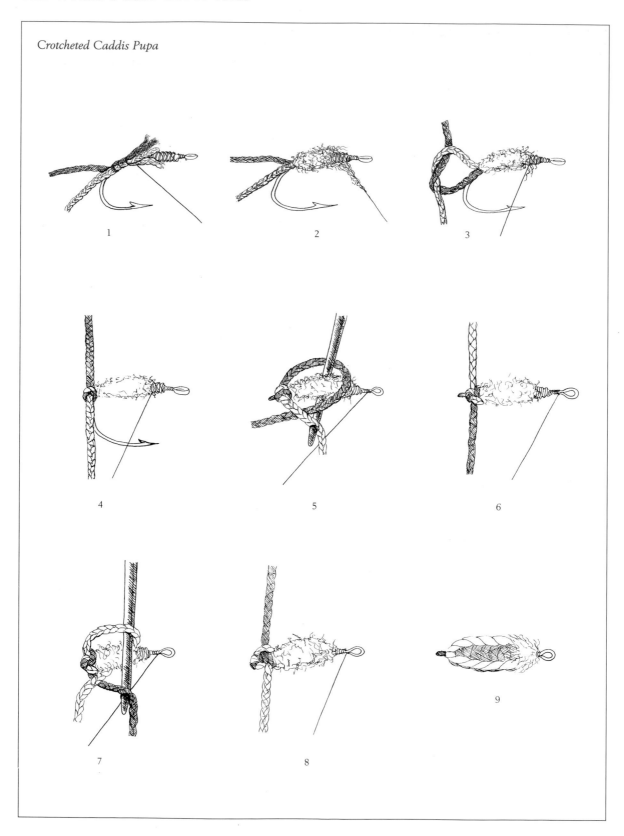

Crocheted Gold Head Brown Stonefly Nymph

Thread the gold head onto the shank, then secure hook in vice. Fasten the antennae, make two whip finish knots, and cut the tying thread. Push the bead to the eye. Fasten the tail and both sections of Antron yard. Dub a tapered abdomen and weave the Antron yarn with a crochet hook. Fasten two of the legs and the wingcase. Dub the thorax, fold the wingcase over and tie it in behind the gold bead. Fasten the two front legs and tie off.

HOOK: Mustad 80000 KEBR

THREAD: Black

TAIL: Brown goose biots

ABDOMEN: Brown dubbing underneath two sections of Antron yarn – one plain brown and one brown with a few black strands of Antron yarn. The darkest section should be on top

WINGCASE: A few fibres of golden pheasant tail feather and brown raffia

ANTENNAE: Stripped brown cock hackles

LEGS: Brown goose biots

THORAX: Brown fox dubbing

HEAD: Gold bead

Damselfly Nymph

This fly is designed to fish upside-down. Heat the mono and tie in approximately 2mm behind the eye and seal with superglue. Fasten the lead wire on top of the shank. Fasten the tail and the two sections of Antron yarn and one olive ostrich herl. Weave the abdomen with a crochet hook and rib it. Trim the rib. Tie in the gills and then the wingcase. Dub the thorax and head, fold the wingcase over and tie off with two whip finish knots.

HOOK: Mustad 80150 KEBR

THREAD: Olive

UNDERBODY: Lead wire laid on top of the shank

TAIL: Olive fox hair

ABDOMEN: Two sections of Antron yarn, one olive and one Green Highlander green, crocheted

RIB: One olive ostrich herl, trimmed on top and underneath

GILLS: A sparse bunch of olive fox hair on each side protruding from the rear of the thorax dubbing

THORAX: Olive dubbing

EYES: Nylon monofilament (appox 3cm, 0.30mm diameter) burnt to a ball at both ends

WINGCASE: Antron yarn from the abdomen

Midge Emerger

Fasten the tail and the two sections of Antron yarn. Weave the abdomen with a crochet hook. Fasten the wing in the upright position, then fasten the hackle. Dub the thorax and wind the hackle round the wing base in parachute style and tie off.

HOOK: Mustad 80100 or 80250

THREAD: Black

TAIL: 3 – 4 fibres of white, short marabou

ABDOMEN: One section plain black and one section black plus a few strands of medium brown Antron, weaved with a crochet hook

WING: A small bunch of white organza with the butts protruding out of the upper rear thorax

HACKLE: One top-quality grizzle cock, wound round the wing base

THORAX: Black dubbing

JUREK KOWALSKI

POLAND

Since 1989 Jurek Kowalski has been the influential captain of the Polish National Team for the World Championships. In this time they have become World Champions in Finland and runners-up the following years in Wales and New Zealand and in 1993 in Canada. Members of the team took individual championship honours in 1989 and 1990, second place in 1990, 1991 and 1993, and third place in 1992. The success of the Polish nymph-fishing methods has made the world of competitive fly fishing take note.

By profession Jurek is a medical doctor and works for the marketing and technical services department of an international pharmaceutical company. He has fly fished for about twenty years.

The World Champion fly fisher for 1984, Tony Pawson wrote in an article in the English newspaper *The Observer* before the 1990 championships that when the competition is organized on rivers inhabited by grayling, then the first two positions should be reserved for Poland and Czechoslovakia, and the rest of the teams may compete for third place downwards. His prognosis was extremely accurate since Czechoslovakia won ahead of Poland and Poles were the top two individuals.

During the championships in Finland, Wales and New Zealand, Polish fly fishermen become recognized as nymph-fishing specialists and competition champions. It would therefore be unusual if I describe flies other than nymphs in my selection. I will concentrate mainly on nymphs suitable for different styles of presentation, beginning with the most successful Polish method of short lining with a weighted fly, and ending with the more traditional upstream fishing with small lightweight patterns.

I fish mostly on the River San which begins on the Polish-Ukranian border and has its most productive part before two reservoirs – Solina and Myczkowce. There is excellent trout and grayling fishing amid the variety of scenery and water types.

My favourite nymph for June and July on the River San is a variant of the Stick Fly, a cased caddis imitation, in Poland commonly called a Bronze Nymph due to its colour not its medal quality, although it gave us our team and individual success in Wales. This fly is tied on a size 8 or 10 standard hook (Partridge G3A) as a weighted pattern to penetrate the deepest parts of the current. I usually fish it with a short (floating) line presentation in fast-flowing waters cast into the likely lies of trout and especially grayling. Sometimes when the current is broad and deep I use a longer line controlling my fly without any drag. It is very important to balance the weight of the fly and the strength of the current so as to let it drift as close to the bottom as possible but avoiding fouling the riverbed. Sometimes slight upwards movement is crucial for the success of this fly.

During the entire season I like to use freshwater shrimp imitations which are successful all year long. My favourites are tied on smaller, size 12 or 14, specially curved hooks (Partridge K4A) which match the size and shape of the naturals. To let them work accurately without too much weight I form the underbody with very fine copper wire, the thinner the better, wound on the shank and

JUREK KOWALSKI

1 Stick Fly
2 Freshwater Shrimp
3 Pheasant Tail Nymph

4 Versatile Nymph
5 February Snow Flake
6 Kowalski's Mayfly

tapered at each end. The sides are then squeezed with forceps or between scissor handles to obtain a flat humpy body. The copper wire is then covered with dubbed grey/brown fur. My preference is for greyish-tan or light brown hare's fur. The stiffer, longer guard hairs imitate the natural's legs whereas the softer fibres give colour and movement. The back of the body is covered with a strip of transparent plastic and reinforced with three-pound nylon monofilament.

The Freshwater Shrimp is mostly fished near the river banks in shallower water and near weed-beds and large rocks where shrimp congregate. Presented in a dead drift on a long line, it works very actively in the water and attracts fish with its shape, appearance and movement. This delicately weighted pattern is fished on a floating line or with a sink-tip line when water conditions require quicker deep presentation of the fly. In slower water I like to increase the attraction of the shrimp by adding more aggressive movement with a series of quick, short pulls.

I use the next nymph patterns for delicate presentations on comparatively slow-flowing waters with a flat surface. I like this kind of nymph fishing and I practise it mainly in my non-competitive fishing. I cast a small fly on a fine tippet to an individual fish feeding very close to the surface or in the film, presenting my nymph just subsurface on a long, partly greased leader. Any movements of the leader knots indicate that the fish has taken my fly and can be hooked. The method requires considerable concentration since the takes are very quick. A fish in slow currents will not hook itself and when it can feel any resistance of the line or leader it rejects the artificial immediately.

For this kind of fishing I use a Pheasant Tail Nymph based on the pattern devised by Frank Sawyer and another small, simple versatile invertebrate imitation. I call the second pattern the Versatile Nymph because when I ask fellow fly fishermen what they think it is, I receive very varied opinions: from mayfly nymphs, sedge pupae or even a freshwater shrimp. It is a very simple, uncomplicated tying but highly effective for trout and grayling. I must emphasize that in this method, skilful presentation and the angler's concentration are much more important than the patterns he or she uses.

Measured across a season I believe the sub-surface approach with a fly is more effective for trout and grayling than the floating fly. I also think that it offers much more scope for development. My favourite early spring wet fly is a pattern of my own, the February Snow Flake. In the beginning of the 1988 trout season I tried to prepare some good fish-fry imitations to provide some fishing at a time when insect life and vegetation is in decline in cold, winter waters. Sitting at my vice I tried to imagine the fry before me. Through half-closed eyelids I looked at the hook and I carefully selected the materials for the fly. I gave it a brown tail and throat, a blue body with flat gold ribbing, dark spotted wings over stiff otter fur fibres. I then tested the fly in widely different waters and I found it very successful. I use a fast-sinking line and a short 1 – 1½ yard leader, casting the fly slightly upstream, then letting it sink and presenting it with a series of short, quick pulls. It's always very exciting to hook a fish from deep water because you never know how big it is until the slack line is retrieved and full contact with the hooked fish is reached.

I have left the cream of fly fishing – the dry fly – to the end. I call it the cream not only because the flies float on the water like cream on milk but because I know of no more pleasurable way of fishing for trout than tying an imitation of a specific insect, giving it good floatability, presenting it with a perfect drift, and observing a fish rising to choose this man-made creation over the naturals. When it all works it is another small proof of man's subtle domination in a strange and unfamiliar environment.

It was very difficult to select any particular dry-fly pattern. I chose the Mayfly imitation which I tie upside-down on Partridge Swedish hooks.

My nymph and wet fly fishing requires considerable concentration of the line and leader and rapid reactions. In contrast I feel very relaxed watching a floating dry fly and rising fish, having enough time to enjoy my surroundings and still hook fish. Sometimes when I change quickly from nymph to Mayfly I try to fish very far away, casting almost the whole fly line to slow down my reactions and delay the strike. It is all too easy to lose fish on the Mayfly by striking too quickly.

Stick Fly

HOOK: Partridge G3A (D/E, standard shank) size 8 – 10

THREAD: Black

UNDERBODY: Lead wire

BODY: Dark brown wool, wound not dubbed

RIB: Fine copper wire

NECK: Yellow wool

HACKLE: Brown hen

HEAD: Black tying thread tied large.

Freshwater Shrimp

HOOK: Partridge K4A (D/E, curved shank) size 12 – 14

THREAD: Black

UNDERBODY: Very fine copper wire tapering at each end

BODY: Greyish tan hare's fur, mixed short fibres and guard hairs

BACK: Clear or coloured plastic

RIB: 3-pound nylon ribbed over the back

Pheasant Tail Nymph

This is tied without tying thread using the copper wire to bind in the materials. The pattern differs from Sawyer's original dressing by including black tying thread to reinforce the head and it is tied on a curved shank hook.

HOOK: Partridge K2B (D/E, curved shank) size 14

TAIL: Cock pheasant centre tail fibre tippets

UNDERBODY: Copper wire

BODY: Cock pheasant centre tail fibres, wound with and ribbed with copper wire

WINGCASE: Pheasant tail fibres, doubled and redoubled

HEAD: Black tying thread

Versatile Nymph

HOOK: Partridge K2B size 14

THREAD: Black

BODY: Yellow wool, dubbed tapering to the rear

WINGCASE: Cinnamon-brown hen wing

HEAD: Tying thread, tied small

February Snow Flake

HOOK: Partridge G3A size 6

THREAD: Black

TAIL: Cinnamon hen wing fibres

BODY: Light blue wool with the tying thread twisted round and wound

RIB: Flat gold tinsel

THROAT: Natural red (brown) hen fibres

WING BASE: Stiff otter fur fibres, just short of the wing length

WING: Mottled mallard flank

HEAD: Black thread

Kowalski's Mayfly

HOOK: Partridge K3A Swedish (long shank for upside-down tying) size 12

THREAD: Black

TAIL: Cock pheasant centre tail fibres

BODY: Natural grey deer hair, bound lengthways along the shank

RIB: Fine silver wire

WINGS: Two mallard breast feathers, tied upright

HACKLE: Speckled partridge and natural red (brown) cock, wound round the angled part of the shank

THORAX: Dubbed brown fur

WAYNE LUALLEN

USA

Few tyers can match the all-round ability of Wayne Luallen. From fully dressed, feather-wing salmon flies which are much sought-after collector's items, down to perfectly proportioned size 28 Royal Wulffs, Wayne is one of the most skilled and versatile tyers in the world. Every year since 1980 he has been invited to the international gathering of the Federation of Fly Fishers (FFF) held annually at various locations in the USA and Canada. He was elected by his peers in the FFF to receive the Buz Buszek Memorial Fly Tying Award and was delighted to join a list of prestigious past recipients including Dave Whitlock, Art Flick, Polly Rosborough, George Harvey, Darwin Atkin, George Grant and many others.

A variety of fishing and fly-tying magazines have featured articles by Wayne or about his tying. Amongst the books in which he is featured is Judith Dunham's The Atlantic Salmon Fly: The Fly Tyers and Their Art. *He demonstrates widely across the USA and has also tied in Canada, Holland, Norway and will be seen in England before too long.*

Wayne and his wife Donna enjoy most of their trout fishing in the Sequoia National Park, California, but begin to get really serious about their fishing on what has become their annual pilgrimage to the waters in and around Yellowstone National Park.

As with almost every tyer I have known, my flies are not unique creations, but rather a culmination of ideas I have put together based on observations I have made of other tyers at work. By observing those aspects of a given fly that make it functional, durable and attractive to both the fly fisher and the fish, I find those things that are eventually incorporated into my work. It has been only on rare occasions when I have felt that I could actually claim credit for an idea. When I have, it seems inevitable that eventually it is discovered that the proverbial 'mouse-trap' had already been invented. Rather than be disappointed I am thankful that there are so many creative tyers who are willing to share what they have learned through trial and error so that we in turn can attempt to improve on what has gone before.

Though I enjoy tying most styles of fly, from small blue gill poppers to large tandem streamers for sailfish, my greatest love remains my first love,

trout flies. I like the simplicity with which some of the most effective flies can be tied. Then, too, I enjoy tying more complex patterns that may or may not prove as effective, but can be educational as well as simply great fun to tie. Since I want my flies to meet those prescribed factors of functionality, durability, attractiveness, and still be copied by others, I generally try to retain simplicity in the design.

The following six flies have been selected because they have been shown through years of service to fit the criteria of what I want my trout flies to fulfil, both at the tying bench as well as on the water. These represent the flies that I find myself turning to time and time again in the fishing situations that I frequent most, as well as being fun to tie. None are beyond the ability of the average tyer.

The B'NL Midge Pupa is a very simple fly, but has proven itself to be worthy for a variety of people in a number of different situations where a

WAYNE LUALLEN

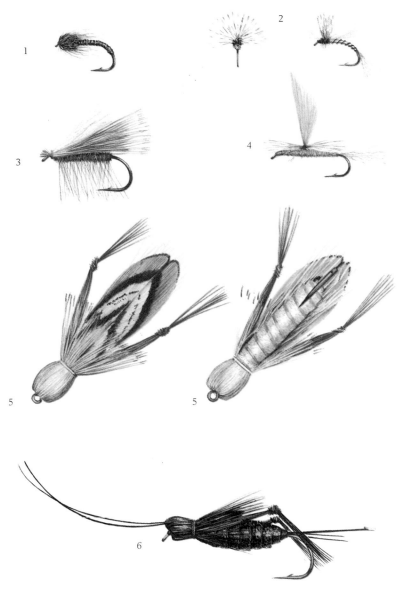

1 B'NL Midge Pupa
2 Stuck Shuck Midge
3 White Top Deer Hair Caddis
4 Sparkle Parachute
5 Whopper
6 Counterfeit Cricket

midge pupa is required. It is equally effective in deep-water situations as well as just below the surface when it is obvious by the appearance of a dorsal and tail that trout are taking just below the surface. It is generally easier to fish with some sort of indicator attached to the leader, whether it is with yarn, a small cork ball, small pieces of fluorescent line, or a dry fly. Most of the B'NL Midge Pupa's time spent in the water has been in the San Juan River of New Mexico, which is known for its big fish that prefer small flies, especially midges. The idea first developed when Gary Borger showed me his midge pupa that has a loose dubbing 'shuck' encompassing the abdomen. (I admit reticence in laying full claim to this fly. The B'NL is identical to Gary's Sparkle Midge Pupa in design concept; the appearance of the gas-filled shuck surrounding the pupa achieved by the use of loose yarn filaments. The only real difference lies in a more distinct thorax and unique abdomen.) He explained that during emergence, the translucent nature of the gas-filled shuck was a factor the tyer should not ignore. My fishing experience proved him correct.

A few years ago our friend, Robert Lobato, my wife Donna and I were invited by two guides to fish the upper reaches of the San Juan River's tailwater fishery. Our purpose was to head-hunt for large cruising rainbows that were randomly sipping small individual adult midges. Donna had first strike and probably the biggest success that day, and I probably had the worst. Our guides had to leave us early in the afternoon. As they were walking away I pulled out my box of B'NLs. Their waders had not reached dry land before I had the first of many large fish. I moved from graduate school back to being a freshman, but I knew it would catch fish. Possibly it was an easier form of fishing. I've learned that under similar circumstances I can always turn to the pupa to save the day.

The Stuck Shuck Midge developed out of sheer necessity. After being frustrated on the San Juan, I decided it was time to make a serious attempt at developing a fly that would be rarely refused, function well on the water, and yet be easy to tie in the small sizes it would be fished in. When midges clump to mate, a variety of fly types (like the Griffith's Gnat) are effective, but effective flies to use over selective fish carefully taking in-

dividual tiny midges, then several seconds or possibly minutes later taking another, had evaded me. The Stuck Shuck Midge has proven durable and attractive to fish. It is easy to tie on size 20 – 14 hooks, turns over well on the long, fine tippets typically used, and has proven nearly as effective as I could have hoped. The fly attempts to suggest a crippled adult. Hook weight and shape as well as the configuration of the trimmed hackle all contribute to the fly being both on and still in the water.

Dave Burns of San Jose, California, tied some of the cripples for the Green River of Utah after I reported the success my wife and I had with it there in late autumn. He fished the same area in June, and reported a first day's release of thirty-one fish on this often difficult river.

It seems that everyone has fished at one time or another the Elk Hair Caddis that Al Troth popularized. I, too, have found it very effective but I also found many situations, especially in the Sierra Nevada mountains of central California, where the caddis encountered were much darker in wing and body. Though the Elk Hair Caddis fooled many fish, it seemed obvious that if the insect could be matched more closely, superior success would be achieved. I have found that the White Top Deer Hair Caddis has filled that void. Body colour was a simple adjustment, but wing colour presented a problem. A friend, Dr Stu Garrison, and I came up with the notion of simply making an overwing of white deer hair on top of the darker hair. This fly has become a standard for local fly fishermen of this area and has been very useful on numerous other rivers we fish. Wing colour and the choice of material for the body are determined by the insect being matched. A general colour for our rivers has a body of peacock herl with a reinforcing rib of copper wire. The useful thing about peacock herl is that it turns a bronze/olive shade when wet, closely matching many of the resident naturals, while still retaining its natural iridescence.

Z-lon is a product first introduced to the tying public by John Betts. I learned of its effectiveness from West Yellowstone's Craig Matthews. In the fly shop he owns, Z-lon is used as a trailing shuck on several fly types, including caddis, adult midges and mayflies. One fly developed there is the Sparkle Dun, which is simply a Comparadun with a tail of Z-lon. Since its introduction a few years ago it has quickly spread in popularity all over the US. Representing a crippled insect, it gives the assurance to the fish that this is a meal that will not get away, and it is therefore more worthy of attention. Numerous materials have been used to represent the trailing shuck of the mayflies, including nylon stocking, Antron yarn and ultra chenille. In fact, it seems rather obvious that the clumped tail of a standard dry fly probably represents a trailing shuck. There is no doubt that it does not represent a tail as such, since there is no resemblance whatsoever to the cerci of the natural insect.

I have always been fond of parachutes incorporating turkey body feather barbs for the wing. After experiencing the effectiveness of the Sparkle Dun I decided to add Z-lon to the tail of my parachutes. My experience has been that in most difficult situations, especially when observation of the fly by the fish may take several seconds, the Sparkle Parachute will be taken when other flies, including the Sparkle Dun, are likely to be ignored. I will however admit that occasionally I have returned to a standard parachute with a short, forked tail when there have been refusals to the Sparkle Parachute.

Terrestrials have always been a favourite fly type for me, to tie as well as fish. If I were to select a favourite day of fishing, it would have to include a breezy August or September day on a Montana stream lined with sage brush alive with the raucous chatter of the grasshopper. The Whopper is a fly which has been successful for a number of seasons. I hesitated in publishing it because I always felt it not to be an especially attractive fly, due to the legs' position purposely being tied out evenly away from the body. The observant angler must admit that this is the configuration of the natural when it lands on the water. The legs nearly always go askew once the insect is trapped and tries to free itself from the meniscus.

This fly has proved to be reliable in every situation, in fast pocket water, slow back eddies, cast in front of the fish, on their noses, a foot behind the trout, and sunken (an extremely effective technique often overlooked). It is aerodynamically sound, turns over well on 4X or 5X tippets, lands properly on the water, lays in the meniscus, not on it, has an instantly recognizable sound and silhouette to the fish, and can be altered in colour at the streamside if desired.

The Counterfeit Cricket has had fewer hours on the stream than the other five patterns. Admittedly, in actual fishing situations I tend to use more simply tied flies. I am more likely to fish, for instance, a Letort Cricket since my cricket takes more than just a few minutes to tie. All the same, I always carry some Counterfeits of various sizes and, when they have got wet, I have been pleased with the results. I suppose what makes the Counterfeit attractive is that 'it looks like it ought to catch fish', at least so say other fly fishers. Though a definite feature of the silhouette and an enhancement to the appearance of the fly, care must be taken when adding antennae since their addition will often lead to twists in the leader. The use of fine, soft material is advised. Most fishers seem to enjoy fishing hopper patterns, but few fish cricket imitations. They do not know what they are missing, especially when casting over waters that are heavily fished. When a trout refuses a hopper, a smaller terrestrial will generally work. Traditionally a small beetle is used, but a size 12 – 14 cricket should not be neglected. I generally use a black cricket, but I would not be comfortable without a tannish brown field cricket as well. Often the latter will be taken and the former ignored.

B'NL Midge Pupa

The yarn strand and Prisma thread, or Flashabou, are tied in at the rear. With hackle pliers, twist these into a tight rope. (For the right-handed tyer, twist the rope anticlockwise to form tighter segments.) Wind to the rear of the thorax area.

HOOK: Mustad 3906, Daiichi 1550, Partridge E6A or K4A size 16 – 22

THREAD: Danville's Fly-Master 6/0 or Uni-Thread 6/0, to match the body colour

ABDOMEN: 8cm of 3-ply, lightweight sparkle acrylic knitting yarn, colour to match the insect. One ply will be subdivided into 2 or 3 strands. Use only one strand which is wound as a rope with an 8cm single strand of $\frac{1}{69}$ inch Prisma thread or Pearlescent Flashabou. The abdomen should begin slightly round the hook bend

THORAX: Dubbed yarn (as for the abdomen) that has been cut into pieces from $\frac{3}{4}$ – $1\frac{1}{2}$ overall hook length and then blended with darker rabbit fur, colour to match the insect. After dubbing pick out long strands to represent a shuck surrounding the pupa

Stuck Shuck Midge

Care must be taken when tying this, and any small fly, in considering the placement and number of thread wraps. Fewer, strategically placed wraps are preferable. Also flat thread covers more area with less bulk than twisted, so periodically untwist the bobbin holder until the thread looks like flat floss.

HOOK: Daiichi J220 size 20 – 24

THREAD: Uni Thread 8/0, colour to match the insect

SHUCK AND ANTENNAE: 15 – 25 fibres of cream or white Antron

ABDOMEN: Flat thread wrapped like floss

RIB: Twisted thread (colour should be dark enough to complement the abdomen colour)

WING: Dun or white cul de canard

THORAX: Dubbing, colour to match the natural

HACKLE: Palmered 3 – 4 wraps through the thorax, the trimmed beneath in a 'V', colour to match the natural

White Top Deer Hair Caddis

HOOK: Mustad 94840, Daiichi 1310 or Partridge L2A size 8 – 22

THREAD: Danville's Fly-Master 6/0 or Uni Thread 6/0, colour to match the body

BODY: Herl or dubbing ribbed with fine copper wire

HACKLE: Furnace, brown (natural red), ginger, grizzly or dun with a 'V' cut into the top where the wing will lie

WING: Well-marked deer hair (natural or dyed) topped with approximately 10 – 12 white hairs from the flank of a white-tail deer

Sparkle Parachute

First tie in the wing without wrapping in front of it. Next, tie in the Z-lon. Then wind back to the wing and in front of the wing. Build a thread taper from short of the eye back to the wing to force it upright. Secure the wing upright and post the wing with flat thread wraps around its base.

HOOK: Mustad 94840, Daiichi 1180, TMC 100, Partridge L3A or GRS3A (D/E, fine wire, wide gape) size 14 – 22

THREAD: Danville's Fly-Master 6/0 or Uni Thread 8/0 to match the body

SHUCK: Z-lon in brown (usually) or dark brown, gold, or olive to match the nymphal shuck

BODY: Natural muskrat or bleached and/or dyed blended fur to match, when wet, the underside of the insect

WING: White turkey body feather, dyed pale to dark dun to match the natural

HACKLE: High-quality cock, to match the natural

Whopper

Never stretch the Evazote foam as it only reduces its floatability. Also note that Pantone pens shrink overly bulky Evazote bodies to approximately the right size.

HOOK: Mustad 9672, 9671 or 94831, Daiichi 1710, Partridge H1A (D/E, long shank) size 8 – 12

THREAD: Danville's Fly-Master 6/0 in cream, tan or grey

BULLET HEAD: Elk or deer body hair, natural or dyed to match the insect

BODY: Evazote, dyed prior to wrapping or marked afterwards with a permanent marker

UNDERWING: 12 – 20 elk or deer hairs matching the wing colour of the insect, usually yellow

OVERWING: Ring neck pheasant body feather, treated with silicone glue or Goop, with the fibres pulled together into a wing shape

REAR LEGS: A clump of ring neck or golden pheasant tail fibres, tied in an overhand knot to represent the joint

Counterfeit Cricket

HOOK: Mustad 9672, 9671 or 94831, Daiichi 1710, Partridge H1A size 10 – 14

THREAD: Danville's Fly-Master 6/0 in black, brown or tan

BULLET HEAD: Elk or deer body hair to match the natural

ANTENNAE: 2 very thin stripped hackle rachis

OVIPOSITOR: Quill and short section of rachis from a stripped hackle, colour to match the insect

TAILS: Tips of 2 peccary hairs

BODY: Evazote dyed or marked with permanent pen, or polycelon

UNDERWING: 10 – 15 dun or white deer hairs

OVERWING: Very short tip of ring neck pheasant body feather in natural colour or dyed

REAR LEGS: A clump of golden, or ring neck pheasant, tail fibres to match the insect, tied in an overhead knot to represent the joint

PAUL MARRINER

CANADA

Paul Marriner is an award-winning, international, outdoor writer. Author of Atlantic Salmon –
A Fly Fishing Primer *and many magazine articles, he is five times a member of the Canadian
team to the World Fly Fishing Championships and the Canadian team captain for 1994 – 96.
He organized the Commonwealth Fly Fishing Championship in 1993.*

*A fly fisher and fly tyer for more than twenty-five years, Paul has cast to a wide variety of warm-
and cold-water species in a dozen countries around the globe. As a senior partner of International
Angling Associates, he is involved in teaching fly fishing, marketing quality angling destinations,
and acting as a consultant to the fly-tackle industry.*

The travelling fly fisher, in addition to acquiring local patterns on arrival, must carry a group of proven patterns in which he has confidence. What follows are six of my group. I put my faith in several others as well, some of which are likely to be found elsewhere in this book. A few of these are: Marabou Muddlers, the Leadhead Nymph, Zonkers, Muskrat Nymph, Pheasant Tail, Montanas, Hare and Copper, Black and Brown Stones, Brassies, and the Elk Hair Caddis.

I chose the following because, first, several are unfamiliar on the world stage; secondly, three are emergers or floating nymphs which I believe imitate the stage most frequently taken during a rise; and thirdly, they include an outstanding subsurface attractor and a terrestrial.

The Usual is a brilliant emerger pattern for all mayflies. A random experiment springing from the talented vice of Fran Betters, a well-known tyer living beside the West Branch of the Ausable River in the Adirondack region of New York State, its success is well documented in North America. Among its many triumphs for me are half a dozen wild browns from the Itchen.

A snowshoe hare cannot afford wet feet in winter; thus, hair on its feet is water repellent. It's also crinkly, reflective, and quite translucent. A tail tied of this material floats well and resembles a nymphal shuck. Add a post wing of the same stuff and a body of the underfur and you have a shimmering imitation that simply keeps on floating. I have tried to collect as many natural colours as possible but when stuck for an available body shade, I use sparkle-blend dubbing.

As this is no place for an extended argument, I will simply state from observation (confirmed by others) that most smaller duns float on their feet with bodies above the water. This implies that the imprint of an insect's feet on the surface film is a strong trigger for trout. Reasoning thus, several years ago I tied, among other experiments, some reverse hackle (a centuries' old concept) flies without bodies or wings. The result lands like a parachute with the bend down and the shank vertical. This simplest of flies has been quite successful when trout are taking duns; however, it is perfectly useless when the fish are selecting emergers or spinners.

Gary LaFontaine spoke highly of a similar fly in his outstanding book, *The Dry Fly*. His version has a hackle tip (simulating the wing) tied parallel to the shank at, and extending beyond, the eye of the hook. My experiences suggest this addition is unnecessary and often destabilizes the fly. Success is improved by using a tippet one size finer than usual and letting the fly drop from a foot higher above the surface than normal – wind is a *bête noire*.

Following logically from my position on duns is a belief that virtually all so-called dry-fly designs (for mayflies) imitate emergers, stillborns or cripples. The sole exception (with all its tying and casting problems) is John Goddard's USD Dun design. Thus, when the Usual fails to perform, I rely on parachute patterns. To ease construction and provide additional flotation when necessary, I developed (independently but not uniquely) the Foam Post Emerger.

Flycraft, an American company, offers a line of foam cylinders for ant bodies. I use these for almost all my foam requirements including the Foam Post Emerger and Suspender midge pupa designs.

The success of the Black Foam Beetle speaks with great eloquence. From Monk Lake in New Zealand to New York's Beaverkill River, from Lake Brenig in Wales to Wyoming's Snake River, wet and dry, this simple pattern has consistently produced. Some swear by an Elk Hair Caddis as a searching pattern, but the Black Foam Beetle has my vote.

The Olive and Black Woolly Bugger would gain the approval of many as today's top streamer. When combined with a Black Foam Beetle on a dropper, this is my standard subsurface searching rig on stillwaters. Eric Leiser, in his authoritive book, *The Book of Fly Patterns*, attributes the design to an American Russell Blessing. Olive and black is given as the original dressing.

The first session of my first World Championships was on Lake Big Jim, part of the London Lakes Fishery in Tasmania. Just before the early start of 5.30am, I spotted a brown trout lurking in six inches of water close to the end of my beat. Several anxious moments passed by as I urged my guardian leprechaun to keep the trout from straying beyond my mark. I tied on a size 10 version of the Thong and within moments of my controller whispering, 'OK, start', I made a cast some three feet in front of the trout. The fly sank slowly, the trout cruised over and sucked it from the bottom, and shortly thereafter my controller entered 54cm (over 21 inches) on the score-card as the carefully released trout scooted away.

The margins of some Tasmanian tarns are cluttered with vegetation. An ordinary nymph will sink to the bottom and lie flat. If you decide to try an attractive twitch, it catches a stick or weed. To combat these difficulties, John Bessel, an inventive Tasmanian fly tyer, designed the Thong. The bulbous foam thorax allows the fly to sink slowly, but the moment the tail touches anything it stops. And there it sits, upright, in full view of the fish. A cunning little twitch is also possible without snagging.

Usual

HOOK: Partridge CS27 (D/E, barbless) size 12 – 18

THREAD: To match the body colour

TAIL: A small bunch of hair from the foot of a snowshoe hare (remove the underfur for the use below)

BODY: Dubbed underfur from the above

WING: A single upright post wing of the same material as the tail

Editor's Note: Ruth Zinck also included the Usual in her original choice of six flies. Her tying included an amendment made by Jack Imhof, an Ontario fisheries biologist. His dressing included bright red tying thread which was visible through the dubbed body. Imhof believed that the red triggered a response from rainbow trout.

Reverse Hackle

HOOK: Kamasan B410 size 14 – 20

BODY: Tying thread

HACKLE: Colour to suit. Attach the hackle to a point on the shank just ahead of the point of the barb. Take 4 or 5 wraps backwards (do not go beyond the straight part of the shank) and then wrap forward again to the starting point and tie off.

Foam Post Emerger

Split the foam post with scissors and tie in the resulting legs fore and aft on top of the shank. Rather than put up with the hassle of winding the hackle and then having to finish the thorax and tie the head with hackle barbs in the way, complete the entire fly and then wind the hackle. Next, take a needle, push it through the bottom of the post, insert the tip of

the hackle in the eye of the needle and pull it through the post. Finally clip the waste hackle and put a little cement in the hole to secure it.

HOOK: Partridge CS28 (D/E, slightly long shank, barbless)

TAILS, ABDOMEN AND THORAX: To suit the natural

FOAM POST: Flycraft foam cylinder in the appropriate size. (The package provides a scale to match hook size to foam cylinder size)

HACKLE: Cock hackle to match the natural, wound around the base of the foam post

Paul Marriner on the Fon du Lac River, northern Saskatchewan.

Black Foam Beetle

HOOK: Partridge CS27 (D/E, barbless) size 10 – 18

BODY: Peacock herl (a turn of black hackle at the front end of the body is optional)

BACK: Black foam tied in at the rear and pulled over the top of the body and tied off behind the eye. A daub of red cement on the back improves visibility

PAUL MARRINER

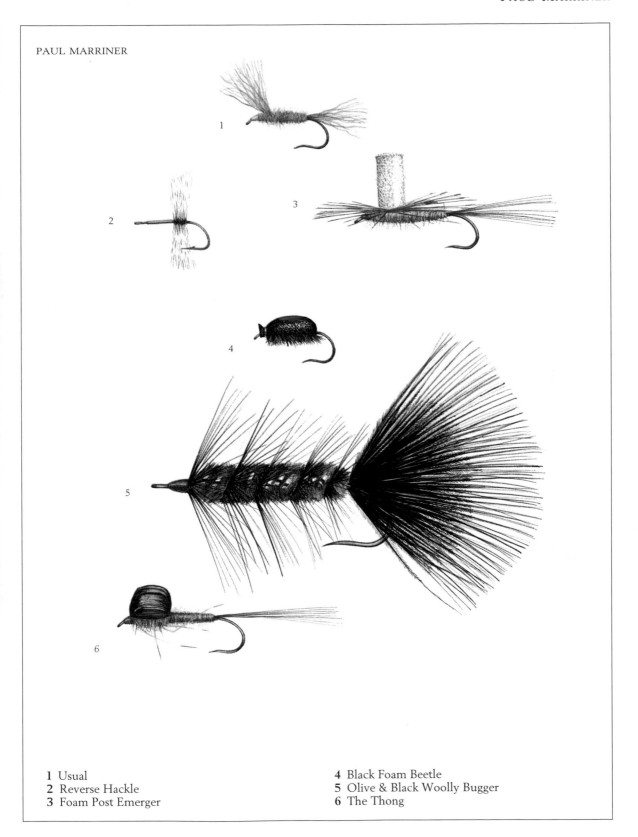

1 Usual
2 Reverse Hackle
3 Foam Post Emerger

4 Black Foam Beetle
5 Olive & Black Woolly Bugger
6 The Thong

Olive and Black Woolly Bugger

HOOK: Partridge CS29 (S/E, long shank, barbless)
size 2 – 8

TAIL: Black marabou blood feathers extending the
length of the shank beyond the bend. Add a few
strands of flashy material such as Crystal Flash,
Flashabou, etc, as an option

BODY: Olive chenille (the pattern shown has chenille
incorporated with silver thread for a little extra glint)
sized appropriately for the hook

HACKLE: Black, palmered through the body

The Thong

The right size of foam is important but difficult to
accomplish. It wouldn't be worth the trouble if the
fly wasn't so effective. Begin by calculating the size of
the foam necessary to float the hook (the effect of
the dressing is negligible). The simplified formula I
developed by calculation and experiment is V + (W
× 0.0004)/60, where V is the volume of the foam in
cubic inches and W is the weight of the hook in
milligrams. Partridge give the weight of some of their
hooks on the packet; for others, check Dick Stewart's
The Hook Book, or weigh the hooks. To make life
easier I use foam strips ⅛ inch wide and ⅛ inch thick
and so vary only the length.

Example: One Partridge CS28 weighs
approximately 35 milligrams. Substituting the
formula gives the length of foam necessary to float
the hook as ⁵⁄₃₂ inch. I cut a dozen pieces this length
and tie the fly. Usually, as it supposed to do, it floats.
Nothing lost, because I will mark it and use it as a
floating nymph. Next I trim a sliver off the next piece
of foam and try again. After one or two tries, the fly
sinks and rests on its tail as desired. If you trim a bit
too much the fly will sink and sit up on its tail and
hook point – not disastrous, but not perfect either.

HOOK: Partridge CS28 (D/E, slightly long shank,
barbless) size 10 – 14

TAIL: Brown (natural red) cock hackle fibres,
extending at least half a shank length beyond the
bend

BODY: Dubbed fur to suit the natural

THORAX: A small piece of dense closed-cell foam
(the right size) cut from a beach or wading sandal
(hence the name) and wrapped in a piece of Swiss
straw (Raffene). Tie in using the twisted ends of the
straw

DARREL MARTIN

USA

Darrel Martin was born in Washington State and raised on the rainy slope of Mount Rainier. He has Bachelor's and Master's degrees in English Literature and has taught literature and philosophy for twenty-nine years. He has also taught various fly-fishing courses at college level and presented programmes at the national level on various aspects of fly fishing. His numerous articles, art and photographs have appeared in many major American and European magazines and he is the contributing editor on fly-tying for Fly Rod & Reel *(USA) and a contributing editor on the American angling scene for* Fly-Fishing and Fly Tying *(UK).*

His four books include the award-winning Fly-Tying Methods *(1987, Lyons & Burford). He has recently completed* Micropattern, *a definitive text on small fly fishing. He has invented various tools for the fly fisher including the Dubbing Whirl, the Fly Tyer's Template, the Martin Brush Spinner and the Martin Leader Furler.*

Darrel has trout fished extensively throughout the American West, Canada and Europe. His passion is the small fly on the spring creeks and chalk streams of the world.

It is often said that the generic Humpy is all insects because it is none. There are, however, few flies in the wallet that match the mottled caddis as well as a Humpy. In miniscule it imitates small terrestrials and mayflies; larger sizes match stoneflies and grasshoppers, as well as a hoard of other insects. The origin of the Humpy, sometimes called Goofus, has been ascribed to several people and several proto-patterns. However, in a discussion of origins, the argument usually leads to a tyer from San Francisco. The late Jack Horner tied the Horner's Deer Fly, which had a folded deer-hair body ribbed with thread while the natural tips of the hair formed the wings. According to Jack Dennis, the term Humpy, which comes from the pattern's distinctly humped body, may have originated near Jackson Hole, Wyoming. The term Goofus, popularized by Dan Baily of Montana, sometimes refers to a Humpy with mixed brown and grizzly hackles. Today, however, Humpy and Goofus are synonymous for myriad variations.

Perhaps the best qualities for the Humpy are its buoyancy and imitative capacity. Although typical Humpy water is quick, heavy and nervous, the small Humpy is realistic enough for slow streams and still waters. Perhaps, as Westerners say, the Humpy is effective because it imitates anything that the trout wants. This popular pattern can constitute over thirty per cent of the total patterns sold during a Western season. A Western angler who has not cast a Humpy is usually an angler without experience.

The Humpy presents interesting tying problems in proportions and material manipulation. If its proportions are wrong, the pattern becomes awkward and gauche. Even a small error in proportion distorts its demeanour. A few tricks make it easier to tie.

The deer body fibre length must account for the underbody, overbody and wings. Long, soft fibres makes this pattern easier to tie. The number of body fibres will determine, to some extent, the body length. The more body fibres that are used, the wider the body bends will be; hence, more length will be required for those bends at the rear and wing base. Fewer fibres bend more abruptly. The deer hair length will constitute the under-body, the overbody and the wings; therefore the correct length is critical. The final problem is the separation of the body fibres from the tail fibres. This is especially critical if a dubbed or floss underbelly is added. Sometimes, especially in the smaller sizes, the underbelly is merely the thread itself.

The Female Adams is a sombre lady, a traditional Adams with a small yellow fur egg sack. It is an elegant pattern, especially effective for spring-creek and chalk-stream trout. Matty Vinceguerra's egg-sack Adams, described in Richard Tal-leur's *Mastering the Art of Fly-Tying*, incorporates a small loop of polypropylene yarn beneath the shank for an egg-sack; the egg-sack actually increases the buoyancy. It is this touch of colour that makes this lady so effective. According to Harold Smedley's *Fly Patterns and their Origins*, the first Adams was tied in about 1922 by Leonard Halladay of Michigan and used by C.F. Adams to imitate, of all things, the flying ant.

The ubiquitous Adams pattern, and its variations, has the neutral colour of a caddis and the silhouette of a mayfly. It is one of North America's leading patterns. It imitates caddis, stoneflies, mayflies, mosquitos, and a wealth of nature's creatures. Its true value lies in its variegated, but neutral, colours. Even the gravid female is dressed in sombre grey. The wound hackle produces a mottled grey-brown mix that effectively suggests a variety of insects, including the Spotted Winged Quill (*Callibaetis*), the Spotted Sedge (*Hydropsychidae*) and even midges and reed smuts. The banded grizzly-point wings may suggest the vibrant fluttering of an insect attempting to fly. It is an excellent pattern, not only for rainbows and browns, but also for grayling. The Adams has been praised on the English chalk streams as an excellent pattern for shy, selective trout. Halladay's original dressing is enhanced by the availability of quality genetic capes. But perhaps nothing improves on this pregnant lady who has a touch of colour and class.

Fishing the midge, sizes 20 to 24, is either angling affectation or supreme sport. For me stalking spring-creek trout with diminutive imitations is the supreme sport. Selective trout are less alarmed by micropatterns. Furthermore, with the strength of modern tippets and hooks, the angler gains some advantage, especially when power gum is used to absorb that take and struggle of large trout. This pattern, rather simply tied, may be effective due to the hidden hook and realistic silhouette. Various wing materials may be used, but a white slip of turkey flat works well. Theoretically the variegated grizzly or cree scatters the light leaving the impression that the insect is buzzing on the surface.

My drifting Midge Pupa pattern obscures the hook point and attracts with a segmented body and a pinch of colour. It is an excellent slow-water pattern for visible, selective feeders. Variations of this pattern, with a dry hackle in place of the cul de canard barb legs, may also prove effective. The CDC suspends the pattern in the surface film.

The RFC Scud is a brush-bug design with excellent entry and sink. The whirled wire gives weight and metallic flash to the pattern. All scud-shrimp patterns should be tied on straight shanks for adequate hook gap and a natural profile. Making the dubbing brush with weighted, single-hook whirlers is simple. First, create a five-inch loop with a length of fine copper wire (wire diameter should correspond to the hook size). Connect a weighted, single-hook whirler to the bottom of the loop, and apply a high-tack wax to both strands. Mount finely chopped synthetic or natural dubbing between the hanging strands. Twirl the whirler to lock the dubbing between the strands and continue to twirl until the wire is tightly twisted. The dubbing brush is then ready for tying in.

The Beaded Pheasant Tail Nymph hides a bead in the thorax, creating a weighted, but realistic pattern, with only a dash of flash to seduce selective trout. The bead puts the pattern down among deep lying trout. Furthermore, it is also possible to slip a bead over the tippet for increased sink. Spirit River double-drilled beads are used. Such beads with double-drilled holes easily slip over a size 18 hook, yet the smaller bead hole prevents the hook eye from passing through.

DARREL MARTIN

1 Humpy
2 Female Adams
3 Midge
4 Drifting Midge Pupa
5 RFC Scud
6 Beaded Pheasant Tail Nymph

Humpy

Full tying instructions for the Humpy are found on pages 175–177.

HOOK: Mustad 94840 size 12 – 20

THREAD: Grey Uni-thread 6/0. Many tyers prefer a flat, multi-strand thread that will not cut the soft fibres

TAIL: Fine moose body fibres or coq de Leon barbs, although hackle fibres or deer hair may be used

OVERBODY: Soft deer body hair, dark mule deer, pale whitetail, and cream elk hair give a variety of natural body colours

UNDERBELLY: Pale yellow dubbing or thread. The underbody can be floss, thread, or dubbing in various colours. Perhaps pale yellow is the most common and effective

WINGS: Deer hair ends

HACKLE: Cree or grizzly cock hackle

Female Adams

Larger patterns, often tailed with moose hair, are heavily hackled for Western waters. On small patterns, especially those under size 18, it may be advantageous to offset the points for better hooking.

HOOK: Mustad 94840 size 14 – 22

THREAD: Black or grey Uni-thread, size 6/0 or 8/0

BODY: Natural grey muskrat or medium grey synthetic dubbing tied slim finishing 1mm behind the wings

WINGS: Paired and divided grizzly hackle points (use feathers with bold barring and rounded tips), tied 'concave to concave' with the darker barring on the outside. The wing length, when mounted, should equal the shank length excluding the head

TAIL: Mixed grizzly and brown, or ginger hackle barbs (fibres)

EGG SACK: Fine, pale yellow dubbing, natural or synthetic

HACKLE: Mixed grizzly and brown, ginger or cree. These are usually tied along the foreside of the shank with the dull side of the hackle pointing towards the tyer. Both hackles are then bent sharply so the dull side is towards the eye. Wind both hackles together, three times behind and twice in front of the wings

Midge

HOOK: Tiemco TMC 101 (1XF, wide gape, S/E) size 20 or smaller

THREAD: Dark orange Uni-thread 6/0

OVERWING: White turkey flat section, coated with Tuffilm, a fast-drying acrylic art spray. Ensure the ends extend beyond the hook. An excellent alternative is fine, folded Antron fibres

BODY: Orange, yellow or dun thread or stripped peacock herl

THORAX: Brown mole's fur, finely chopped, dusted on the high-tack waxed thread and wound over the wing roots

HACKLE: Grizzly or cree cock

Drifting Midge Pupa

The pattern is tied backwards with the head-thorax over the hook gap. Mount a strip of pheasant tail for the pupal case; tie in the CDC barbs in a dubbing loop – only a few bars are needed. Spin and wrap in. The barbs should extend slightly beyond the hook gap. Fold the pupal case forward and tie in. Add a band of red CDC for a narrow collar. Finally, tie in and spiral forward a stripped peacock herl body and whip-finish at the eye.

HOOK: Tiemco 947 BL or Daiichi 1190, size 18 – 20

THREAD: Grey 8/0

BODY: Stripped peacock herl

COLLAR: Bright, blood red CDC dubbing

PUPAL CASE: Pheasant tail barbs

BREATHING TUBE AND ANAL BRUSH: A short, white CDC breathing tube may be added prior to mounting the pupal case. The anal brush is attached before wrapping the body. Both the plumes and the brush assist in suspending the fly in the film

RFC Scud

Lay the end of the dubbing brush (pointing towards the eye) along three-quarters of the shank. Wrap securely. Spiral the dubbing forward, pulling the fibres of the previous wrap back so as not to trap them. When completed secure the dubbing brush with wraps, cut the excess and whip-finish. Crop the top fibres and fold all others beneath the shank.

HOOK: Orvis 4641, Mustad AC 8000BR, Tiemco 101 (wide gape, 1XF, S/E) size 12 – 18

THREAD: Light Cahill (light tan) Uni-thread

UNDERBODY: Tag end of dubbing brush, three-quarters of shank length

BODY: Short-fibred, sparse dubbing brush; cream or pink underfur blended with Antron or Z-lon

Beaded Pheasant Tail Nymph

Slip the bead over the point of the hook, entering the smaller of the two holes in the bead. Tie in the pheasant tail fibres for the wingcase and wrap firmly and whip-finish. Remove the thread. Push the bead over the wingcase foundation. Re-attach the thread behind the bead and tie in the wingcase and wind the thread to the rear. Tie in the tail. Twist the fibres and wrap forward, finishing behind the bead. Add a dusting of mole's fur and whip-finish behind the bead. The mole's fur collar covers the final wraps, creating an invisible whip-finish.

HOOK: Orvis 4641, Daiichi 1560 or Tiemco 101 size 12 – 18

THREAD: Brown Uni-thread 6/0

BEAD: Spirit River Brite Beads, silver or gold, with dual-diameter holes, sizes $3/32$ inch to $3/16$ inch

WINGCASE: Dyed or natural pheasant tail fibres

TAIL AND BODY: Dyed or natural pheasant tail fibres

VÁCLAV MAZURA

CZECH REPUBLIC

Dr Václav Mazura is an expert in environmental impact assessment at the Czech Environmental Inspection Agency. His doctoral thesis was entitled The Nutrition of Brown Trout and Grayling *and the subsequent four years were spent working for the Fishing Department at the College of Agriculture in Brno.*

Václav has been fishing since 1964 and fly fishing since 1979. He is currently the President of the 60,000-strong Moravian Anglers' Union. In 1990 and 1992 he was a member of the winning team in the Czechoslovak Fly Fishing League and in 1990 he won the individual championship and was nominated for the national team. He fishes widely in Moravian and Czech rivers for brown trout, rainbow trout and grayling. Perhaps his most unusual catch on fly was a 97cm, 9.8kg wels. Václav has written for a number of Czech journals and is a member of the Editorial Board of Sportovni rybarstvi (Sports Fishing).

There is a long tradition of fly fishing in the Czech Republic with many of the original flies and methods introduced from England. The conditions of fly fishing are comparatively good. Although the number and length of rivers may not be great, we have a large quantity of fish. This is due to the activities of Anglers' Unions who are engaged in fish breeding and stocking, and environmental river work.

Our fly fishing is rather unusual because of some specific conditions. The first is that a great number of our trout rivers have been created below large reservoirs. This is reflected in the bentos, the basic food for fish, and must be taken into account when deciding on the right fly. The situation is further complicated by periodic fluctuations of the water flow during the day caused by peak-load operation of hydro-electric power plants. This has a great influence on the feeding activities of fish.

Another significant factor is the considerable influence of eutrophization – the result of excess quantities of macrobiogen elements in the water. As a consequence, rivers are overgrown with water plants and the pH level changes frequently.

These conditions have an effect on the food composition and fish feeding behaviour. Changes in trout and grayling feeding behaviour have been observed in recent years. Surface feeding has reduced and feeding close to the river bed or from water plants is increasing. Fly fishers have been obliged to adapt their methods and patterns accordingly.

Fly fishing on Czech rivers is always very interesting and technically demanding. Even on the small rivers and streams, of which there are many, a surprising catch can always be expected.

In recent years competition fly fishing has developed considerably. The Czechoslovak national team has gained notable international achievements, including the World Championships where our competitors are considered among the world's best.

My first fly selection is a *Gammarus* or shrimp. This small crustacean represents an important part of trout and grayling diets. In some rivers it is completely dominant and often accounts for over ninety per cent of the contents of the alimentary canal of fish that are particularly attracted to it by its size, number, considerable nutritional value

VÁCLAV MAZURA

1 Gammarus
2 Baetis Nymph
3 Emergent Caddis Pupa

4 Dark Olive Dun
5 Grey Dun
6 Yellow Caddis

and comparatively easy accessibility.

The artificial is used as a heavy nymph as it is necessary to make it move on or close to the river bed. Its efficiency is increased by active movement caused by lifting the rod tip. It is suitable for fishing in the streamy and quieter parts of the river. It ranks amongst the most successful and is effective all the year round, especially so for grayling.

The colour of the body is very important since colour of the natural *Gammarus* varies depending on the locality and time of year. Pink, orange, light green and brown are the most frequent and successful.

Flies belonging to the *Baetidae* species (particularly *Baetis rhodani*, *B. alpinus* and *B. lutheri*) form one of the most important parts of trout diets. Research into feeding habits of fish has revealed that the most attractive evolutionary stage is the nymph at the moment that it prepares for the transition to dun. In some seasons fish undoubtedly prefer the flies at this stage of the life cycle.

This particular nymph can be used as a heavy pattern for fishing near the riverbed. It is most effective when the nymph is being raised through the water and this is the moment trout usually attack the fly.

A lightweight floating nymph hanging under the surface is even more effective because it imitates the moment just before the birth of the adult *Baetis*. It is an easy fish target. It is advisable to apply floatant to the fly when fishing this way. When the fish take the fly it is usually with the minimum disturbance and on some water surfaces it is difficult to detect. This method is highly effective during a heavy hatch of flies.

My third fly also imitates one of the evolutionary stages of a fly's life, this time the caddis which is very often a trout and grayling favourite. Perhaps the most attractive stage is the pupa – at the moment immediately before the adult emerges and leaves the water. At this point the pupa is hanging close under the surface and is easily accessible to fish. During caddis hatches trout rarely pick the adults off the surface but take the ascending pupae or more often the pupae under the film. The success of the imitation is increased considerably when the line is pulled from time to time making the pupa drop deeper in the water and rise again when the line is loose. The fly will only do this when it is a buoyant pattern and my imitation uses closed-cell Polycelon to achieve this.

My next two flies are dry flies, to be fished in the classic dry-fly manner, and are imitations of some of the commoner duns. A dark olive dun imitation is one of the best-known flies and it is a favourite and widely used fly. Probably it is because dark olive duns are found on trout streams right across the world. The imitation can be tied in many ways with the help of a wide range of materials. I think here I am offering one of the most successful patterns. It utilizes the excellent cul de canard feathers which I have been using since 1984.

On our Czech and Moravian rivers the Grey Dun is one of the most common and popular flies for both trout and grayling fishing. Unusually the wings are made from pigeon wing feathers. These are very appropriate as the wings are firm and keep their form perfectly. One variation is to tie it with a parachute hackle.

An adult caddis is a significant part of fish's diets, particularly for trout. It is the mass emergence and returning egg-laying females that takes place over a short period, mostly in the evening that attracts attention. A large number of adults become available. The fishing efficiency is increased considerably by actively moving the fly. The fly can be pulled to make it plough through the water surface. By pulling strongly the fly will sink but due to the materials used it quickly comes up again. That is the moment when fish most often attack. Of all the ways of tying caddis, this type has proved the most successful for me. I usually fish the pattern across or downstream, the latter offering much closer control of the fly's behaviour.

Gammarus

To complete the fly, comb out the bottom of the poly dubbing body with a fine brush to imitate the natural's legs.

HOOK: Tiemco TMC 9902, Partridge K4A or Mustad 37140 (wide gape, curved shank) size 10 – 16

THREAD: Light tan

UNDERBODY: Wound lead wire (0.5 – 1.5mm depending on hook size) covered with polypropelene floss

BODY: Poly dubbing in various colours (pink, orange, various green shades and brown)

BACK: Translucent yellow, green or light pink latex about 3 – 5mm wide

RIB: Black nylon monofilament, wound over the back

Baetis Nymph

HOOK: Tiemco TMC 102Y (D/E, 1XF, wide gape) size 15 – 17

THREAD: Black

TAIL: Eagle-owl fibres

ABDOMEN: Wound eagle-owl fibres

WINGCASE: Turkey feather fibres in a loop over the thorax

THORAX: Silver tinsel

LEGS: A single grizzle hackle tip

HEAD: Black thread

Emergent Caddis Pupa

A bunch of Antron strands is tied in at the rear of the shank, then a Spectraflash strip and turkey fibres are tied in. The Antron body is added and the turkey fibres pulled forward and fastened by the wound Spectraflash. The bunch of Antron fibres is pulled forward and tied in to envelope the abdomen.

HOOK: Tiemco TMC 2487 (D/E, curved shank, 2X wide, 2X short, fine wire) size 10 – 14

THREAD: Beige

ABDOMEN: Yellow Antron dubbing

ABDOMEN BACK: Turkey feather fibres

RIB: Spectraflash, wound over the back

LEGS: A small bunch of roebuck hair

THORAX: Black Antron dubbing

THORAX BACK: Beige Polycelon about 3mm wide

Dark Olive Dun

The wings are tied in first about 2 – 3mm behind the eye. The tail and then the body are added, finishing off with the head.

HOOK: Tiemco TMC 102Y size 15 – 19

THREAD: Beige

TAILS: Sandy brown Metz hackle fibres

BODY: Olive-green poly dubbing

WINGS: Cul de canard feathers bound in an upright 'V'

HEAD: Beige tying thread

Grey Dun

HOOK: Tiemco TMC 102Y size 15 – 19

TAIL: Grizzle hackle fibres

BODY: Grey heron fibres

WING: Two pigeon wing feathers set upright or slightly rear-sloping, in a narrow 'V'

HACKLE: Generous turns of grizzle cock hackle

Yellow Caddis

HOOK: Mustad 94840 size 10 – 14

THREAD: Black

BODY: Yellow poly dubbing tied fairly bulky and palmered with a Metz sandy brown cock hackle

WING: Cul de canard feather over the back

HACKLE: Metz sandy brown cock over the wing base

MARCELO MORALES

ARGENTINA

In the early 1970s few people in Argentina were involved in fly fishing for trout. Books and fly tackle were very difficult to find. In common with other Argentinian fly fishers, Marcelo Morales pays tribute to Jorge Donovan and Jose 'Bebe' Anchorena, the fathers of Argentinian fly fishing who had the generosity and vision to share their knowledge and experiences with everyone who expressed an interest.

Marcelo Morales first taught fly casting and fly tying in 1979 in Jorge Donovan's fishing store which became the meeting place for Argentina's fly fishers. He was, at one time, a director of the Argentine Fly Fishing Association but now spends time as an instructor for that association. He also writes for various Argentinian magazines. Marcelo won all three of the Argentine Fly Casting and Fly Tying Championships, but the fly fishing aspect is no longer organized because so many fly fishers feel that such competitions are incompatible with the spirit of fly fishing. Marcelo now is one of the judges of the fly-tying competition.

Marcelo spends about five months of the year guiding in the south of the country for his outfitting company. He also organizes fly-fishing clinics in the south and in Buenos Aires where he and his partner have their fly-fishing store, Urban Angler Buenos Aires, in partnership with the store of the same name in New York.

My favourite fishing rivers are Quillen, Alumine and Malleo in the San Martin and Junin de Los Andes area of Neuquen province. These are the best for dry-fly fishing and nymphing with light equipment for trout. The average brown trout size down here (one to three pounds in rivers, three to five pounds in lakes) is pretty good when compared with the rest of the world. The rivers are pollution free and it is still hard to see another fisher while you are on the river. In addition to my migratory sea-trout fishing and guiding in Rio Grande (Tierra del Fuego) I head for the north of the country which is one of the few places in the world you can catch dorado, ranging between two and fifty pounds, that are easy to catch with big bucktails and strong rods (#7 and 8) in clear water.

If I had to choose just one exciting dry fly, without doubt this would be the Skating Spider. It has a long history in Argentina ever since the first ones were introduced by the American, Joe Brooks in the 1950s.

One of the more exciting moments of my life was one early morning in the mouth of the River Chimehuin. There was very little light and no wind at all, and there was no surface activity, so I decided to try the Spider to see if I could tempt them up. I was casting something like twenty-five yards across the stream, keeping the rod high and mending the line, making the Spider skate all around the river. At the moment I started skating it under the far bank a huge brown trout attacked the fly three times, and missed it as many times. So on my next cast I made a slower retrieve and hooked it. The only problem I had was that I had all my line out of my reel and had a big knot in the backing line. Then when the fish started running like hell, the knot ripped through the low rod

Marcelo Morales with a fine brown trout caught from the Malleo River.

rings and it stripped the upper three rings off the rod. It took twenty minutes to land that beautiful ten-pound brown trout.

The feathers for the Spider are the spade hackles located at the sides of the neck, but the problem is that genetic capes don't have long enough fibres for that fly. A few years ago a friend of mine from Spain sent me what were the perfect feathers, from a Cock de Leon. They are very stiff and long, with excellent mottled colours. These feathers are available in Europe and the United States.

Like any other fly tyers, I'm always trying to tie different flies for a special purpose, and for a long time I was trying to find a good stillborn dun with the shape and translucency of an attached nymphal shuck. By accident one day I found a piece of Furry Foam that had already been used and cut the wrong way. This gave me the idea to use it as a detached abdomen.

As a fishing guide I'm always trying different flies on the rivers, and this stillborn, which I tie in a variety of patterns, proved to be very effective, especially with selective trout. The significance of the Furry Foam is that it has tiny hairs along the edges, and it has the capability to maintain its shape and translucency in the water. I've been trying this model on standard patterns like the Adams, Humpy and Quill Gordon with fantastic results.

It is always extremely frustrating to fish for selectively feeding trout. When they get like that, no matter what you put on it is really difficult to fool them. Many years ago I was tying emergers and trying to make something that gave me the chance to fish it in the surface film and below. The answer for my Emerging Nymph was to use closed-cell foam for the wingcases, a cul de canard immature wing, and Easy Dubbing or New Dub material for the abdomen because of its perfect segmentation. The CDC wing holds it in position in the film.

I often fish it right below the surface with a dry fly on a dropper as an indicator. Alternatively, I dress it with floatant so that it fishes in the film, where it has become my favourite fly when the going gets tough.

Caddis are one of the more abundant insects found in almost every water. The Cock de Leon Caddis is the imitation I've been using for many years. There is no other feather with the natural stiffness and translucency of the Cock de Leon. It also has the advantage of far less web, so I can stack it and make a perfect wing. The fly is of European origins but I have introduced biots on it to improve the wing shape, and the duck tail fibres in the body for their water repellent properties. The antennae add a touch of realism.

Because we have a good population and a number of species of *Leptophlebia*, it is important to have a very good imitation of them. I believe that the colour of the streambed should have a big influence in the colour we choose for an imitation of these crawling nymphs. Using peacock herl in the abdomen and ostrich for the gills I get a very realistic imitation, especially for slow waters where the trout have the opportunity to be more selective.

The most satisfying way of fishing it is upstream and without any drag at all. The fly is very effective just below the surface before a hatch. Using a dry-fly dropper or a strike indicator helps considerably to detect the takes. To match the correct colour I used different dyed hairs and dubbing but kept the gills grey. It is important to cement the herl for durability.

I've always been attracted to salmon flies since I started tying many years ago. Their elegance and symmetry are in one way or another present in all my flies. Not only does it make them more pleasing to the eye but often more effective too. If you like the look of the fly you are fishing with it gives you more confidence and usually better catches.

From all the salmon flies, the Spey type has very adaptable materials and a tying style that makes them very effective for trout flies. As the original pattern used heron and eagle feathers no longer available, I have replaced them with marabou feathers that are available in a wide range of colours.

It has always interested me that all Matuka-style flies have had the capacity to imitate the shape of a minnow, but the problem was that the original style is almost motionless. The marabou hackles make it much more lifelike, especially in slow water. I've devised and tried a number of models of this fly and this one has consistently given the best results over the years.

Skating Spider

Tie in the thread at the centre of the shank and wind back in loose turns level with the barb. Here tie in a hackle with the concave side facing the eye, and take the thread to the centre of the shank. Wrap the feathers one at a time at this point and secure, cutting off the surplus. Tie in the last two feathers with the concave side facing the bend. Secure each feather separately to a point next to the eye. Finally, coat the feather tips with Flexcement or Goop so the fly will look like a star with all the fibres facing a little bit to the front.

HOOK: Daiichi 1510 size 10 – 12

THREAD: Black or brown 8/0

HACKLES: 4 Cock de Leon spade hackles

Foam Stillborn Adams

The body, wing and hackles may be tied to match a specific pattern or natural. The detached body is tied by tying the tail end of a piece of Furry Foam over a needle, onto which the three tail fibres are tied. The needle is withdrawn and the fibres are secured with superglue. The fly illustrated is based on the Adams.

HOOK: Tiemco TMC 900BL size 12 – 20

THREAD: 8/0 to colour-match the pattern

TAILS: Three long and widely spaced Cock de Leon fibres

NYMPH SHUCK: Grey or light brown Furry Foam

BODY: Dubbed blue-grey fur

WING: Grizzly hackle tips in an upright 'V'

HACKLES: Brown (natural red) and grizzle cocks wound together

Emerging Nymph

After winding on the Easy Dubbing, fasten a piece of closed-cell foam in the centre of the shank, making a hole in it with a needle suitable for the CDC feathers to pass through.

HOOK: Tiemco TMC 3761 (D/E, 2X heavy) size 12 – 18

THREAD: Black 8/0

TAILS: Widely spaced Cock de Leon fibres

ABDOMEN: Easy Dubbing or New Dub to match the natural

WING: Cul de canard fibres

WINGCASE: Closed-cell foam

THORAX: Wild boar dubbing (hare's ear is a suitable substitute)

LEGS: Hungarian partridge

Cock de Leon Caddis

Forming the wing: stack the Cock de Leon fibres and tie over the abdomen, pressing lightly with the thumb so fibres form tent-shape wing. Add the biots in a narrow 'V'. Tie fibres over the centre for the perfect shape.

HOOK: Tiemco TMC 2302 or 2312 (2XL, slightly humped shank) size 10 – 26

THREAD: 8/0 brown

BODY: 6 or 7 fibres from a duck tail feather (or ostrich)

WING: Cock de Leon fibres and tan goose biots

ANTENNAE: Cock de Leon fibres

HACKLE: Mixed grizzly and brown (natural red) cocks

Leptophlebia Nymph

Form a cigar-shape thread underbody and wind the abdomen quill. Laquer with superglue, then make five turns of ostrich herl for the gills.

HOOK: Tiemco TMC 2312 or 2302 (2XL, slightly humped shank)

THREAD: 8/0 black

TAIL: Two parted jabalina (peccary) hairs or moose body hair

ABDOMEN: Stripped peacock eye herl

GILLS: Grey ostrich

WINGCASE: Mottled turkey fibres

THORAX: Tan Antron dubbing over fine lead wire

LEGS: Grey partridge

HEAD: Varnished thread in a conical shape

Spey Matuka

When making the tapered mylar braid body, leave space for the gills and marabou hackle. The wing is formed in the Matuka style. Wind four turns of red hackle for the gills. Tie in two marabou feathers by the tips, being careful to select two with a fine quill and perfect fibres. Force all the fibres to the back and wind four turns. Jungle cock eyes will finish the fly.

HOOK: Partridge CS10 Bartleet, single salmon hook

THREAD: Black 8/0

TAP AND RIB: Fine gold oval tinsel

UNDERBODY: Turns of lead wire

BODY: Pearlescent mylar braid

WING: Four saddle hackles, colour to match a minnow or fry

GILLS: Four turns of red saddle hackle

FRONT HACKLE: Two marabou feathers, wound together

EYES (optional): Jungle cock

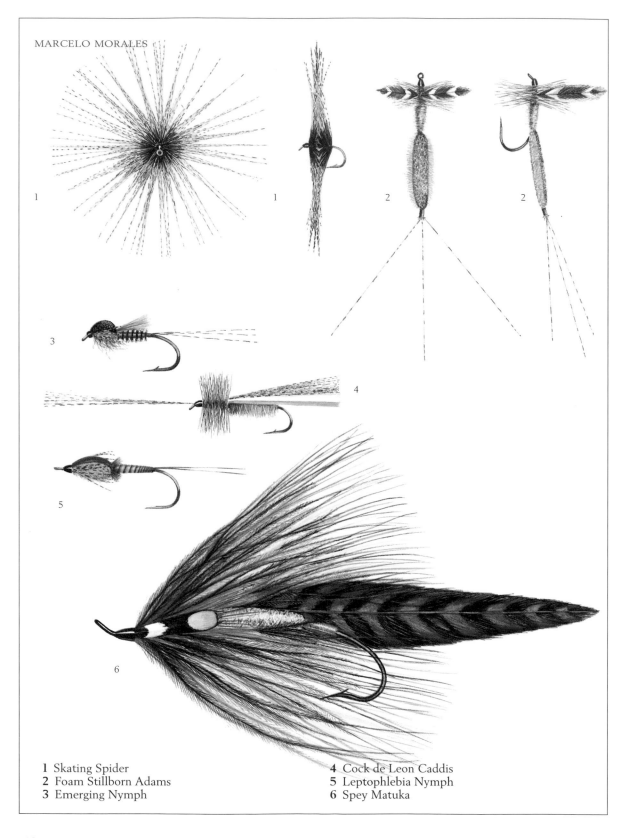

MARCELO MORALES

1 Skating Spider
2 Foam Stillborn Adams
3 Emerging Nymph

4 Cock de Leon Caddis
5 Leptophlebia Nymph
6 Spey Matuka

ROMAN MOSER

AUSTRIA

Roman Moser is one of Europe's best-known fly fisherman. He travels extensively throughout Europe giving casting and fly-tying demonstrations. He has fly fished from the age of fourteen and started tying semi-commercially aged twenty-five. With Hans Gebetsroither, guide and river keeper of Charles Ritz, he started the Gebetsroither School of Fly Fishing. Roman later developed new fly-tying materials and braided leaders with Traun-River Products based in Germany. He left that company about nine years ago to form Innovative-Flyfishing-Products, during which time he has further developed his leaders and introduced new materials and created new patterns.

Roman writes extensively for German magazines and made a highly successful video New Ways with the Caddis *which has been followed up with a further three-part video series,* New Ways of Fishing the Mayfly.

He lives in Gmunden, Austria, on the banks of the crystal-clear and fast-flowing River Traun, one of Europe's premier fly-fishing rivers. By profession he is a teacher of Geography and Physical Education.

I don't know why but most tyers imitate caddis pupae with a light abdomen and a darker thorax. I used to do the same but with poor success until I discovered the unbelievable success of the gold- or brass-head pupa many years ago. The logical step was to create a gold-headed pupa fished dry on top of the water – so the Swimming Caddis Pupa was born. I also tried to imitate the *Rhyacophila* colour with an olive abdomen, but with minor success. The best was and still is the orange type.

In spring caddis pupae appear in larger quantities when the water warms up during the day about noon and in summer in late morning and in the evening before dark. It is always important when you fish this fly to have shadow on the water – caddis don't like bright sunshine.

One of the best parts of a river where most pupae appear are riffles and the stretch below, and rapid river flow. Pupae are agile swimmers. As soon as they reach the surface they swim pretty fast for a short while with or across the current before they pop through the film and emerge as adults. They often try to leave the surface before their long wings have fully dried so they skitter and cartwheel until they can take off to the bankside bushes.

The fish will follow the fast-swimming fly up to the surface with great speed and because of the quick take-off the rise form is quite spectacular. Swirls, boils and splashy takes are common. Sometimes the whole fish shoots out of the water because of their speed.

In these situations I fish my Swimming Caddis Pupa, either in a quarter downstream cast and a wet-fly swing technique or greased and dry in a quarter upstream presentation. In the wet-fly technique it is important to slow down the swing of the fly, either by mending out into the current or by lightly feeding line by the pull of the current. The slack line should slide through the fingers creating drag so the fly has not the same speed as the current. In the case of a take, this will happen in a sharp pull. Because the fish is taking the fly in a curve most people will react instinctively and lift the rod. But the fish has not closed its mouth yet and you feel only the pull and the fish is gone. To avoid this you have to concentrate and learn to develop a different reaction. The rod tip must be dropped to the water surface when you feel the slightest pull and after that you strike upwards. This needs some initial training and practice.

The method of fishing the fly is as a floater and the takes are spectacular. I cast a quarter upstream. The current will create a bow in which I feed in line to slow down. At each feeding mend the fly will skitter and speed up slightly and so I let the imitation drift downstream in short jerks. If there is a take, set the hook by bringing the rod tip parallel to the surface in an upstream movement.

Baetis rhodani mayflies are one of the first up-winged flies to appear each year. I have seen them as early as February but their main emergence is in April. This medium-sized dun with its olive-brown body and oversized buff-grey wings sometimes emerges in tremendous numbers in the early afternoon. They provide fish with the first big surface meal of the year. Early in the hatch any olive imitation will catch a few fish but later on it will be refused more often despite the fish feeding as avidly.

Baetis rhodani emerge quite quickly in, or slightly under, the surface film and you can see only the fully developed fly sitting on the surface. The struggling shredder-emergers with their wings spread out sideways to fill the veins with body liquid is much more interesting to the fish than the already developed upright winged dun which will drift motionless for a long time before take-off. At this stage the fly is mainly ignored by fish.

To be successful I always cast a quarter downstream in a 'stopped-back' manner or with a reach cast. I moisten the fly so it will be presented just under the surface. I follow according to the current speed with the rod tip, jiggling the fly slightly to imitate the natural's struggling movement and it breaking through the surface. You will be astonished how carelessly and confidently fish will attack this imitation.

There are three advantages of the cul de canard feathers that we in Europe have used for many years. It is not so much the oil, as most people

think, that give the fly tied with this feather its buoyancy; it is the incredible amount of surface area this fly creates. Each side stem of the feather is full of hundreds of barbules, like the needles of a pine tree branch. This keeps the feather on top of the water surface.

The second advantage is that a single fibre is thin and limp. There is always some breeze over the water because the current moves the air, and these fine fibres always move and therefore create life in the fly itself; life you could never imitate with the rod tip.

The third advantage is the appearance from underneath. It could be all or nothing – wings, legs, body, all together. It is a dull grey misty view that moves.

When the mayfly is hatching in, or just below, the surface film it blows up its thorax to almost a ball shape. Then the upper side of the thorax back splits and the wings appear. Some fish can be very selective on the different emergent stages of the fly; some can really concentrate on just this shape and stage of the emerger. I call it the 'key shape'. The Balloon Emerger is also a fairly impressionistic example but in fact the over-emphasis is the key to its success.

The Silver Sparkle Bottom Caddis Pupa is a simple pattern enjoying the same sort of success as the Gold Head or Hare's Ear Nymph. At first glance you would think the pattern is an imitation of a freshwater shrimp and could replace Sawyer's Killer Bug, but when fished under certain circumstances I found out that fish will take the fly as a caddis pupa as it leaves the gravel bottom and drifts downstream trapped in the slow current close to the bottom stones. The silver Krystal Hair imitates the gas bubbles and gives the fly an added attraction, and is far more effective and durable than a silver wire rib.

It is very important to fish this very close to the bottom. If there is fast riffle water or fast deep runs I use one of my nymph leaders which has metal inserted inside the braid to get the fly down fast. In slow even flows I use a very long parallel mono leader of about 4 – 5 metres because it is important to have a very small angle to the bottom. When the line is pulled the fly lifts just a little.

I cast a quarter upstream and let the fly sink, then I mend downstream to create a narrow loop.

Slack line is then mended upstream and at each mend the fly will rise a little in a downstream direction. In this way it can be drifted over a long distance very close to the bottom until it swings around and rises to the surface.

My Spent Mayfly (*Ephemera*) floats extremely well because of the deer hair dubbing. The semi-transparent wings give the right appearance to the fish. If you watch female *Ephemerae* near the water you can see them fluttering around, sometimes touching the surface and releasing eggs, then flying away and repeating the process. Eventually the spinner falls to the surface and is carried downstream still fluttering its wings occasionally before dying. The imitation should be fished in the same way with a natural drift and the occasional shiver or jerk with the rod tip.

My final fly is a Plushille Trout Fry which utilizes a new synthetic material ideal for tying lures and fish-imitating flies. When wet the fly appears semi-transparent, glassy and is an unbeatable naturalistic imitation for selective predator fish. It can be marked and coloured with a Pantone pen to imitate different fry or to provide exciting new variations on the streamer theme.

Swimming Caddis Pupa

I secure the initial wrap of tying thread on most of my flies with a droplet of superglue. The finished fly is fluffed up with a piece of Velcro, the fluffier the better.

HOOK: Partridge CS27GRS, barbless, size 10 – 18

THREAD: Yellow 6/0

ABDOMEN: Orange carpet wool mixed with some SLF (Synthetic Living Fibres) from Partridge to give a sparkle effect

LEGS: Two turns of light brown cock hackle, 2nd or 3rd grade. After the fly is finished trim away the lower fibres

THORAX: Golden Yellow SLF fibres, tied fairly bulky

Delta Wing Emerger

The shiny rear extension of the wingcase imitates the split and parted wing shuck of the fly.

HOOK: Partridge CS27GRS barbless, size 12 – 14

THREAD: Light brown 6/0

TAIL: Tip of a cul de canard feather, tied in flat to imitate the empty nymph shuck

ABDOMEN: Light brown hare's ear mixed with white Antron or SLF fibres

WINGS: Dun-coloured cock hackles

THORAX: As for the abdomen

WINGCASE: Pearl plastic lurex strip (Krystal Hair – Flashabou Pearl) with a rear-facing and slightly upward-pointing 2mm stub at the back of the thorax

Balloon Emerger Small Olive

HOOK: Partridge CS27GRS barbless size 14 – 18

THREAD: Orange 8/0

EXOSKELETON: Point of a cul de canard feather tied rear-facing in the middle of the shank

ABDOMEN: Tying thread, 2 layers secured with superglue

THORAX: Olive fine poly, thinly dubbed

BLOWN-UP THORAX: 5 – 10 strands of olive, light grey or light brown marabou fibres, tied in by the tips and brought forward over the thorax

LEGS: Cul de canard feather fibres. The legs are created by the rest of the CDC feather after the tip has been used for the exoskeleton. This is laid flat, rear-facing, so that the single herls are sideways. The herls are pressed close to the fly, tied down and sealed with a small head of thorax dubbing

Silver Sparkle Bottom Caddis Pupa

HOOK: Partridge CS27GRS barbless, size 12 – 16

THREAD: Dark brown 6/0

UNDERBODY: Double layer of lead wire over a drop of superglue

BODY: Dubbed medium-grey carpet wool mixed with some silver Krystal Hair, wound from the front with a second layer finishing at the eye. The fly is finished by combing out the fibres with a piece of Velcro

The fast waters of the Austrian River Traun are where Roman Moser develops many of his patterns.

Roman Moser prepares to release a large River Traun rainbow trout.

1 Swimming Caddis Pupa
2 Delta Wing Emerger
3 Balloon Emerger Small Olive
4 Silver Sparkle Bottom Caddis Pupa
5 Mayfly Spent (Ephemera)
6 Plushille Trout Fry

Mayfly Spent (Ephemera)

HOOK: Partridge CS28 barbless long shank, size 8 – 14

THREAD: Orange 6/0

TAIL: 3 widely spaced cock pheasant tail fibres

BODY: Rear third – dark brown carpet fibre dubbing; middle third – creamy white deer hair dubbing which has been mixed in a blender with poly fibres

THORAX AND LEGS: Dark brown calf hair dubbing which has been blended with fine rabbit underfur, wound in a figure of eight round the wing base

WINGS: White Ghost fibres (100% polypropelene) secured horizontally with figure-of-eight turns, trimmed to shape and marked with a permanent marker pen

Plushille Trout Fry

The full instructions for using Plushille come with each packet. It is easy to use and produces very realistic fry imitations. It is produced by Innovative-Flyfishing-Products of Gmunden, Austria, and is distributed in the UK by Partridge of Redditch Ltd.

HOOK: Partridge CS29 barbless, long shank, size 2 – 8

THREAD: White

EYES: Krystal glass eyes 5 – 7mm

TAIL AND BODY: Plushille trimmed to shape and Velcro brushed

COLOURING: Pantone pens

LARS-ÅKE OLSSON

SWEDEN

Lars-Åke Olsson has been fly fishing for thirty-five years in Sweden, Norway, Denmark, England and the USA. He is a member of the Flyfishers' Club of London, the Grayling Society and the Federation of Fly Fishers. Between the years 1976 and 1988 he took part in the restoration of the River Gim after its timber logging, and in 1989 he leased the Idsjöströmmen, just below the village of Gimdalen, from the local landowners, and there created the first catch-and-release river in Sweden.

He is a casting instructor and a fishing guide, and teaches fly fishing and fly casting in Sweden, Norway and the USA, and has given fly-tying demonstrations in Sweden, Norway, at the Fly Fair in Holland and at the Federation of Fly Fishers' conclave in the USA. He has written two books, From My Flybox *and* Flyfishing in Swedish Lapland, *and has contributed to other books and written numerous articles for European fishing magazines.*

He spends from June to September each year in Gimdalen, Sweden, fishing and guiding on the Idsjöströmmen and in Swedish Lapland, and October to May fishing and teaching fly fishing and fly casting in the USA, where he lives with Jennifer Smith in Bozeman, Montana.

It was a quiet, windless and beautiful morning in May, the time for the large dark olive of spring. I was walking the banks of the Itchen in the south of England with Roy Darlington, the riverkeeper of the legendary Abbots Barton stretch and John Roberts, the editor of this book. John was equipped, not with a fly rod this time, but with a camera, to take fishing pictures of me, if I could get into some action. Roy was guiding us for some time, giving us good advice, before returning to his daily duties in the town of Winchester.

When we came to one of the carriers and crossed it, Roy spotted a nice trout from the bridge. I decided to try for it and went downstream so I could cast upstream. There were no flies on the water, but I needed to fish a dry fly and not a nymph. No flies, no rising fish, so I used a big fly to convince the fish to come up. I tied on a suitable large dark olive imitation, a size 12 Green Gimriver Dun and cast upstream to a point where Roy had seen the fish. My fly landed on the water

and the trout, spooked by my cast, came down in a short nervous rush, saw me, turned quickly upstream and stopped, ten yards from me and ten inches from the bank – my bank!

How do you cast to a trout which lies ten inches from your bank? I could see the trout, the broad back with its spots and the slowly moving tail. It was beautiful and exciting. I false-cast a couple of times over land to measure the distance and let my fly line and half the leader land on the ground. The rest of the leader and the fly landed on the smooth surface, a yard above the fish. Since no fly line was pulling the leader downstream the fly floated drag free in a straight drift, towards the trout. I watched the fly and the trout in knee-deep water; everything was visible. The fly floated into the trout's small window but he didn't move. Of course not, he had been spooked; besides he was not in a feeding mood. He wouldn't take. Then suddenly he rose slowly and standing on his tail, absolutely vertically, he sucked the fly in. It was

A three-pound brown trout completes its final struggles for Lars-Åke Olsson, on the River Kaitum, Swedish Lapland.

OPPOSITE
Lars-Åke Olsson returns a fine grayling to the River Kaitum in Swedish Lapland.

an unforgettable picture which I will carry with me for the rest of my life. He was a beautiful golden Itchen trout, 3lb, and the fly was the irresistible Green Gimriver Dun!

The fly, which I tie in two versions in grey and olive shades, has been with me for a long time and proved its efficiency in Norway, Sweden, England and the USA. I have the greatest confidence in it and there isn't a trout in the world, in any stream, feeding on newly hatched duns, which can resist it!

The Gimriver duns are two flies in the Gimriver series which I devised some years ago using my marrow spoon and the fly trap of Idsjöströmmen in the Gim in central Sweden. I wanted something simple and practical to match the hatch, so I designed two duns to match ninety-five per cent of all the duns, especially *Baetis* and *Ephemerella*.

When reading about the Catskill area in the USA, the birthplace of American fly fishing, I could see the similarity between the American and Swedish environment. The Catskill fly was to become a model for my fly, with some 'improvements'. By placing the wing and the hackle close to the middle of the hook, the balance of the fly was so perfect that it was riding the water, sometimes without touching the surface with the tail. The Gimriver duns are based on the Catskill models.

It was in the middle of June, one week before Midsummer weekend. Stoneflies, upwinged flies and even the sedges, the latest of the three, had begun to hatch. It was warm, the sun was shining and the sky had that perfect blue colour. I was watching one section of the Idsjöströmmen, the rapid just below the village of Gimdalen. Between the main stream and my bank was a shallow part of the river which was fast, straight and smooth. A fish was rising once or twice every minute ten yards in front of me. I tried dry flies of several patterns and colours, nymphs and wet flies without result. I stopped fishing and ceased the somewhat mechanical search through my fly box and studied carefully the smooth water surface and the rises. The surface was bare; I saw nothing. The rises were fast and splashy like when fish take a dun or a sedge pupa, but there were no duns on the water and the time for hatching pupae seemed a little odd – in the middle of the day in bright sunshine!

Suddenly I remembered my floating nymph, which had been efficient now and then during the years, tied it on my leader, greased the tail, legs and body with floatant, and waited for the next rise. When it came I cast my nymph a yard above and watched it float on the smooth surface. The rise came, as usual, on the first cast. I struck and after some time I netted an eighteen-inch grayling. I killed the fish and checked the contents of the stomach. It was crammed with olive nymphs and sedge pupae!

I tie the Green Gimriver Nymph in two versions. The floating version is tied on the lightest dry-fly hook, has longer tails, and a thicker dubbed thorax to create better floatability. I always fish it well oiled or greased.

The Green Gimriver floating nymph and the dun imitation are excellent during a hatch of olives. When the numbers of duns are large enough the fish seem to prefer the duns. If the hatch is sparse they take the nymph fished under the surface, either in a dead drift or with movement. During a steady hatch I have seen the fish change between the dun and the floating nymph, mostly preferring the floating nymph, possibly aware that the hatching and struggling nymph on the surface stays longer at the surface, and is easier to take than a dun which might fly away at any second.

The Black Spider is a small, simple little wet fly which is absolutely indispensable in my fly box and has saved many blank fishing days whether it has been a representative of a small (hatching) nymph, ant, micro caddis pupa, midge pupa or midge. Fished in the middle of the day, the afternoon, or evening, alone on the leader or together with one or other spiders, it is one of the most efficient flies I have ever used. Sometimes I fish it upstream just under the surface on a well-greased leader; sometimes dead drift downstream, mending line where necessary. It is very successful in April and May on the river when trout feed on midge pupae and adults. I have had great success with it for brown and rainbow trout in April on the spring creeks and the Madison River in Montana.

The Green Caddis Worm is a representation of the net-building caddis larvae of the *Hydropsyche* species. It is a fat, clumsy worm, which does not swim but crawls between the stones of the riverbed. The imitation is leaded and is best fished upstream with a short line to make it sink as fast as possible and stay close to the bottom. Even though it is quite possible to catch fish when fishing across and downstream, the most efficient way of fishing the nymph is upstream.

The less line on the water, the less drag of the fly from the line. That's why a long rod is the perfect nymph rod for fishing upstream. It is easier to lift the line off the water, and the necessary fast strike is faster with the long rod. On a smooth water surface, with the right light, a short line, and a shallow river, it is enough to grease the leader or the butt of the leader and use it, or the tip of the fly line, as a strike indicator. When the light or the surface conditions change, it becomes necessary to use one of the many types of strike indicators.

My way of fishing upstream is to cast no more than eight to ten yards of fly line and then mend downstream to create a little bend in the fly line a few yards from the tip of the line. I keep an eye on the bend which must be neither too deep nor to flat, just 'enough'. Depending upon the speed of the current I mend upstream or downstream and watch the signals from the bend in the fly line, the tip of the line or the greased leader.

In the rivers of northern Sweden, and I think also anywhere else in the fly fishing world, the sedges hatch later in the summer than stoneflies and upwinged flies. When they do, they completely dominate the insect life for weeks onwards. The emerging pupae come in thousands and thousands and the show during late afternoons, early nights or in the middle of the nights is fantastic. The fish move fast to chase fast-moving emergers, and the rises are splashy and loud. Fish are everywhere. The whole river is alive, like never before. Empty shucks are floating on the surface, adults are in your hair, behind and on your glasses, in your shirt, your car and in the kitchen next morning. The enormous number of emerging sedges makes it difficult to compete with yours – the fishing is very, very difficult!

One morning on the Idsjöströmmen, in bright sunshine, there were thousands of newly hatched adults in the air, on the bridge, banks and trees, but the water surface was smooth. Not one rise could be seen and there were hardly any sedges on the water because of the speed with which the pupae hatched into adults and immediately took flight. I tried everything – dries, wets, small, big, black, green – but nothing happened. I was sure what was happening below the surface but I wanted proof. After two or three hours of fishing I managed to hook a small grayling and decided that it had to sacrifice its life for science. The stomach contents of that eleven-inch fish yielded 165 sedge pupae and nothing else.

It's not easy to compete with nature. The pupa dressing I have used over the years has never brought me a lot of fish during the intense hatches but it has been the most successful pattern of all the ones I've tried. It can be fished with a wet fly downstream swing but, as usual, the most efficient way with a pupae or nymph is upstream, with the shortest possible line.

The Squirrel Sedge has really got the right name because its body is tied with fur from a squirrel's body and the wing from its tail fur. It is one of my very best flies when the sedge season has started, and trout and grayling look out for emerging pupae and egg-laying females. It is also a perfect fish-finder during those days when fish are lying deep because of the weather, an absence of hatching or egg-laying insects, or high water, and I still want to fish the dry fly.

To me the fish-finder has to be big, to convince the fish to come to the surface when it is lying deep and close to the bottom. There must be a real reward for the journey upwards, an opportunity for breakfast, lunch and dinner at the same time. A fly tied on a size 8 or 12 long-shank hook is the perfect advertisement.

The Squirrel is the oldest of the Gimriver flies. When I tie it I want it to do two things for me: float and show a distinct sedge silhouette. It is a very good floater because the long-haired body which I spin on a spinning block traps a lot of air. The wing, which is double and folded back over the body contains a lot of air, so when the body eventually sinks, the fly still floats on the thick air-filled wing. I also add a palmer hackle which I trim above and below the shank because I want the wing to lie flat along the body.

I fish the Squirrel in a dead drift. It is one of my favourites for pocket water or fast riffles. The faster and more turbulent the water, the more I cast and fish across and downstream, using a parachute cast often combined with a reach cast. The downstream technique offers several advantages compared to fishing upstream. I can use the same length of line, there is no feeding and stripping line, the fish sees the fly first before the leader and

line, and I can lift or pull the line, leader and fly upstream one or several yards and then let it drift down again.

Green Gimriver Dun

HOOK: Tiemco TMC 103 BL size 13 – 19

THREAD: Olive

TAIL: Four Microfibetts, in two 45-degree groups

WING: A single bunch of male mallard mottled breast feather

BODY: Olive-green dyed natural fur

HACKLE: Blue dun cock with a 'V' clipped in the underside, wound over the thorax

Green Gimriver Nymph

Over a built-up tapering thread underbody wind the olive dubbing from the eye towards the bend. I use dubbing spun on a Darrel Martin dubbing whirl which gives a thin, strong and slightly hairy body. Rib with thread to the middle of the thorax, put the capercaillie feather on the thorax, stem towards the bend, positioned so that the fibres give the right leg length. Secure and divide the legs with figure-of-eight turns of thread and cut off the tip section of the feather. Double and redouble the feather for the wingcase.

HOOK: Partridge CS27 (D/E, fine wire, slightly long shank) size 12 – 18, and for the floating version Tiemco TMC 103 BL

THREAD: Olive

TAIL: 4 mottled brown fibres from the primary wing of a male capercaillie (or wood cock substitute), 2 pointing sideways, 2 backwards

BODY: A well-tapered body of olive fur (more thickly dubbed at the thorax for the floating version)

LEGS AND WINGCASES: As for the tail fibres

Black Spider

HOOK: Size 16 – 22

THREAD: Black silk or nylon

BODY: Tying thread

SHOULDER: Black or dark brown fur or peacock herl, as a little knob behind the hackle

HACKLE: Black-green metallic neck or shoulder feather from a starling, or alternatively a black hen hackle will suffice

Green Caddis Worm

Start the fly at the eye by tying in the slip of feather fibre for the shoulder over the eye. Dub the fur and wind well down into the hook bend; use the thread as ribbing, go forward and stop one-third from the eye. Fold the feather fibre backwards and with the thread form three distinct segments and finish off.

HOOK: Partridge GRS6A or K4A (D/E, curved shank) size 10 – 16

THREAD: Olive

UNDERBODY: Wound lead or copper wire

BODY: Natural olive-green fur ribbed with tying thread

SHOULDER: Slip of black or dark brown feather fibres

Brown Sedge Pupa

HOOK: Partridge K2B (U/E, curved shank, sedge) size 10 – 16

THREAD: Brown

BODY: Dubbed fur from the darkest part of a hare's mask or ear

LEGS/ANTENNAE: Brown speckled fibres from a male capercaillie's wing (substitute brown partridge) tied at 45 degrees to the shank

Squirrel Sedge

HOOK: Partridge E1A (D/E, 4X fine, long shank) size 8 – 16

THREAD: Brown

BODY: Reddish-brown summer squirrel fur (substitute hare's ear or mask) spun on a spinning block

HACKLE: Brown (natural red cock) palmered and the upper fibres cut away and the lower section with a 'V' cut out

WING: Reddish-brown squirrel tail, tied in behind the eye, roots behind the hook bend and points in front of the eye and then folded backwards over the first part of the wing. Make a big head of the upper part of the wing and whip-finish behind the head

LARS-ÅKE OLSSON

1 Green Gimriver Dun
2 Green Gimriver Nymph
3 Black Spider

4 Green Caddis Worm
5 Brown Sedge Pupa
6 Squirrel Sedge

Francesco Palu

ITALY

Francesco Palu lives in Campoformido, a small town close to Udine in the north-eastern area of Italy. He has fly fished for almost thirty-five years and has made a career out of developing fly rods and producing fly-tying materials and tools. He regularly fishes and demonstrates in Italy, Austria, Switzerland, Spain, Slovenia and Croatia, and writes for Italian fishing journals. As well as devising an extraordinary dubbing material which is utilized in the patterns below, he has developed a telescopic fly rod which can be adjusted to be used at different lengths. Francesco firmly believes that the advantages of the telescopic rod provides better and more versatile fly-fishing techniques than the traditional fly rod of a fixed length.

I believe there are three important and inseparable aspects to successful fly fishing. Needless to say, I also believe that the flies I have devised and my method of fishing them fulfil these criteria.

The first is that the dubbing material and its tying method should give the artificial the appearance of a real insect. It has to be a credible imitation of the natural. Secondly, a rod of an appropriate length is needed to impart a natural motion to the artificial. To this end I use a telescopic rod which is quickly adaptable to various lengths as I change patterns and face different fishing circumstances. In many opinions my ideas are revolutionary, and I am having to fight for the acceptance of the concept of the telescopic rod. I believe that it has considerable benefits as it offers the flexibility to change fishing styles very quickly and alter the imparted movement to a fly. Thirdly, for maximum effect, artificials should be fished at the time and in a place most appropriate to where and when the natural insects appear.

Crucial to each of these flies is the dubbing material which I have devised. The idea for the dubbing came about after a long and frustrating delay in receiving some high-quality hackle necks from a well-known company. I set about developing my own alternative. The resulting dubbing may be used for bodies to replace the usual dubbing material, or to create legs in the place of the standard hackle. The new material is easier and faster to use, and it is more reliable than buying a neck of an unknown quality. Most of all, the legs and bodies created by the new dubbing are, under most circumstances, much more natural than the alternatives.

The Surface Polyphemus is an emerging *Ephemera* imitation. It is a system pattern to be colour- and size-matched to the natural emerging insects. In addition to being perfect for trout and grayling it has also caught very many salmon. It is extremely buoyant because of the ethafoam ball. I fish it in four fishing styles.

The first is rather like the English Booby nymph style. It is fished on stillwater or in a slow-moving river, and cast downstream where it sinks on the end of a weighted braided leader. It is retrieved by progressive twitches to give it the up-and-down motion typical of an emerging insect.

The second style involves two nymphs fished in tandem on a four- to five-metre leader. The point fly is a weighted Polyphemus, larger than the dropper fly. I suggest the following sizes: size 16 dropper with a 12 – 14 point fly; size 10 with a 8 – 12; size 8 with a 6 – 10. The dropper should be 25cm. The point fly is the one being fished. It is cast upstream and the dropper fly monitored as a strike indicator. When cast across and downstream, and retrieved by raising the rod tip, the dropper fly is made to imitate the skating motion of some sedges and the point fly will be moving enticingly up and down.

I also fish two Polyphemus nymphs in tandem on or close to the surface with a wiggle-like motion. The surface nymphs will have drag typical of the struggling insect in the film. The second and third styles of fishing are best achieved by my two-handed telescopic rod which extends to 5.3 metres to give considerable control over the flies.

The final method is to fish a single nymph upstream in a non-hatch situation. The best results are achieved in riffle water or where vegetation overhangs the bank.

The second in the Polyphemus series is this weighted imitation of the emerging mayfly nymph. It was named after the mythical one-eyed Cyclops killed by Odysseus. The nymph was born on the River Gacka for sight fishing to visible fish. I had been used to fishing nymphs with coloured beads at the head but the beads will not fit on many hooks because of the barb or the hook bend. After a long period of testing and trials on the sphere positioning I came up with the idea of the position on top of the shank and secured by a central pin. The outcome is a weird, but deadly artificial.

On clear water I cast it between the weed lanes or at the head of deep inviting pools where the big trout lie. It is cast upstream and fished in a dead drift. This versatile pattern works on any kind of water. In the appropriate sizes, colours and techniques it is also great for salmon.

Mayflies of one sort or another are probably the most widely imitated natural flies. This is my interpretation which, with the exception of the wings and tails, is made exclusively from my dubbing fur. The wings are synthetic, lightweight and transparent. It is tied to represent the surface emerger erecting its wings and struggling from the nymphal shuck.

It was born out of some frustrating grayling fishing on the River Unec in Slovenia about fourteen years ago. Fish were freely rising in a hatch of duns but for this embarrassed professional fly tyer it was an unsuccessful day. The failure of a pattern sometimes spawns the success of another and so I forgot the rules and tied a size 16 imitation, an insignificant thing compared to the hatching naturals. The outcome was that these so-called canny and unpredictable grayling ended up liking these small flies better than the real thing. The Grey Dun may be colour-matched to whatever naturals are about.

My two chosen nymph patterns are simply known as No 9 and No 11. The colouring and sizes can be amended for different rivers and different naturals. I fish them in tandem and they have the devastating knack of depopulating the water of trout. They imitate the emerging nymph early in its ascent to the surface. The silver sphere in its under-thorax is representing the gas build-up under the natural's nymphal skin. The most productive style of fishing them is directly upstream in a dead drift, retrieving the fly line to keep pace with the drift. I use a 2.5 metre leader with a dropper placed about 40cm above the point. The dropper should be only about 5cm and of stiff nylon to avoid it twisting round the rest of the leader.

I tie my dry Cinnamon Sedge to imitate erratically behaving ovipositing females when they return to the river's surface. They skitter in long or short bursts across the water dragging the tips of their abdomens as they go. This peculiar motion is an irresistible invitation to trout and grayling, and even to chub and carp. It rings a bell of crazy uncontrolled desire to rise and catch the insect.

To imitate the wiggling motion of the naturals I use my two-handed telescopic rod of 4 to 5.4 metres in conjunction with one or two imitations on a five- to six-metre leader. The dropper fly should be tied about two to three metres from the point on a 25cm dropper. The rod tip can be wiggled from side to side to imitate the erratic movement of the naturals.

Surface Polyphemus

HOOK: Tiemco TMC 2310 size 6 – 20

THREAD: Polyester thread to match the dressing

HEAD: White ethafoam ball enclosed in a nylon mesh

TAILS: Hair fibres of a darker colour than the body

BODY: Palu dubbing fur wound, colour to match the natural

Weighted Polyphemus (Black and Yellow)

HOOK: Partridge GRS12ST (S/E, L/S sedge hook) or K12ST size 4 -14

THREAD: Black polyester

SPHERE: Metallic silver Palu ball secured with small gold-coloured nail

UNDERBODY (optional): Fine lead wire as required

TAILS: Two stubs of black Palu dubbing, ref 106, iris tinsel

BODY: Black Palu dubbing fur, ref 106, size II, wound

RIB: Yellow Palu dubbing fur, ref 106 LO

Grey Dun: Surface Emerger

Using the Palu dubbing the fly is tied without tying thread. Coat a fine smear of varnish on the shank. Wind on the body dubbing and tie in the tails. Wind towards the eye, stopping about a third from the eye. Make four turns of the hackle dubbing for the thorax. Cut out the wings and fix in position with a drop of fast-setting glue. Continue to wind the dubbing to secure the wings and secure with a drop of fine varnish at the head. Pick out the hackle fibres with a dubbing needle.

HOOK: Partridge L3A (D/E, wide gape, fine wire) size 12 – 20

TAILS: A few fibres from a doormouse tail

BODY: Palu dubbing fur, ref 106 LA (silver tinsel)

WINGS: Transparent Palu winging material, ref 186 L, grey

HACKLE: Smokey grey Palu dubbing fur, ref 106 H

Nymph No 9

HOOK: Dahiatsu 0240 size 6 – 16

THORAX: Metallic silver bead positioned one-third from the eye and secured by figure-of-eight turns of thread

TAILS: 2 small stubs of maroon Palu dubbing, ref 106 LI (iris tinsel)

BODY AND WINGCASE: Palu dubbing as for the tail, quadrupled over the top of the bead

WINGS: Transparent Palu winging material, ref 186 L, cut in a wide 'V' shape

HEAD: Fine copper wire

Nymph No 11

HOOK: Dahiatsu 2040 size 6 – 16

THORAX: Metallic silver bead positioned one-third from the eye and secured with figure-of-eight turns of thread

TAILS: 2 small stubs of black Palu dubbing, ref 106 LI

BODY: White Palu dubbing, ref 106 copper wire, size II

WINGCASE: 4 strands of black Palu dubbing, ref 106 LI, over the top of the bead

LEGS: Speckled partridge back feather secured over the bead by the wing case fibres

HEAD: Fine copper wire

Cinnamon Sedge

HOOK: Tiemco TMC 2312 (S/E, 2XL, slightly humped shank) size 6 – 14

THREAD: Orange polyester

BODY: Reddish Palu dubbing fur, ref 108, size 0, wound

WINGS: Transparent Palu winging materials in a tent-shape

LEGS: Reddish Palu dubbing fur, ref 108, wound

ANTENNAE: Dubbing fur fibres tied facing forward

Note: Some of the materials referred to may not be easily available to all readers. Francesco Palu can be contacted at Via Silvio Pellico 88, 33030 Camporformido (UD), Italy.

FRANCESCO PALU

1 Surface Polyphemus
2 Weighted Polyphemus
3 Grey Dun: Surface Emerger

4 Nymph No 9
5 Nymph No 11
6 Cinnamon Sedge

MASAO SAKAGUCHI

Masao Sakaguchi is a regular contributor to the Japanese fly-fishing press. Many of his articles have been on the results of his surveys into the relationship between aquatic insects and trout in Japanese rivers. Since 1989 he has been a regular demonstrator at the conclaves of the International Federation of Fly Tyers and has participated in programme demonstrations with fellow-countryman Nori Tashiro on three occasions.

One of Masao's concerns is that Japanese fly fishers have tended to accept imported ideas, methods and fly patterns from the USA and Britain rather than devise their own strategies and patterns for Japanese rivers. Rather as Halford, Gordon and others created national styles and imitations through their interest in entomology, Masao's close interest in aquatic entomology should be one of the catalysts for Japanese trout fishers to develop techniques and patterns of their own.

Masao was born in 1950 and by profession is a marketing analyst for an oil company.

Japan's game fish species are largely a well-kept secret and perhaps it is appropriate that I should enlighten you.

In Japan, we have two native trout families, Yamame and Iwana. The Yamame is very quick and extremely wary. They do not grow very large and a twelve-inch fish is regarded as big. There are more species in the northern part of Japan and Hokkaido, the northern island of Japan. Some of these are catadromous, going down to the sea before returning to spawn. They are called Sakuramasu or cherry salmon, and they grow to between twenty and twenty-four inches. The Amago belongs to the Yamame family and has red spots on its flanks. They are found mainly in the south-west of the country, and grow to about twelve inches.

Iwana is a species of the char family. Along with the Yamame, Iwana are keenly sought after by fly fishers. Their habitat is at the highest altitudes of all Japanese freshwater species. They eat anything that is edible, from insects to small snakes and frogs. They average twelve to fifteen inches in streams, but those that live in lakes grow up to twenty to twenty-four inches. Also in Hokkaido, we have a slightly different Iwana called Amemasu with white-spotted flanks. Another catadromous char species with red spots, similar to Dolly Varden of Alaska and Canada is found only in Hokkaido Island and grows to between twelve and twenty inches.

Additionally, there are brown trout, brook trout and rainbow trout. They were all transplanted from abroad and all are enthusiastically sought after by fly fishers. Brook trout are found only in two or three streams. The brown trout mainly inhabit lakes but rainbow trout are more widespread. The latter reproduce well in Hokkaido but rarely elsewhere in Japan. As a result rainbow trout are mainly a stocked fish. Fish that survive a season without capture become more like truly wild trout, strong and spectacular. They are highly valued by fly fishers and have become the number-one target by Japanese fly fishers.

Many Japanese rivers are precipitous; flowing from high mountains through V-shaped ravines, they often look more like cascades than rivers.

We have a tremendous variety of aquatic insects, mayflies, caddis and stoneflies, the same flies that are important to trout fly fishing across the world.

The fundamental principle of fly fishing is one of matching the trout behaviour. I have made several surveys of aquatic insects at the major trout streams in Japan with my friends, Nori and Tada Tashiro who are pace-setting fly fishers in Japan. Identifying the species and their numbers, as well as their emergence activities, is directly connected to fly fishing. Trout fly fishing is becoming increasingly popular in Japan, and many anglers are putting an undue emphasis on the numbers of fish caught, and have been too willing to accept the influences of American or European fly fishers. Anglers who understand the significance of insect life cycles on trout behaviour are increasing, but we lack any hatch charts for the major trout streams. It seems to me that the development of hatch charts through on-stream research is the responsibility of fly fishers. I firmly believe that the starting point of fly fishing is to understand precisely both the aquatic insects and trout behaviour towards them.

An important issue facing Japanese fly fishers is to save the native trout. The increasing number of fly fishers has had a serious impact on the trout population, especially of bigger trout. Many of us believe that the catch-and-release concept must be the only way to reverse this trend. The potential of our rivers can match some of the world's best and we are appealing strongly to fishing co-operatives, and local government who actually manage the rivers, to adopt a longer-term view.

The six flies I have chosen are very important ones in Japan and all six patterns are based upon Nori Tashiro's original designs. The *Siphlonurus* is a typical swimming mayfly nymph. *Siphlonurus* species hatch out on rocks and stones sticking out of the water or along the bank side after climbing there. Therefore, the dun of this mayfly type is rarely taken by trout. It is in the early spring, prior to emergence, that trout take advantage of these nymphs. They are relatively large with a body of about 20mm.

The swimming nymph pattern simulates the natural's kicking swimming action. The dubbing furs are picked out after ribbing, then trimmed flat and slightly oval to imitate the gills. Soft synthetic furs are easier to pick out than natural fur. The hook is the TMC400T designed by Nori Tashiro specifically for swimming nymphs. I recommend two different types: point-down and point-up. For the point-down type, lead wire is wound at the elongated neck. For the point-up type, lead is wound at the hook bend to keep the hook point up. The size of the wire and number of turns, which depend on the hook size, are very important for realistic swimming. This pattern type is also very good for imitating *Ameletus* and *Isonychia* species in different materials.

The best fishing method is to cast upstream and allow the fly to drift drag-free. When it reaches the fishing zone, gradually lift the rod or move it upstream parallel with the surface to make the nymph swim attractively. The natural's swimming speed is four to eight inches per second. Jiggling the rod tip or varying the retrieve speed is more effective than the dead drift. The combination of a point-down type with a point-up type on the dropper is the most effective.

The *Baetis* species are very important trout food on streams throughout the world although individually the nymphs of many species are tiny, between 6 – 9mm in length. Most emerge in the surface film. The several seconds when they drift down to emerge are the most vulnerable in all their life stages. The imitation should be fished in a drag-free drift. My chosen nymph has a body colour similar to the blue-winged olive in North America. This pattern has worked very well both in Japan and the USA, and can be colour-adapted to local species.

Our surveys revealed that it is probable that caddis flies, at various stages of their life cycle, are the most important aquatic insect measured over the year. The *Stenopsyche japonica*, a large species about 40mm (1.6 inches) long is a typical and abundant species in most Japanese trout streams. It is similar to the *Hydropsyche* species in that it makes nets between rocks using its own silk and collects tiny life-forms for food. Through our researches with stomach pumps, we have often found them in trout and know them to be an essential item on the trout food menu.

At the pupal stage almost all caddis species can be easily taken by trout. I tie a pupal imitation of the *Cheumatopsyche* species, often referred to as the Little Sister Sedge, which is abundant on many American and Japanese trout streams. Trout feed frantically on these, like many other pupae, just beneath the surface with typically splashy rises.

I fish this most successfully in the down-and-across style but lifting it towards the surface and then allowing it to drift with slight drag just beneath the surface. This is very effective because the pupae swim to the surface and then drift during emergence.

The *Stenopsyche* is a very common genus of net-spinning caddis in Japan. The more widespread *Hydropsyche* species behave in a similar manner. Because the larvae usually live within their silken nets in the narrow gaps between stones, you could be forgiven for ignoring this as an important trout food. These large larvae are often caught by trout when leaving their net shelters. They drift in the current, bending their bodies, thorax upward, as they change shelters. The dead drift is the most effective presentation with additional weight on the line to get down deep.

Stonefly species are also an important trout food. I have tied two examples of stoneflies, large and small. Like similar rivers the world over, our clear water freestone waters usually have many stonefly nymphs. These imitations work very well and I suggest they can be colour-matched to your own local species.

The first is a simple but effective imitation, the Hare's Ear Stonefly. It has a shabby look, but this fuzziness seems to be attractive to trout. The pattern doesn't set out to imitate a specific species but its combination of a dark brown body and a yellow thorax is typical of a number of species. I also use this for Yamame (landlocked cherry salmon) and Iwana (Japanese char) in freestone streams.

The *Amphinemura* (small black stonefly) is a very numerous genus in early spring. When they emerge, they are sometimes forced to drift in the current and consequently frequently end up being taken by trout. Both stonefly nymphs are best fished in a dead drift. Riffles, pools and pocket water are the most likely places. Since I usually use a floating line, some split shot or other sinking aids are indispensable in sinking the fly quickly.

Siphlonurus Swimming Nymph

POINT-DOWN TYPE

Hook size	Lead wire size (mm)	Number of wrappings
8	0.90	13
8	0.45	13 – 2 layers
10	0.90/0.45	10 – 2 layers*
12	0.55	13
14	0.55	10

POINT-UP TYPE

Hook size	Lead wire size (mm)	Number of wrappings
8	0.55	20
10	0.55	15
12	0.45	20
14	0.45	15

*of narrower wire

HOOK: Tiemco TMC400T (1XF, bent shank) size 8 – 14

WEIGHT: Depending on hook size, see above

THREAD: Olive Flymaster 6/0

RIB: Gold round tinsel (Veniards #20)

TAIL: Amherst pheasant tippet fibres

BODY AND THORAX: Dubbed pale green synthetic fur

OVERBACK: Barred wood duck flank feather

WINGCASE: Crow quill for the emerging season; dyed olive goose quill for the rest of the season

LEGS: Natural grey partridge flank feather

Baetis Nymph

HOOK: Tiemco TMC2687 (2X wide, 2X short, fine wire) size 16 – 18

THREAD: Uni-thread 8/0 olive

TAIL: Dyed olive partridge fibres

BODY AND THORAX: Synthetic olive dubbing fur

WINGCASE: Dyed dark brown turkey quill

RIB: Super-fine French round tinsel

LEGS: As for the tail

Cheumatopsyche Caddis Pupa (Little Sister Sedge Pupa)

HOOK: One-Up 3846 (wide-gape, 1X short, strong wire) size 14 – 16

THREAD: Uni-thread 8/0 olive

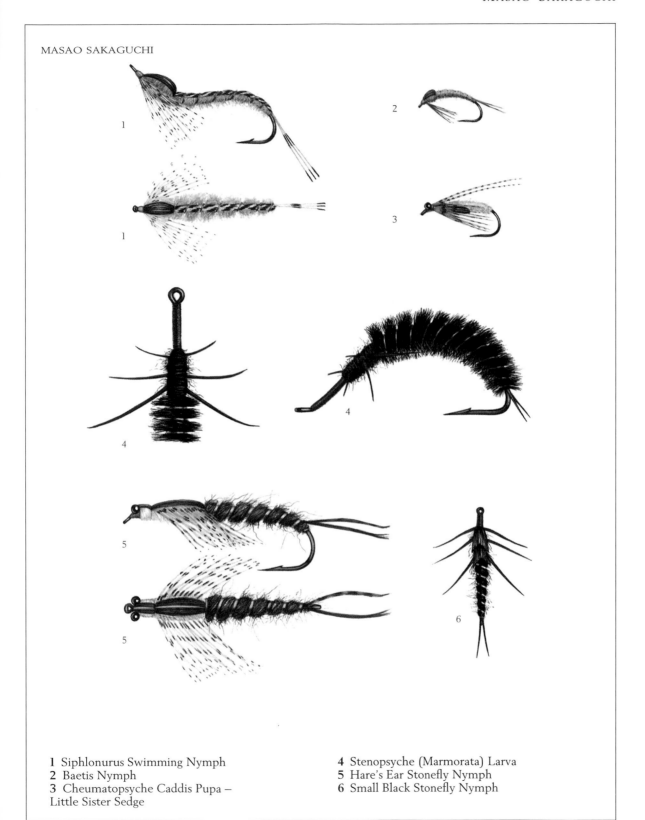

MASAO SAKAGUCHI

1 Siphlonurus Swimming Nymph
2 Baetis Nymph
3 Cheumatopsyche Caddis Pupa –
Little Sister Sedge

4 Stenopsyche (Marmorata) Larva
5 Hare's Ear Stonefly Nymph
6 Small Black Stonefly Nymph

BODY: Bright green synthetic fur with Crystal Flash
WINGCASE: Dyed black duck quill
LEGS: Brown partridge feather
THORAX: Dark brown fur
ANTENNAE: Wood duck fibres
EYES: Burned monofilament (approx 10lb b.s.)

Stenopsyche (Marmorata) Larva

HOOK: Mustad 37160 size 6 – 10
THREAD: Flymaster 6/0 brown
WEIGHT: Lead wire (0.55mm)
TAIL: Stripped brown goose quill
BODY: Black ostrich herl
THORAX: Blackish brown dubbing fur
LEGS: Stripped brown goose quill
RIB: Oval gold tinsel
HEAD: Brown thread

Hare's Ear Stonefly Nymph

HOOK: Tiemco TMC2302 (2XL, slightly curved shank) size 6 – 10, or TMC200R

THREAD: Flymaster 6/0 brown
TAIL: Dark brown grouse feather
BODY: Dark brown hare's ear fur
THORAX: Yellow fur
RIB: Round gold tinsel (Veniards #20)
WINGCASE: Brown partridge feather with white stem at the centre
LEGS: Brown partridge feather

Small Black Stonefly Nymph (Amphinemura species)

HOOK: Tiemco TMC 3761 (1XL, 2X heavy, sproat bend) size 12 – 14
THREAD: Flymaster 6/0 brown
UNDERBODY: Lead wire (0.45mm)
TAIL: Brown stripped goose quill
BODY: Blackish brown synthetic fur
THORAX: Blackish brown dubbing fur
WINGCASE: Black goose quill
LEGS: Brown stripped goose quill
RIB: Varnished French tinsel
HEAD: Clear varnished brown thread

ERNEST SCHWIEBERT

USA

Few anglers will ever achieve the worldwide reputation and status of Ernest Schwiebert. He has travelled the world trout fly fishing with his flies and tackle and taking his paint boxes for nearly fifty years. His first book Matching the Hatch *was published in 1955 and has been reprinted more than a dozen times. In addition to his seven other books of fishing writing and painting his major book on stream entomology,* Nymphs *(1973) is outstanding. His* magnum opus *is his two-volume* Trout, *published in 1978 after fifteen years of research, writing and illustration. Almost 1,800 pages in length, it is an unparalleled masterpiece on its subject.*

Ernest Schwiebert is an architect and planner who has played a major role in a number of famous projects around the world. Profiles of his several careers have appeared in many magazines including Life, Esquire, The New York Times *and* The Washington Post. *He lives in Princeton, New Jersey.*

Fifty-three seasons have passed. It seems improbable that I taught myself to dress flies, working from the slim little book that Elizabeth Gregg published at the threshold of the Second World War, but that is how it started. Those boyhood attempts were frustrating and troubled. The diagrams in such handbooks seldom explain the full spectrum of skills involved, and I often put my head down and cried when the working silk broke at a critical moment, or wing feathers split and hackles suddenly came unwound.

Help arrived before I abandoned these first attempts, when a teacher discovered those fly-tying struggles (my father never attempted to learn) and showered me with advice and scraps of first-rate materials and criticism. The old teacher also bought me the useful fly-tying book that William Bayard Sturgis published in 1940. It still stands on the library shelves, although I cannot remember what happened to Gregg.

The flies coming from my vice in those days were fishable, but those early efforts were scarcely works of art. Their wings were clumsily matched, their hackle diameters were erratic, and there were always fibres trapped in heads that were too bulky. Such flaws are common.

Before the war years were finished, I was already tying for my father and his friends, although there were few trips possible in those days. The quality of my flies had improved considerably, just enough to generate a measure of unwarranted pride.

It was a beautiful copy of *Flees, and the Art of Artyfichal Flee Making* that forced me to understand that fly dressing might be something more than a mere craft. The beautiful gilt-cloth quarto belonged to a retired physician who lived nearby, and I was awestruck when I studied the copies of Carroll and Ronalds and Walton in his collection. But it was the thickly bound Aldham quarto, with its actual flies and their materials displayed in their sunk mounts that were unforgettable. Its flies were quite beautiful, delicate, flawlessly tied and exquisite, and were attributed to the British tyer James Ogden in 1875.

His work had shaken my youthful pride. Those nineteenth-century flies seemed so perfect that I was no longer content with my boyhood skills, and the opportunity to improve came when I met

William Fitzgerald Blades in 1947. Blades had come to the United States shortly after the First World War, intending to work as a highly skilled mason in Chicago, but his knowledge of construction itself soon led to a lucrative career as a construction manager and contractor. Blades prospered building the great mansions that line Lake Michigan north of the city itself, and he retired at a relatively young age to devote his time to fishing and dressing flies. His flies were also works of art. Blades became perhaps the finest amateur fly tyer of his generation, since he never dressed flies commercially, and was a remarkable and demanding teacher.

Blades was a legend among knowledgeable tyers in the 1950s, when he published *Fishing Flies and Fly Tying*, and was best known for his remarkably detailed nymph patterns and detached-body mayfly imitations. James Ogden had included detached-body drakes among the patterns dressed for *Flees, and the Art of Artyfichal Flee Making*, perhaps tied on pale hog's bristle cores like the detached bodies described by Frederick Halford in 1886. Blades dressed his extended bodies on cores of silkworm gut, and later experimented with stiff cores of nylon. These several detached-body styles, and the steel-shanked Yorkshire flybody hooks used today, all share a common flaw: their rigid armatures seem to keep trout from getting hooked. But their lifelike silhouettes did seduce difficult trout, and I still treasure the Blades mayflies in my collection, with their gracefully curved bodies and trimmed-hackle legs. His flies, and the detached-body dressings from the nineteenth century, did simulate the big mayflies called drakes (after their matched wing feathers of wood duck and Egyptian goose and Rouen drake), tended to conceal their hooks in their hackles, and I experimented with them for many years.

Forty years ago, when I was working on a large construction project north of Colorado Springs, I accepted a commission to design a small residence for a local hardware dealer. I visited his lumberyard and store often during its design and construction, and discovered several spools of fine corrosion-resistant wire. I was also teaching a fly-tying class for the City Parks Departments in Colorado Springs, and had just received a shipment of twenty-five vices for the students. There was a spool of stainless wire lying among the vices, and I suddenly understood that detached bodies might be prefabricated with their tail fibres and the wire, stretching it tight between two vices.

I started experimenting immediately, dressing three tails and bodies on tightly stretched wire. These prefabricated bodies were finished and set at each end with head lacquer. Trimmed at the tails and cut free, with a quarter inch (8mm) of wire at their butts, these bodies were simply tied in on up-eyed hooks, with their wire folded back and seated firmly in place.

These first experiments tried several winging styles: soft hen hackle points selected for their roundness, rolled wings of wood duck and mallard and teal, cutwings in the style found in *Sunshine and the Dry-Fly* (1924) by John William Dunne, and Marinaro tool-shaped wings made with the Bennett wing-cutter.

Gamecock hackles were conventionally wound and mixed, masking the upright wings and concealing the hooks. The fine stainless wire was durable and springy, and it deflected easily to hook the fish. I had seen large drakes dressed by the American master Preston Jennings, as well as the detached-body mayflies that Blades had tied. There were also the drakes and spinners dressed at Garnett's and Keegan's in Dublin, flies I admired for their elegant workmanship, as well as their effectiveness on Lough Sheelin and Lough Corrib. But I also liked their masking face hackles of mallard and brown mallard and teal. Such mottled body feathers have a wonderful 'bugginess', aesthetic echoes of the nineteenth century, and perfectly imitate several of our large American mayflies.

European anglers have been familiar with their three Green Drake species for nearly two centuries; the beautiful *Ephemera danica* and *Ephemera lineata* found on the clear-flowing chalk streams, and the widely distributed *Ephemera vulgata* found from Yugoslavia to the British Isles. Our continent has a similar mayfly species in its *Ephemera guttulata*, but our trout waters are blessed with a number of other large drake species, including a few much larger than the famous Green Drake mayflies indigenous to either Europe or the United States. Their annual hatches can trigger remarkable sport, with blizzards of mating spinners over the water, and the

ERNEST SCHWIEBERT

1 Great Yellow Spinner
2 Great Brown Spinner
3 Coffin Fly
4 Brown Drake Spinner
5 Yellow Drake Spinner
6 Golden Drake

largest fish losing their caution to feed greedily.

Our big drakes range from the nocturnal species called *Hexagenia limbata*, with its twenty-eight millimetre wings, to the yellowish *Potamanthus distinctus* with wings that measure sixteen millimetres. *Litobrancha recurvata* is only slightly smaller than its better known *Hexagenia* cousins. Our indigenous Green Drake has twenty-millimetre wings. The closely related Brown Drake, classified *Ephemera simulans*, and our most widely distributed drake species, has slightly smaller wings. The little-known Yellow Drake, its taxonomic designation *Ephemera varia*, emerges later than the golden yellow *Potamanthus* flies. These two species are similar in both size and their nocturnal habits.

Freshly hatched drakes of these species sometimes emerge too sporadically to trigger any serious rises of fish, trickling off to moult in the streamside foliage. But their mating swarms collect these sporadic flies thickly above the current, rising and falling in the twilight, and dipping down to oviposit their egg sacs in the water. Such large mayflies will not always fall spent after mating, and both upright and spentwing patterns are useful. Some tyers might find that adding a fat tuft of egg-sac dubbing to their upright imitations is effective too, since fat egg-filled spinners often fall helplessly. These large mayflies all develop golden yellow egg sacs, except for *Potamanthus* spinners, which have ova that are bright yellowish orange. Although their season is quite brief, seldom lasting a full week on most waters, these spinner falls of big mayflies are often the high point of the year.

These are my favourite dressings for these big drakes. A number of the bodies can be tied on a single strand of stainless wire, tightly secured. The tail fibres are tied in and secured and the tinsel rib is tied in. The lower body is conventionally dubbed on tying thread and wound onto the wire. The dorsal section is spun on a core of strong, slightly coarse button thread of the same colour as the dubbing. This should taper to the rear. It is laid on top of the body dubbing and secured with the rib and drops of Flexament at each end. In the larger flies two dorsal layers may be laid three-quarters of the way up each side so that the body dubbing is exposed as a strip along the very top of the abdomen. The body is then secured to the hook shank with tying thread and flexible cement.

Great Yellow Spinner (*Hexagenia limbata*)

Female, 28mm wings

HOOK: Partridge K2B (curved body sedge hook, U/E) size 8

THREAD: White nylon 6/0

TAIL: Dark brown mallard fibres

BODY DUBBING: Primrose scintilla 17

DORSAL DUBBING: Dark cinnamon scintilla 12

RIB: Extra fine oval gold tinsel

WINGS: Pale dun hen saddle hackles

HACKLES: Pale honey ginger and pale grizzly mixed

FACING HACKLE: Brown mottled ptarmigan

HEAD: Brown nylon 6/0

Great Brown Spinner (*Litobrancha recurvata*)

Female, 25mm wings

HOOK: Partridge K2B, size 8

THREAD: Brown nylon 6/0

TAIL: Dark brown mallard fibres

BODY DUBBING: Medium chocolate scintilla 14

DORSAL DUBBING: Dark rusty scintilla 28

RIB: Extra fine oval gold tinsel

WINGS: Dark blue dun hen saddles

HACKLES: Dark brown olive and dark grizzly mixed

FACING HACKLE: Brown mottled ptarmigan

HEAD: Dark olive nylon 6/0

Coffin Fly (Ephemera guttulata)

Female, 20mm wings

HOOK: Partridge K2B, size 10
THREAD: White nylon 6/0
TAIL: Dark brown mallard
BODY DUBBING: Chalky white scintilla 22
DORSAL DUBBING: None
RIB: Extra fine oval silver tinsel
WINGS: Dark grizzly hen saddles dyed olive
HACKLES: Dark grizzly and natural black mixed
FACING HACKLE: Brown mottled ptarmigan
HEAD: Dark olive nylon 6/0

Brown Drake Spinner (Ephemera simulans)

Female, 18mm wings

HOOK: Partridge K2B, size 10
THREAD: Yellow nylon 6/0
TAIL: Dark lemon wood duck
BODY DUBBING: Golden brown scintilla 40
DORSAL DUBBING: Medium hare's mask scintilla 44
RIB: Extra fine oval gold tinsel
WINGS: Brown mottled ptarmigan saddles
HACKLES: Dark furnace and dark grizzly mixed
FACING HACKLE: Brown mottled ptarmigan
HEAD: Dark olive nylon 6/0

Yellow Drake Spinner (Ephemera varia)

Female, 16mm wings

HOOK: Partridge K2B, size 12
THREAD: Yellow nylon 6/0
TAIL: Pale lemon wood duck
BODY DUBBING: Pale primrose scintilla 16
DORSAL DUBBING: Light chocolate scintilla 13
RIB: Extra fine oval gold tinsel
WINGS: Pale dun hen saddles
HACKLES: Pale grizzly and yellow mixed
FACING HACKLE: Brown mottled ptarmigan
HEAD: Dark olive nylon 6/0

Golden Drake (Potamanthus distinctus)

16mm wings

HOOK: Partridge K2B, size 12
THREAD: Yellow nylon 6/0
TAIL: Pale lemon wood duck
BODY DUBBING: Pale amber scintilla 4
DORSAL DUBBING: Bright apricot scintilla 20
RIB: Extra fine oval gold tinsel
WINGS: Pale dun hen saddles
HACKLES: Pale grizzly and orange mixed
FACING HACKLE: Brown mottled ptarmigan
HEAD: Dark olive nylon 6/0

ADAM SIKORA

POLAND

Adam Sikora lives in Krakow, the town of his birth and the cradle of Polish fly fishing. Fly fishing in Poland really did not develop until the 1970s and from this infancy it has developed into a thriving sport. Adam is an active member of the Polish Angling Union and, like many of his fellow countrymen, is a keep participant in competitive fly fishing. In 1988 and 1992 he won the individual Polish title. In 1989 he was appointed to the Polish national team and competed in the World Championships held in Wales in 1990. There he finished in the silver-medal position in both the individual and team classifications. The following year in New Zealand the team won a silver medal and in Canada in 1993 the Polish team repeated their success with silver medals and Adam again took the individual vice-championship title.

Adam writes for a Polish fishing magazine and is working on a book, one of the few which will be available in Polish. He jointly owns a company, Test-Fly, which produces and sells angling equipment.

It is a real delight for me to present some of the flies I use every day. Selection was not an easy task and it has cost me several grey hairs. It is difficult to present something new and interesting to Western fly fishers where the history of fly fishing is so long and where so much has been published. Many of our flies are similar to other European patterns but I have noticed a growing interest in our Polish nymphs and how we fish them. This interest stems from our national team participation in the World Fly Fishing Championships especially in Poland and Finland. Therefore I hope that my contribution will be of interest and may help to dispel some of the myths that have grown up around our techniques.

The nymph method most popular in Poland is best known as the 'short nymph', contrary to the fallacious name 'rolled-nymph'. Many anglers are of the opinion that the construction of the nymph is the most important. In fact, the correct way of controlling flies under water is of greater importance than their colour, size, shape and construction details. However, one significant feature of the dressings is their lead wire underbody and the

absence of hackles to ensure that the nymphs sink quickly.

The main idea of the short-nymph method is to register the maximum number of delicate takes and enable the dead drift of the nymph. Therefore we shorten the distance and we fish just under the end of the rod so that the line does not touch the water surface. The leader should be longer than the water depth and very fine, which makes the flies sink more quickly and provides a better contact with them. Usually we put two nymphs on. These sink more quickly and aid a faster penetration. Sometimes when we use a small nymph, it is fished with a bigger one which will pull the smaller to the bottom.

Apart from several variations, this is the essence of the short-nymph method in the traditional form. We stand sideways to the current and cast the nymphs upstream, then we lay the line on the water surface for a couple of seconds so that the nymphs sink and then lift it several centimetres or more, depending on how deep the nymphs are. Keeping in touch with the nymphs, we follow them downstream in as natural a drift

ADAM SIKORA

2

1

1

3

1

4

1

5

6

1 Woven Nymph
2 Mackerel Nymph
3 Little White Head Nymph

4 Pink Nymph
5 Catgut Nymph
6 Cul de Canard

as possible. Remember that the surface layer of water flows faster than the bottom layer. This is why, in the majority of cases, we cannot follow the leader at the water-surface speed but a little slower. We follow the nymphs along the current for a short distance, without side drag but in a totally natural drift. Before the next cast we make an energetic strike. If the fish takes the fly impetuously and perceptibly, we make the distance of presenting the nymph longer.

The distance the nymphs are being fished under close control is about 1.5 meres or even shorter. It happens that you cannot see takes because they are very delicate. In such cases we present the nymphs for a shorter distance of half to one metre. When this happens seventy per cent of the hooked fish come from the final strike. The whole trick is to let the nymphs drift for a short distance only, in a very narrow current lane, allowing a natural drift but maintaining close contact with them.

You might think that the method appears to be an easy one but learning it may take some time. I was being taught the method of two excellent fly fishers, Krzysztof Sasula and Leazek Frasik. In order to show me the method with maximum precision they placed themselves in such a way that I could watch one of them sideways and the other from the front. We fished together, one opposite and the other following me. Although I watched very carefully, I could not make a fish even nibble my fly, whereas my friends were catching fish one after the other. I was trying very hard but without any effect. On the following day I went to the same place alone and, to my surprise, I had a fine catch of fish. The technique fell into place. Today I realize that I was controlling the nymphs at too fast a speed by pulling them downstream. This is a common mistake during the learning period. Another mistake is not being thorough enough when searching likely water.

Every metre of water should be examined thoroughly even at the risk of soaking your trousers when the current is rapid. With these methods we can fish only just in front of us, thus the method is most efficient in rapid currents and riffles because there you can take the fish unawares. The calmer the water, the deeper it needs to be to make the method possible. The short-nymph method is more effective for grayling, a

less timid fish than brown trout. It is impossible to use the method in calm rivers where you fish from the bank. Such is the short-nymph method, but if this fails, you can try lifting the nymphs a little or drifting them sideways.

The Woven Nymph is typical of the patterns used for the short-nymph method. The features of the Woven Nymph are the body of smooth thread and the wingcases of feather fibres. The back is usually darker. The green-yellow and the dark grey-beige are particularly good.

The Mackerel Nymph is very effective in various colours and shades of dubbed body. The mackerel skin is used because it makes it look very natural and it might be more efficient because of the natural aromatic material. To prepare a Mackerel Nymph, you should remove the skin from a smoked mackerel, clean off the remainder of the meat and soak the skin in water. Then remove the white inside part of the skin from the belly and the skin becomes slightly transparent with a golden tint. The dark stripes on the mackerel's back give darker points, which should be placed at the head of the nymph. When tying in, the strip of skin should be wet. The nymph with beige dubbing is the most effective.

My next fly was largely responsible for my success in the World Championships on the River Dee in North Wales. The Little White Head, devised by Franciszek Szajnik, is a very efficient summer pattern, especially for grayling. It is excellent on the dead drift, but it sometimes requires a slight control across the current.

The Pink Nymph is a wonderful fly for brown trout and grayling, efficient in all seasons, with best results in autumn and winter. In spring and summer its success varies depending upon location.

It is most important that the Pink Nymph should preserve its colour when soaked. That is why a synthetic underlay which does not change colour should be put under the wool. Personally I use a piece of plastic tape. Its very simple construction is to its advantage.

The Catgut Nymph was devised in 1979 by Krzysztof Sasula. Plastic, tinsel and Swannundaze, despite their nice looks, proved to be ineffective as elements of this pattern. They were replaced by a natural material, catgut, which is a surgical cord made from the intestines of a ram.

This material swells when wet, becoming soft and slightly transparent, and so imitates the segments on the caddis larva's back perfectly well. Catgut cord is round, so when using the thicker sizes it can be cut in two with a razor blade. It should be dampened before it is wound round the abdomen. To obtain the desired colour, an underlay of the chosen colour should be used. If the required colour is intensive, the catgut can be dyed. Size No 2 is the most often used.

My final pattern uses the cul de canard feather. The fly is very effective, particularly for our Polish grayling in the River San, where it has appeared to be a revelation.

Woven Nymph

HOOK: Tiemco TMC 2302 (2XL, slightly humped shank, D/E) size 6 – 12

THREAD: Black

UNDERBODY: Lead wire

BODY: Plaited synthetic fibres; viscose or floss silk; the upper fibres dark grey, the lower white

WINGCASE: Black hen fibres coated with clear varnish. This is laid on top of the body after the rest has been tied

RIB: Black silk wound over the wingcase

HEAD: Black thread

Mackerel Nymph

HOOK: Tiemco TMC 2457 (2X wide, 2X short, 2X heavy, curved, D/E) size 6 – 12

THREAD: Black

UNDERBODY: Lead wire

ABDOMEN: Olive-green dubbing for 80% of the length

THORAX: Black wool

RIB: 0.16 mm monofilament wound over the back

BACK: A strip of smoked mackerel skin

HEAD: Black thread

Little White Head Nymph

HOOK: Tiemco TMC 100 (1XF, wide gape, D/E) size 10

THREAD: Pale beige

UNDERBODY: Lead wire

RIB: Red copper wire over the abdomen

ABDOMEN: Rust or copper-coloured wool

THORAX: Cream-coloured wool

HEAD: Beige thread

Pink Nymph

HOOK: Tiemco TMC 2302 (2XL, slightly humped shank, D/E) size 8 – 12

THREAD: Black

UNDERBODY: Lead wire

BODY: Pale orange-pink wool

RIB: Gold wire

HEAD: Black thread, varnished

Catgut Nymph

HOOK: Tiemco 2457 (2X short, 2X wide, 2X heavy, curved D/E) size 8 – 12

THREAD: Black

UNDERBODY: Lead wire

ABDOMEN: Green-dyed catgut

THORAX: Black wool

WINGCASE: Black plastic

Cul de Canard

HOOK: Tiemco TMC 102Y (1XF, wide gape, D/E) size 17

THREAD: Black

BODY: Beige wool

WINGS: Cul de canard feathers

ROBERT SLOANE

AUSTRALIA

Robert Sloane is English by birth but his adopted home is Tasmania, Australia's trout-fishing Mecca. He has a Ph.D in fish biology and his professional involvement with trout culminated in a six-year stint as head of Tasmania's Inland Fisheries Commission. He is known to fly fishers in many countries through his involvement with the World Fly Fishing Championships, having been responsible for securing and organizing the 1988 event held in Tasmania. Robert fishes widely in Tasmania and regularly elsewhere in Australia and New Zealand. He has fished as far afield as the UK and Finland.

Robert works as a fisheries consultant and is dedicated to fishing writing and photography. He is a regular contributor to Australia's fishing journals and edits the Australian Fly Fishers' Annual. *The first of his books,* The Truth About Trout *was recognized as an Australian classic and encouraged a new and innovative approach to fly fishing, emphasizing the 'functional' importance of flies.*

Robert acknowledges that many of the flies he uses were developed in close collaboration with his father Tony Sloane — Tony providing much of the experimental impetus, and Robert largely responsible for their testing and refinement.

Wild brown trout, derived from English stocks introduced in the 1860s, form the backbone of the Tasmanian fishery, though rainbows are locally plentiful in many of the larger hydro-electric storages. An abundance of shallow, clear-water lakes and lagoons offers exceptional fly fishing to rising and 'tailing' trout. 'Tailing' fish are a Tasmanian highlight; trout show their tails and fins as they fossick in the extreme shallows. I helped popularize the art of 'polaroiding' — wading the shallows or walking the banks and spotting cruising trout with the aid of polarized glasses. This emphasis on sight-fishing, as opposed to blind-fishing, has provided an ideal field laboratory for close observation of trout, particularly their response to various flies and presentations.

Each of my six patterns is very easy to tie. The first, the Fiery-Brown Beetle is a killing pattern which is effective in all sorts of situations. I have probably caught more trout on the Fiery-Brown Beetle than any other wet fly. This versatile hoodwinker can be fished inert in front of tailing fish in the shallows, or drawn slowly across the path of smutting trout. Fished inert, it is my favourite pattern for fussy snail and amphipod feeders. The ideal presentation is aimed to land just close enough to catch a trout's attention without spooking it, then the fly is simply left for the fish to find and pick up.

It is always my first choice for early morning wind-lane fishing. When cast well in front of a midging rainbow, then drawn to the surface in several firm pulls as the trout approaches, it rarely fails. Presumably it bears sufficient resemblance

OPPOSITE
Rob Sloane polaroids a big brown trout from the shallows of Lake Jindabyne, New South Wales.

to a hatching midge to trigger a favourable response. There are certainly more sophisticated patterns for these situations, but I doubt that any is more effective.

My second beetle pattern is a dry fly specifically developed to match the summer falls of gum (*Eucalypt*) beetles which account for good rises along forested shores in Tasmania. Even so, the pattern is very versatile and the soft 'plastic' body can be coloured to match any terrestrial beetle. The body can also be hunched, elongated or trimmed to suit any beetle shape.

Its most endearing feature is that it always floats, no matter how rough the water, and is consequently ideal for windy conditions, fast rapids and fishing in the half-light. The crunchy texture of this fly must be very like the real thing because trout rarely reject it once committed to the take.

The ideal body material is Plastazote, but any buoyant high-density soft-foam plastic will do, provided it is white or pale in colour and will accept waterproof marker pen and nail varnish. Preparation involves cutting the plastic sheeting into strips, about 5mm thick and 7 – 8mm wide. The strips are then coloured to match the natural. The Tasmanian gum beetle tends to be fawn-yellow on the underside and yellow-green on the back.

The Western Lakes Nymph evolved out of a recognition that hatching insects, and mayflies in particular, are most vulnerable as they emerge. A floating nymph represents the most reliable pattern because it will take trout which are feeding on nymphs, emergers or duns, and it still offers the satisfaction of responding to a surface take. This is a simple but effective mayfly emerger. Size and body colour can be varied to match the local hatch. The body is a conventional silver ribbed nymph, whilst the generous burst of hare's fur which forms the thorax gives the confused appearance of an emerging dun. The thorax provides the buoyancy and is surprisingly visible on the surface. I simply dunk the fly in Permaflote occasionally to keep it floating.

The curved Tiemco nymph hook provides for an elongated body and orientates the fly correctly at the surface, with tail slightly tilted down and thorax in the meniscus.

Though somewhat of a departure from my 'functional' theme, the fourth fly is an imitative

pattern to highlight the usefulness of blue dun hackles in mimicking the natural sheen of the wings of adult mayflies — something that seems to have been appreciated far more in bygone days. I'm not talking about some ghastly blue-dyed monstrosity, rather I'm referring to that very subtle sheen that characterizes the rare, well-bred hackle.

I source my hackles from Nigel Harris, a river-keeper in the English Lake District, who convinced me of the importance of the true colour and has spent many years breeding suitable birds. I have tried the modern genetic capes but have found their blue dun hackles too chalky, lacking that vibrant sheen.

There are various theories about the trout's keen eye for mayfly spinners — even the tiniest Caenids are eagerly sought. It has been suggested that trout may see this blue wing sheen far better than we do, possibly by virtue of a greater capacity to differentiate light at the ultra-violet end of the spectrum. Whatever the reason, I am convinced that a dark blue dun hackle is far superior to black in the tying of any black spinner, and imitations of paler varieties of spinners can be enhanced through the use of pale blue dun hackles, either alone or in combination with other hackle colours.

The Tassie Spinner, in various sizes, effectively imitates a range of natural black spinner adults, with the dark blue dun hackle being the most important characteristic. The pattern also features dark moose-mane fibres, which make ideal mayfly tails – they are soft and buoyant, whilst being relatively strong. The stripped peacock herl ribbing gives the characteristic mayfly body segmentation. The hackle should be tied sparsely, to let the light shine through.

The Rabbit Fur Fly is the epitome of functional design and simplicity in fly tying and it is a versatile and effective wet fly. It is little more than a tuft of rabbit fur tied to a bare hook, but its semi-buoyancy, natural colour and lifelike action make it a deadly pattern for fishing shallow lake margins.

Though the fly may have little to commend it when held wet in the hand, the rabbit fur flares out as the fly slowly settles in the water, and the fibres pulse and wave in a most lifelike manner as it is retrieved slowly in short pulls. It may appear bulky enough to disguise the hook under water, but when a fish takes hold it effectively grabs a bare hook, and striking is a mere formality.

If it is allowed to settle on the bottom, trout will often pick up the inert fly – testimony to its attractive appearance. If the leader is greased the Rabbit Fur Fly can be fished in the surface film, giving a realistic impression of a spawning frog or hatching dragonfly. This buoyancy can be very handy when fishing weed-choked shallows. It also works well when fished down and across in slow-flowing streams, and has caught its share of sea trout at night. Though the Rabbit Fur Fly may not represent anything in particular, it catches fish, and that's what counts.

Variants are unlimited – any type and colour of fur can be used. But always use natural dried pelts in preference to dyed or tanned ones. The untreated fur gives the fly a positive scent and flavour, which may be far more important than we generally appreciate. Likewise the head can be varied to suit. The secret of the pattern is its simplicity. I have tried just about every conceiv-

able addition and have found the simplest version works best.

The Sunset Fly is the only genuine lure or 'exciter' in the collection. It is without doubt the most successful evening and early morning wet fly I have used, and is particularly effective on rainbow trout. It is an ideal sunk-line lure for rivers and lakes, and for stream-mouth fishing in particular.

The name reflects both the vibrant colours of a Tasmanian sunset and the fly's usefulness at that time of day. The use of bright orange and yellow was derived from earlier successes with the Red & Yellow Peril, a Matuka pattern formerly quite popular on Tasmanian rainbow trout waters.

The fly should be cast out, allowed to sink a little, then retrieved in steady pulls. It is always savagely taken and is rarely tapped or bumped by half-hearted fish; they just hook themselves. Its success can largely be attributed to the inherent colour-contrast between black, hot-orange and yellow. It also swims well and looks equally appetising from all directions.

Fiery-Brown Beetle

This is one instance where exact body colour seems critical – orange, brown or claret just won't do. Veniards fiery-brown dye is ideal.

HOOK: Mustad 9980 or 94838 (D/E, short shank, fine wire) size 10 – 14

THREAD: Black

BODY: Fiery-brown seal's fur

BACK: Crow or cormorant feather fibres

Plastic Gum Beetle

The pre-coloured plastic strip is positioned above the hook, the tail end level with the bend and the longer end extending over the eye. The tail is pinched firmly and tied in with several turns and a half hitch. The loose end is held up while a few turns of ginger hackle are wound at the centre of the hook and clipped off above, leaving only a sparse hackle below the shank. Next, apply a clear nail varnish coat to the underside of the plastic strip. Press it down firmly on the hook and tie off behind the eye. The excess plastic is trimmed at the front and rear, and the cut surfaces are touched up with a marker pen. Finish by

giving the back and sides two coats of clear varnish. The hackle fibres can be spread out underneath to help the fly sit flat, and trim if necessary.

HOOK: Mustad 9980 or 94709 BR size 10 – 14

THREAD: Yellow

BODY: Buoyant foam-plastic, coloured to match the natural

LEGS: Small ginger cock

Western Lakes Nymph

HOOK: Tiemco TMC 200R (S/E, 3XL, slightly curved shank) or Partridge MM3B size 10 – 14

THREAD: Black

TAIL: Furnace hackle fibres

BODY: Brown seal's fur or substitute

RIB: Embossed silver tinsel

THORAX: Generously dubbed hare's fur

Tassie Spinner

A very effective red spinner variant is tied by substituting orange floss silk for the body and mixing a ginger and a pale blue dun hackle.

This big wild brown trout took a Tassie Spinner, in the Monaro region of New South Wales.

1 Fiery-Brown Beetle
2 Plastic Gum Beetle
3 Western Lakes Nymph

4 Tassie Spinner
5 Rabbit Fur Fly
6 Sunset Fly

HOOK: Mustad 94709 BR or Partridge Arrowpoint CS20 (D/E, fine wire, arrowpoint) size 12 – 14

THREAD: Black

TAIL: 3 or 4 dark moose-mane fibres

BODY: Black floss silk

RIB: Stripped dark peacock herl

HACKLE: Dark blue dun cock, tied sparsely

Rabbit Fur Fly

Select a good, thick winter pelt and use the darker, long-staple fur from the lower back. Cut a narrow strip of skin (with fur attached) by cutting *across* the pelt. A segment about 4mm by 15mm is ideal. This is then folded in half, end to end, and then in half again. The folds are made keeping the skin inwards, retaining the darker fur on the outside. The folded skin is pinched hard together and the fur tuft is tied in like a feather fibre wing. The thread need only be whipped from the eye to half way along the shank to provide a base for the fur. The prepared fur segment is held in place with the folded skin collar centred more or less over the eye, then tied down firmly behind the skin and pulled tight with a half hitch. The surplus skin collar and hair roots are clipped off.

The trimmed roots can be daubed with a little clear varnish and whipped with extra turns of thread for strength. The fly is completed with a head of ostrich herl.

HOOK: Mustad 9980 size 8 – 10

THREAD: Black

BODY: Grey-brown rabbit fur

HEAD: Black ostrich herl

Sunset Fly

Each successive hackle is swept back by overlaying with thread; this effectively forms the underbody. When the front, black hackle is laid on, a yellow-on-black eye can be created by exposing a portion of the black hackle root between wraps of yellow thread.

HOOK: Mustad 9672 size 6 – 8

THREAD: Yellow

TAIL: Black squirrel tail

HACKLES: 3 large white saddle hackles, dyed jet-black (front); hot-orange (middle); bright yellow (rear)

HEAD: Yellow on black

JENNIFER SMITH

USA

As a teenager, Jennifer spent her summers fly fishing the Madison River, in Montana. She became her father's shadow during those formative years when hand in hand they crossed swift currents and slippery rock bottoms. In tennis shoes with old pieces of carpet glued to the soles, and a handed-down vest containing the minimum of tackle she never guessed that she would become so captivated by the sport and that eventually her love of fly fishing would lead her into becoming a professional casting instructor and guide.

Jennifer is a licensed Montana and Yellowstone National Park outfitter/guide and teaches fly fishing and fly casting. In 1991 she taught at the first all-women's fly fishing school in Sweden. Her fishing travels have also taken her to Canada, Argentina, Mexico, Florida and Alaska. She has written for a number of journals and is a contributor to the first published anthology of women's fishing stories, Uncommon Waters.

During my years of guiding I have learned that one of the problems beginners have is being able to see their dry fly on a fast, rippled surface. An Elk Hair Caddis or Goofus Bug would remain invisible. On opening my fly box all I could see were little white flags of calf tail. The solution: a Parachute Adams. The white parachute stem is perfect for training novices to see their fly on the water. The fly is a great fish catcher in Montana from April through until the end of August.

Today, I grab a handful of Parachute Adams at the beginning of every season in sizes 12 – 18. I always have at least a dozen tucked away in my fishing vest. Last year (1992) the Parachute beat all other flies on the small creeks of the Gallatin, and on the rivers I fish in Yellowstone National Park. On days when the sun seemed to keep the fish down in the dark, cooler pools I worked like a madman changing flies trying to get a pattern that worked. I even had to retire to the Royal Wulff on several occasions before finding success with the Parachute Adams.

I think a fly with a white calf tail, or polypropelene, top offers a great advantage to the fly fisher. I do not feel that it diminishes the experience in any way, or that you are cheating. The angler can see the white stem, the fish see the fly, both strike, and everyone is happy.

Not all white calf tail winged flies can be expected to work on all waters, but another such pattern, the Wright's Royal works consistently and is a standard in my fly box. I love this fly because it looks like a Royal Wulff, but has a flared elk-hair wing giving it the profile of a caddis. I feel like I am fishing several flies in one. This easy-to-see pattern is buggy looking. It can be seen on the surface longer and far further than almost any other fly. Because of its unique profile I have also fished it as a hopper in larger sizes.

I like that fact that its creator, Phil Wright, took a chance and augmented the classic legendary Wulff pattern with his own inspiration. I met Phil Wright when he walked into a shop where I was working. This fresh-from-college girl blurted out 'Are you Phil Wright of the Wright's Royal?' His expression changed so suddenly it was if he had found a long-lost friend in a foreign country. We sat down to discuss the fly, where it worked, why we liked it, and how it was tied. All other con-

The Idsjöströmmen in Sweden where Jennifer Smith spends some of her summer months.

cerns were ignored while we examined the possibilities of a Wright's Royal floating over our favourite trout streams.

Wading or fishing from a boat, I usually fish the Wright's in sizes 12, 14 or 16. I have used it on the Madison, Gallatin and Yellowstone Rivers from July to September. The Wright's in smaller sizes is excellent on small creeks. It is perfect when caddis are on the water and when you are searching the stream to rise a trout. It is versatile as an attractor, caddis, ant, flying ant and hopper.

I am a secret devotee of the Woolly Bugger.

This is not a nice fly with a nice name. Fishing the Woolly Bugger in the company of match-the-hatch fly fishers is like asking to be kicked off the stream. The Woolly Bugger is a staple pattern in my fly box. Black, olive or with shiny tinsel strips dressed in the tail, the Woolly Bugger is a seductive fish magnet. It is supposed to imitate a small fish, minnow, or it could pass for a leech. The Bugger's marabou tail undulates in the water irritating browns or perking the curiosity of rainbows. Trout chase it and they ferociously attack it. Sometimes they nip at it and all you feel is their firm tug.

Depending on the river, I like to fish the Woolly Bugger in sizes 4, 6 and 8. There are several different ways to fish it, and often you must test all of

JENNIFER SMITH

1 Parachute Adams
2 Wright's Royal
3 Woolly Bugger

4 Black and Orange Beetle
5 Brassie
6 No-Hackle Dun

them to see which will work. My favourite method is to cast and strip the fly through the current. I learned to fish Woolly Buggers from a drift boat, and casting to the bank and stripping the fly back became second nature. Often you can dead drift it in the current while you mend for drag. You have to experiment. In fast or deep water I weight the fly with split shot right at the eye. Some people weight the fly with split shot 12 – 20 inches up the leader. This gives it another action in the air and in the water. I prefer the weight at the eye because it does not hinge in the air while casting, and it sinks immediately.

As a Montanan, a Woolly Bugger is the fly you turn to when the wind and weather dictates wet-fly fishing. It is also the pattern you use when the fishing becomes difficult and you need to search the water and create some activity in slumbering trout. Because I have always used a Woolly Bugger it never occurred to me that it might offend anyone. I have fished in Canada and Argentina where the Woolly Bugger was welcome and took fish. In Sweden, my hosts of the Idsjöströmmen and Kaitum Rivers watched me tie on a black Woolly Bugger with a pinch of lead. They coughed politely and turned away.

Perhaps this dark fly may have a question mark hanging over it in proper fly-fishing circles, but as long as you can answer the questions, a little lead and a Woolly Bugger can be very effective!

The beetle imitation became one of my favourite flies almost by accident. I used to own a fly shop and discovered early on that the best way to sell a product was to know something about it. When restocking I noticed that the beetles we carried in three sizes had not sold. I had never fished a beetle and wondered if they were any good. The next time I went fishing on the Gallatin River I cast a black beetle above a fallen log and let it drift along its slippery moss-covered side. The rainbow I hooked sipped the beetle as casually as if beetles came by that spot every day. Most of the time beetles are taken without the commotion that distinguishes many dry-fly takes. A victim of circumstance, a fall off a leaf, an untimely wind, a rising river, beetles are helpless in water and the trout seem to know it.

I have the best success when casting alongside obstructions such as fallen logs, brushy banks and near boulders. I have also found them to work on spring creeks when the fishing has slowed and trout refuse to rise even to the current hatch. Because of my success under these conditions I like to test the waters with a black beetle when other patterns fail. Unfortunately a beetle is very difficult to see on the surface but this can be remedied. The dressing I prefer has a piece of bright orange polypropelene tied on top.

The spring creeks in Montana are enormously popular with fly-fishing pilgrims making their sojourn to the wide open spaces and wild rivers. These are challenging waters with selective trout feeding on size 18, 20 and 22 hatches. I liken the fishing on the spring creeks to a game of chess because it requires accuracy, skill and good strategy. It also requires the right fly in the right place at the right time. Many fly fishers have stood in the waters of DePuys watching trout rise steadily all around them while all presentations were ignored. They just did not have the right pattern at the right time fished in the right way.

One of the patterns I use throughout the year is a simple one called a Brassie. It is a midge larva imitation and I fish it in sizes 16 and 18. At first glance the fly does not give the fly fisher much confidence. No fancy wing, no undulating tail, no individual legs, no buggy body. It is just fine-gauge copper wire wrapped round the hook shank and topped with a black dubbed head. Small and unassuming, the copper wire body flashes in the sun as it dances down and through weeds where big trout hide. I am amused that this little fly can catch anything, but most amused because it catches large 18- and 20-inch trout.

I prefer to fish the Brassie upstream in feeding lanes and riffled water. The strikes are barely discernible so I use a strike indicator half way up the 9-foot 6X leader. I do not weight it, although some do in deeper water. I have most success when fishing the Brassie near the bottom and letting it drift naturally with the current. The spring creek is where the Brassie is taken consistently. Try it if you fish a spring creek or stream where the water is slow and clear, and alive with aquatic vegetation. You will be pleasantly surprised.

My favourite fly has been chosen because of its fragile appearance and accuracy in imitating a pale morning dun (in yellow) or a *Baetis* (in olive shades). The Harrop's No-Hackle's parents were art and genius. This is a noble fly with the quality and perhaps the symbolism of fly fishing embodied in its looks and in the way it is fished.

I was introduced to the No-Hackle late one June while fishing the pale morning dun hatch on a Montana spring creek. Its accurately shaped quill wings made it a perfect match for the naturals. I fished size 18 on a 7X tippet – yes, the trout are that leader-shy. I learned that it is best not to cast willy-nilly into the hatch or suspected trout lies, but to wait and watch for a specific trout to rise regularly. The reason I became so particular about where I placed my fly was because, first of all, I love the challenge of selective trout, and secondly, I did not want my No-Hackle to drop into the mouth of just any trout. For me, the

No-Hackle is really a one-fish fly, and you don't want a scrappy ten-incher when you can have its 18-in brother. Once the wings are crushed and separated by being bitten and dragged underwater the fly is never quite the same. The ephemeral quality of the No-Hackle is what endears it to me. I like its fragility and knowing that I have only a chance or two to succeed with it. For me, the No-Hackle is the art of dry-fly fishing in a nutshell: immediate and fleeting, one chance in the right place, requiring skill, patience and accuracy.

I have also fished the No-Hackle in Argentina on the Malleo River where it took 20+-inch rainbows. Its profile is uniquely a dun, and it is successful where mayfly hatches occur.

Parachute Adams

HOOK: Size 12 – 20
THREAD: Grey
TAIL: Light or medium blue dun cock fibres
BODY: Dubbed grey muskrat fur
WING: White polypropelene yarn or calf tail, tied upright
HACKLE: A grizzled and brown (natural red) cock hackle, wound together around the wing base

Wright's Royal

HOOK: Size 10 – 16
THREAD: Black
BODY: Peacock herl with a pronounced thorax, with a broad band of red floss in the centre
WING: Light elk
THORAX: Peacock herl
HACKLE: Brown (natural red) thorax style through the front third of the body

Woolly Bugger

HOOK: Size 6 – 10, long shank
THREAD: Black
TAIL: Large tuft of black marabou
BODY: Black chenille
HACKLE: Palmered black cock

Black and Orange Beetle

HOOK: Size 14 – 18
THREAD: Black
BODY: The shank is wrapped with Flashabou. Black deer hair is tied in behind the eye, folded back and tied in at the rear of the shank. The tips of the fibres are tied widely spaced at the top of the body at the place where the tuft of bright orange polypropelene yarn is tied in

Brassie

HOOK: Size 14 – 20
THREAD: Black
BODY: Fine copper wire
HEAD: Fine black dubbing

No-Hackle Dun

Tie in tails and wings first and body last.
HOOK: Size 16 – 20 Tiemco 100
THREAD: Olive 6/0
TAILS: Three light dun cock hackle fibres, divided by a small ball of dubbing
WINGS: Paired light grey mallard quill slips, mounted on the sides of the hook
BODY: Fine poly dubbing (see text)

Editor's Note: Jennifer Smith places the Royal Wulff top of her short list of six patterns. Because the Royal Wulff has also been selected by Al Beatty, Jennifer kindly agreed to a substitute.

JUHA VAINIO

FINLAND

When Juha Vainio isn't fly fishing he practises dentistry in the city of Espoo near Helsinki. His main fly-fishing interest lies in the brown trout and grayling of central Finland. Lest you think his interest is parochial, he also has extensive experience of the rest of Scandinavia and Europe, including the UK and Russia, and has fly fished in the USA, Canada, New Zealand and Caribbean. He has five times been a member of his national fly-fishing team and is currently its captain.

Juha has contributed to a number of books and is Field Editor of a Finnish fly-fishing magazine. He is a fly-fishing, fly-tying and entomology instructor for the Finnish Sportfisherman's Federation and is International Affairs Secretary for that organization.

My tying style is not a very complicated one. I'm often busy and need flies which are fast and easy to tie and long lasting. My experiences in international competitions have also modified both my tying and my fishing methods towards fairly simple and effective flies. If one fly can be fished in different ways to represent several insects or stages of insects I like it even better. However, I have no wish to trade the art of fly tying and the charm of casting solely in favour of better catches. I favour natural materials, but also like to mix them with man-made fibres. Dry flies are very close to my heart, even though they don't always produce as big fish as some other methods might. The flies in my selection are tied on barbless (actually, compressed barbs) hooks, which I prefer in all my fishing except when using very heavily weighted nymphs. The tyings selected have been most successful for me and many of my friends.

The February red (*Taeniopteryx nebulosa*), a species of stonefly, is the first fly to hatch in the budding Finnish springtime. The main hatch normally occurs in late March or early April and is one of the most important of the whole season. The size and fishability of the hatch depends greatly on the fast-shifting weather of the late winter but usually you can get one or two totally marvellous days of dry-fly fishing. After the long winter this heavy hatch of clumsy stoneflies drives normally difficult trout into a feeding frenzy. For some reason or another there is often an uncommonly large percentage of crippled or stillborn emergers involved in this hatch and many trout prefer these easy tidbits over normal flies. Some are selective to the right colour (which really is light orange in the emerging insect, the more mature adults are quite dark) but most just want a low-floating imitation. I usually catch some of the best (and biggest) trout of the season on this particular tying. As a bonus, it works well as a caddis imitation too. The hackle is optional; I find myself tying it in and then, in the fishing situation, clipping it away.

Caddis or sedge flies are the most important insects in Finland for both trout and fly fishers. They occupy almost all waters and many of them are sufficiently large and plentiful enough to attract even the big fish-eating trout. Larval imitations of free-living species (such as *Rhyacophila nubila*) are basic tools for many skilled nymph fishers through the whole season. After mid-June many important species start hatching and then the vulnerable pupal stage is a staple food for most trout.

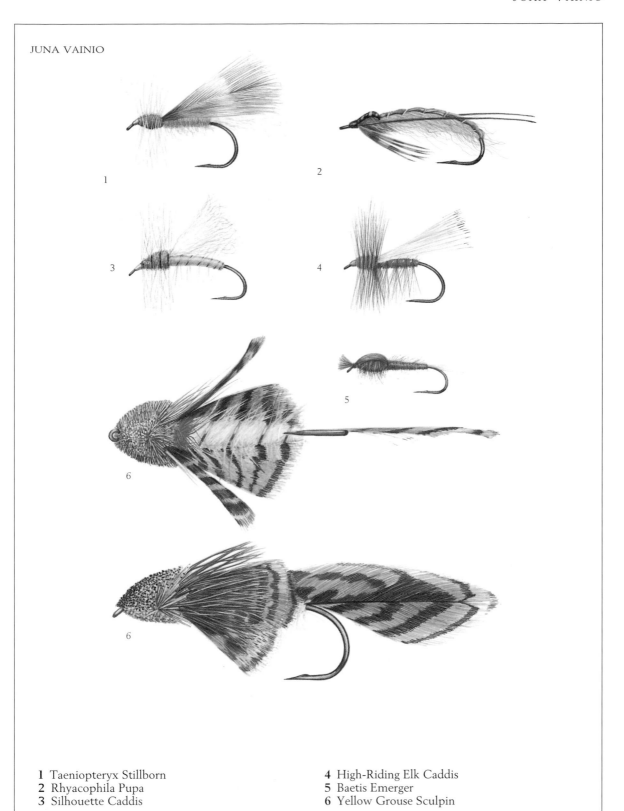

JUNA VAINIO

1 Taeniopteryx Stillborn
2 Rhyacophila Pupa
3 Silhouette Caddis

4 High-Riding Elk Caddis
5 Baetis Emerger
6 Yellow Grouse Sculpin

I fish the Rhyacophila Pupa to represent both phases: cast upstream and fished without drag close to the bottom as a larva, then allowing it to swim to the surface on the downstream swing. I often use two similar flies of different sizes at the same time. This way I get enough weight for the tumbling currents and give the fish a choice of two flies at different levels. A small strike indicator is often of great help in detecting subtle takes. This approach has been very successful both before and after the main hatch which takes place quite late in the evening, often at midnight. When flies are hatching very heavily on the surface an emerging pupa pattern is without doubt the best choice.

My Silhouette Caddis represents the newly emerged adult fly. It also has some of the key characteristics of an emerging/stillborn insect. Most species display quite light colour when newly emerged; this is represented by the yellow Antron body and the wonderfully translucent snowshoe hare wing. A flush-floating imitation as this one is often superior when dealing with selective trout. The qualities of snowshoe hare add quite a lot to this basic fly, as it resists matting very well and is easy to keep floating for long periods of time even after several fish. It also forms a background against which the body of the fly is well visible for the fish and a kind of halo around the fly which might suggest the emerging caddis. Of course, it's clearly visible for the fisherman in the gathering shadows of late summer evenings.

My next fly is modified after one of the best recipes ever devised, Al Troth's Elk Hair Caddis. That superior imitation of most caddis species has been one of my true favourites for years, but in many of our fast and turbulent waters I wanted a little extra buoyancy – so the extra hackle. The light, contrasting wing gives good visibility in low light and difficult currents. I've sometimes taken the modifications a little bit further and added an elk hair tail (which actually gives us a miniature Stimulator). I consider the balance of the fly a very important factor in its fishability. Our rivers are often wide and difficult to wade, forcing the angler to employ long casts to reach the fish. It's reassuring to use a well-balanced fly which cocks well on every cast even though it's too far out to see properly. Another important part is that little amount of dubbing under the hackle collar. It gives a truer shape and supports the hackle. Nowadays I tie almost all of my dry flies with this small but significant improvement.

Upwinged flies are usually of minor importance in the caddis-filled Finnish rivers but there are areas and times, especially in the north of Finland, where mayflies provide satisfactory sport. In these areas we'll mainly be dealing with grayling, but my fifth pattern, this Baetis Emerger has proved itself with the most selective brown trout as well. It's not too visible when hanging in the surface but you usually watch the rise and react to that. This emerger also doubles as a chironomid imitation in its smaller sizes.

Finnish brown trout are piscivorous at a relatively early stage of their life. This results in rapid growth and good-sized fish are usually very much in evidence. Big trout (above 2 kilos or 4.5 pounds) mainly follow shoals of dace and smelt in lakes, but there are always many fish of this size in rivers and rapids, too. Usually it's not before mid-June when waters warm up enough and dace, smelt and perch move into running water. Before that, ie in April and May, about the only bait fish available for trout in rivers is the sculpin or miller's thumb. During and after spawning (a week or so after the ice-melt) sculpins are quite vulnerable and trout seem to favour them over most other food items. At the end of the season in autumn sculpins are again an important part of the diet of bigger trout.

There are two effective fishing methods: upstream with a floating line or downstream with a fast-sinking one. I prefer the upstream approach in fast pocket water and fish the sculpin imitation very close to the surface. This is a very exciting method as you can see even all the inspection rises in addition to the real banging ones, of which there will be many.

Taeniopteryx Stillborn

I recommend that you save all the fibres of the CDC feathers not used for wings and use them for the head. It's often good to have several shapes and shades of these stillborns as trout can be maddeningly selective.

HOOK: Partridge L3A (D/E, fine wire, wide gape) size 10

THREAD: Grey

NYMPH SHUCK: Light Z-lon, as long as the body

BODY: Light orange dubbing such as Ligas 46

WING: Whole (tip of) light speckled cul de canard feather, two if very small

HACKLE (optional): 2 – 4 turns of light blue dun cock, wound over the thorax

THORAX AND HEAD: Roughly dubbed CDC

Rhyacophila Pupa

This pattern is usually weighted with an underbody of lead wire.

HOOK: Partridge GRS12ST (S/E, long curved shank, fine wire) size 10 – 14

THREAD: Green 8/0

RIB: Fine (2lb b.s.) monofilament, wound over the latex back

BACK: Green marbled latex, coloured darker with an indelible felt-tip pen at the two head segments

ABDOMEN: Green Antron dubbing, lateral parts well-picked out to represent gills

THORAX: Hare's fur, well picked out

HACKLE: Grouse, a bunch of fibres as a beard hackle

ANTENNAE: Two cock pheasant tail fibres, placed laterally

Silhouette Caddis

The upper body hackle fibres should be cut away before tying in the wing, which can be shaded with Pantone pens to harmonize with the body colours. A variant has a dark olive front hackle.

HOOK: Tiemco 2302 (D/E, 2XL, slightly humped shank) size 10 – 14

THREAD: Yellow 8/0

RIB: Fine gold wire

BODY: Yellow Antron dubbing

BODY HACKLE: Short-fibred sandy dun cock

WING: Snowshoe hare foot hair, not too dense

HEAD HACKLE: Dark blue dun cock, wound sparsely over the thorax

THORAX: Antron/Hare blend

High-Riding Elk Caddis

The fly should balance well when finished. If not, cut a 'V' from the underside of the hackle. Colours should be varied to match the naturals.

HOOK: Partridge L3A, size 10 – 14

THREAD: Orange 8/0

RIB: Fine gold wire

BODY: Rusty orange Antron dubbing

BODY HACKLE: Dark ginger, furnace or brown (natural red), saddle hackle

WING: Black-tipped elk hair, also coastal blacktail deer, Texas whitetail, etc

THORAX: Body material mixed with hare's ear

COLLAR HACKLE: As for body, with longer fibres

Baetis Emerger

The wing sac should extend from both sides of the body, not only from the top. It is better for trapping air if it isn't pulled down too tightly.

HOOK: Tiemco 2302 size 14 – 18

THREAD: Olive 8/0

TAIL: Z-lon or Antron, amber or any other light colour, sparse

BODY: Fine Antron dubbing, shades of olive to match the natural

WING SAC: Brownish cul de canard feather over the thorax

THORAX: Antron/Hare blend

HEAD: Stumps from the wing sac

Yellow Grouse Sculpin

Use gold tinsel only to segment the body, tie in the wing with the monofilament just behind the gold tinsel. Monofilament can be used in tying the deer hair head too. The top of the head may be coloured black with permanent felt-tip marker pens.

HOOK: Partridge D4A (long-shank streamer) size 2 – 6

THREAD: Yellow, fine kevlar for the head

RIBS: Medium gold oval tinsel and fine monofilament

BODY: Yellow Partridge SLF (#20), seal, angora-goat or similar long-fibred dubbing

WING: Two grouse wing feathers (ptarmigan and similar feathers also work well) in matuka-style; 2 – 4 smaller, soft feathers at the shoulders of the fly

THROAT: Fiery red Partridge SLF (# 18) dubbing

PECTORAL FINS: Grouse feathers, curving down and away from the body

HEAD: Spun deer hair, large and quite wide

A stony Scandinavian river where caddis and stoneflies abound.

Hans van Klinken

HOLLAND

The editor once described Hans van Klinken as 'a grayling junkie who overdoses with uncanny regularity'. If there are grayling in a stream, Hans van Klinken starts as the odds-on favourite to find those fish. Each one of his flies also is as effective for trout as it is for grayling.

As a largely self-taught fly fisherman and fly tyer, Hans approached the river and the empty vice with few preconceived ideas. Out of his own ingenuity, tempered by his repeated trials and experiments, he has produced some wonderful trout and grayling flies; none better, in the editor's view, than the Klinkhamer Special. The parachute style has always appealed to Hans and many of his dry flies and emergers incorporate this feature. Hans has never been one to tie on a size 20 hook when a size 12 will do. It is wise not to question his patterns because of their size. They have usually answered the critics for themselves. The Culard is an exception to the van Klinken rule that only big flies attract big fish.

Hans contributes to Dutch and English fly-fishing and fly-tying magazines and has assisted a number of authors in their researches, including the editor's books. He fishes widely in Holland (fly fishing for non-salmonids) and for trout, grayling and salmon in Scandinavia, Eire, Germany and the UK. He has lectured and gives tying demonstrations in Holland, Scandinavia, Germany and England.

It was in 1980 on my summer visit to the Swedish River Klara that I met an angler who was enjoying much more success than me. I was a fan of the traditional shoulder-hackled dry fly but the pattern that this fly fisher gave me was to be a watershed in my fly-fishing and fly-tying life. He gave me a Rackelhanen, an unusual Swedish sedge pattern made entirely from polypropelene. After great success with the fly and losing it I attempted to make my own. In subsequent seasons I experimented with poly yarn until 1984, when fishing in Norway, an angler departing the river advised me to use big flies deep in the surface film. So incorporating my preference for a parachute hackle and the poly yarn, I created a large parachute fly on a Partridge grub hook. This fly was much like an iceberg and gave the best results when ninety per cent under water. The body was fine and tapered and taken as close as possible to

the barb, and a peacock herl thorax proved more attractive than the dressing without it. I called it the L.T. (Light Tan) Caddis for the simple reason that it did well in a caddis hatch. It was later to be renamed the Klinkhamer Special by Hans de Groot.

Without any of us being aware of the other, Thomas Olssen and, in the United States, Roy Richardson developed very similar flies at about the same time.

Whereas many British and European ideas about grayling fly fishing are based around small patterns, the Scandinavians have other ideas. In Britain wherever I fished the Klinkhamer Special and others of my patterns I was met with incredulity. Scepticism was soon replaced by pleas for sample tyings as the Klinkhamer out-fished all the local standard patterns. Today it is accepted as an excellent all-round fast-water fly throughout

Europe for trout and grayling. It has also gone on to be highly successful for dry-fly fishing for salmon and sea trout in Scandinavia.

The basic pattern can be varied to accommodate emerging sedges, mayflies, midges and some terrestrials. It is also very effective when there is nothing rising and no hatch in progress and consequently makes a very useful search pattern. The abdomen hanging below the film is an obvious target for watching fish. The upright poly yarn wing makes the fly very visible for the angler.

In the large Scandinavian rivers I fish mainly downstream for grayling because it is possible to get longer drag-free drifts. The longer drifts give grayling hugging the bottom in deep water time to rise. It is possible to exercise more control of the fly, keeping it in the correct current lane from an upstream position. Also I have observed grayling following the fly to take it at the last moment. Fishing downstream means that the fly is seen first before the leader or tippet.

The Caseless Caddis series owes its inspiration to Oliver Edwards who urged me to think about imitating the naturals more closely. I have tied and tried the pattern in twelve to fifteen different colours but my yellow and green are the best two by far. On the German River Kyll my friend Jack Tazelaar caught more than a hundred fish with these two in just one day. We had searched the river, turning stones before breakfast to discover the *Rhyacophila* larvae. He (and the fish) had no doubt about the choice of imitation.

It is usually fished blind in a dead drift but when conditions are right I love to fish to sighted fish. I caught a 54cm (over 21 inches) and a 51cm (20 inch) grayling on sight with this pattern. They remain my records from German and Danish rivers. It has proved its success in Norway – with a 56cm grayling – Sweden and on the northern English rivers of the Ure and Wharfe. It will do well wherever caseless caddis larvae abound.

In the middle 1980s I made some real improvements to my cul de canard patterns. I named this variant the Culard. It was first developed as a dark grey sedge with a normal sedge wing extending just beyond the bend. I experimented with shorter wings, with the result that the pattern with the shortest wing gave me the best results by far. It is now one of the best patterns in my collection. It has been excellent in the rivers of central

Europe and it also works well in the high summer and low-water conditions I've met in Scandinavia.

Instead of using it as a normal dry fly, I often moisten it and fish it just under the surface as an emerger. If the conditions are right it is great sport to fish it to visible fish. On stillwater I use it first as a dry fly but if success eludes me I pull the fly down and use it as an emerger at slow retrieving speeds; however, in this style it works best in the smallest sizes.

The Once and Away is one of my best emerger patterns and is almost unsinkable. The pattern arose because I found some stillwater rainbow trout feeding in the film on something I couldn't see. I fished the Culard as an emerger and managed nine fish that afternoon, but I wasn't satisfied that I had got everything right. I returned next day to catch some of the emerging insects. They had thin abdomens and larger than usual thoraxes. I still don't know what they were. I had very few materials with me in the car, but minus a bobbin holder and hackles I eventually managed to put together a fly with some cul de canard feathers from a dead duck I had found at the roadside that morning. With this I went on to catch many more fish than on the previous day. It is called the Once and Away because it proved reluctant to float again after a fish had taken it. It has subsequently been improved by the way I tie the cul de canard and now the pattern always hangs in the surface film. I prefer to fish it in or close to a wind lane and allow it to drift to the feeding fish.

The method of fishing my Remerger was established by my wife Ina when fishing in Norway. Contrary to the normal upward swim of a natural nymph the Remergers are best fished 'on the drop'. This is quite the opposite to how a nymph intent on surface emergence would behave. Nymphs sometimes migrate to the surface and back to the riverbed again on days before emergence so perhaps this is what is being imitated here. The fly is allowed to sink without further movement or retrieval. With a sink-tip line and a short leader it is a deadly pattern in deep pools of Scandinavian rivers. Back in central Europe it is a killer on most rivers I fish and has proved very effective in its unweighted version for grayling feeding in low water.

The Leadhead is probably the most successful deep-water nymph I have ever used. I originally developed it for Scandinavian grayling in deep lies but it can also be used in other parts of the river. It has gone on to be highly successful for trout and salmon in Europe and North America. It has been an evolving pattern which I originally based on a nymph shown to me at a riverside in Sweden. Over four or five seasons I arrived at the finished model.

There are a number of important features to the dressing: the placement of the lead-substitute shot which allows the nymph to fish upside-down, point uppermost to avoid snags and achieve better hooking; the highly visible fluorescent green butt for which Flexibody has given the most spectacular results; and the long-fibred mobile tail fibres.

There are three main fishing methods for the Leadhead, all with a floating line. For the dead drift the fly should be cast upstream and across and left to drift as naturally as possible. In this way the nymph is being taken for a drifting cased caddis. In this and the third method it might be necessary to use a bite indicator to see the takes. The second technique which I call 'looping the line', is mainly for use on fast water. I cast downstream and mend the line; then I retrieve the fly by looping in line with my left hand. In slower waters this is achieved by a figure-of-eight retrieve. It is important to experiment with varying the speed of the retrieve. The third technique is the lift-sink-lift method. Cast upstream, the fly is then left to sink to the bottom. It is lifted briefly by raising the rod tip and allowed to sink again, repeating until the cast is fished out.

Caseless Caddis Larva

HOOK: Partridge GRS12ST or K12ST (S/E, long-shank emerger hook) size 12

THREAD: Black

UNDERBODY: Wound lead wire, a single layer at the abdomen, two layers at the thorax

RIB: Nylon mono, 20mm; at least 12 wraps, wound over the back

BODY: Dirty yellow or olive green Furry Foam

BACK: Transparent grey Flexibody over the body and thorax

THORAX: Fitch (polecat) or dark brown mink wound in a dubbing loop, well picked out after ribbing

HEAD: Black thread

Culard

Against popular opinion as to the use of cul de canard feathers, I cut them and retain the stiff central quill. The wings on the fly are stiffer and the fly is very easy to dry with one or two false casts.

HOOK: Partridge E1A (D/E, 4X fine, long shank) size 18 or E6A size 16

THREAD: Black

BODY: Herl fibres from a black wing feather of a peacock (for grayling) or dark grey or dark blue dun synthetic dubbing (for trout)

RIB: Extra fine gold wire or yellow Pearsall's silk, at least 6 turns wound in the opposite direction to the body

WING: 4 cul de canard feathers, pulled together and cut half way along the body length

HACKLE: 2 turns of a very small dark blue dun (dry) or starling body feather for the emerger

Once and Away

HOOK: Partridge GRS12ST 12 – 18, given a further downward bend

THREAD: Fine black

BODY: One peccary fibre or any stripped quill as a substitute taken well round the bend

THORAX: 3 strands of peacock herl

WING: 6 or 7 large cul de canard feathers, secured in the upright position; place a tiny drop of varnish at the base, avoiding the fine rump fibres; trim to a tuft

WINGCASE: Same feathers as for the wing

Remerger

The colours and materials can be varied to suit the natural nymphs.

HOOK: Partridge H1A (D/E, 2X long shank) or E1A, size 12 – 14

TAIL: 3 Chinese boar fibres

ABDOMEN: Natural ostrich herl ribbed with light brown transparent Swannundaze

Hans van Klinken plays a spirited Norwegian fish.

HANS VAN KLINKEN

1 Klinkhamer Special
2 Caseless Caddis Larva
3 Culard

4 Once and Away
5 Remerger
6 Leadhead Nymph

WINGCASE: Olive-dyed heron herl over the thorax and legs

LEGS: Dark blue dun soft hackle tied in at the rear of the thorax and laid flat over the thorax

THORAX: Dubbed natural hare's ear mixed with No 2 Hare-tron

HACKLE: Small starling body hackle

Leadhead Nymph

The lead or lead-substitute spilt shot is crimped onto a piece of strong monofilament (25 or 30mm) and bound onto the shank with the split towards the eye to make it more secure.

HOOK: Partridge H1A or G3A size 8 – 14

THREAD: Black or brown

TAIL: Brown partridge tail fibres, partridge back fibres or a mottled soft wing feather from a hen pheasant, wound as a collar between the butt and the body; one or two turns only as the butt must shine through

BUTT: Fluorescent green Flexibody or fluorescent lime-green wool

BODY: Shaggy brown rabbit fur, in a dubbing loop and wound

HEAD: Lead-substitute shot, strongly bound in a looped piece of monofilament (the split towards the hook eye)

Klinkhamer Special

Even though the suggested hook is a bent long shank it is often more successful if the shank is bent even more before starting the dressing. After winding on the thread well round towards the barb, tie in the wing and fully secure along the shank with thread. Tie in the hackle and then dub a slim tapered body, stopping behind the wing. (1) Tie in three peacock herls and wind three turns behind the wind with further turns in front. (2) Tie off and secure with varnish. (3) Turn the hook in the vice 45 degrees to face downwards. (4) Wrap a base of Spiderweb at the base of the wing. Wind the hackle and secure the hackle tip between the wing and the body with half hitches or a whip-finish. (5) Secure with varnish.

HOOK: Partridge GRS12ST or K12ST size 10 – 12 (smaller sizes work well in low water)

THREAD: Sparton Micro grey for the body; Spiderweb around the base of the wing and tying in the hackle

BODY: Fly-Rite light tan poly dubbing, or dark tan or rusty olive

WING: White poly yarn

THORAX: 3 strands of peacock herl

HACKLE: Blue dun (preferred), chestnut brown or light ginger cock

Klinkhamer Special

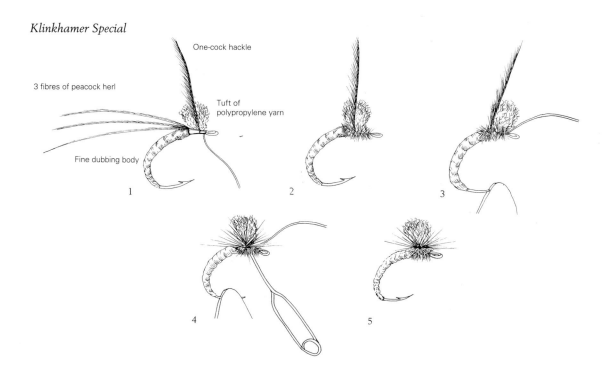

HANS WEILENMANN

HOLLAND

For many years Hans Weilenmann has been teaching fly tying in classes and exhibitions in Holland. He has also been a guest tyer at the Federation of Fly Fishers in Livingston, Montana. He claims that his membership of DAAFT (Dutch American Association of Fly Tyers) aptly describes his mental state. He contributes to British and German fly-fishing journals. Hans used to compete internationally in casting tournaments and, whilst no longer active in tournaments, he continues studying and teaching various casting techniques.

Due to the absence of trout in Dutch waters most of Hans' trout fishing takes place in rivers and streams in Germany and the British Isles. Other fishing exploits have taken him to the USA, Canada and New Zealand and he gratefully acknowledges that through the generosity of other anglers he has enjoyed some of the finest fishing those countries have to offer.

Hans' other fly-fishing interests include entomology, photography and collecting vices.

Most tyers have their 'pet' patterns. If I had to indicate my personal favourite among the various styles of mayfly patterns the Thorax Fly would surely come out on top. It embodies all of the qualities on my 'must have and must do' list.

The tying criteria are the use of cheap, easily obtainable materials, and ease of tying. The fishing criteria are durability, the correct blend of realistic and impressionistic features, great flotation, and visibility.

The Dark Kyll, although a fine general-purpose pattern, was designed by me to imitate one of the important flies of the early season throughout Europe, the large dark olive, *Baetis rhodani*. It was first used on the Kyll, a medium-sized rain-fed stream in Germany. Since then it has produced generously on most of the rivers I have fished across three continents. Whereas the natural it attempts to imitate has a much lighter olive body, this dark brown pattern has consistently come out on top.

A creature bearing the name *Tricorythodes* may suggest images going back to the Jurassic era, when dinosaurs roamed the world. Not so, this mayfly of diminutive size is a far cry from any such scene. Ranging in size from 3 to 4mm, hook size 24 – 26, it is nevertheless of great importance to fly fishers on those streams where it occurs. In size it is similar to the *Caenis*, a fly which can frustrate British anglers and which is commonly dismissed as the 'Anglers' Curse'. The trico is much more agreeable to the anglers fishing the eastern rivers of the United States where it hatches. And what hatches they are: awesome numbers of tricos will hatch daily without fail from late June until October, and sometimes even longer. The flies emerge in the early morning, transform from dun to spinner usually within the hour, moulting in mid-air, mate and become available to the trout again in a massive spinner fall. Amongst so many naturals, you must try to get the edge. My answer in attempting this is to offer an imitation of a female trico, complete with a bright green egg sac.

As spinners are notoriously difficult to see I tie the Trike with an oversized badger cock hackle, then clip the bottom half flush with the body. This results in the imprint of spread-out spinner

Late-season trout fishing on the River Wylye.

wings, but still leaves a round collar hackle to promote visibility.

Soft-hackled flies, although longstanding favourites in the north of England, have been long underestimated in most parts of the fly-fishing world. Deceptively simple in their appearance, they are, when fished properly, consistent producers on streams the world over. Quite deservedly they are staging a revival.

My version of the traditional Partridge & Green has a fine copper rib, both to suggest segmentation and to improve durability. An ostrich herl thorax provides additional bulk and movement within the dressing, complemented by a sparse hackle. If you deliberately try to underhackle this

type of fly, you probably get about the right amount of hackle. 'Lean and mean' aptly describes this fly. My favourite hook type for soft-hackle flies is the Partridge sedge hook with its fine wire and nicely curved shape. Fish it in either a dead drift just under the surface or quarter downstream and retrieve with a gentle figure of eight.

Sometimes it is necessary to fish with a buggy nymph which has to get down deep very fast. A quick glance at the material list for the Westward Bug will make clear how this is achieved: use enough lead wire – for a size 14 use 4 inches (10cm); size 12, 6 inches (15cm), and size 10, 8 inches (20cm). I don't tie this in smaller sizes.

The fly was devised by Bob Church. I first came across it when fishing several years ago in Kent. Other than the weight in it, it is really pretty nondescript. The only other thing I would like to say

HANS WEILENMANN

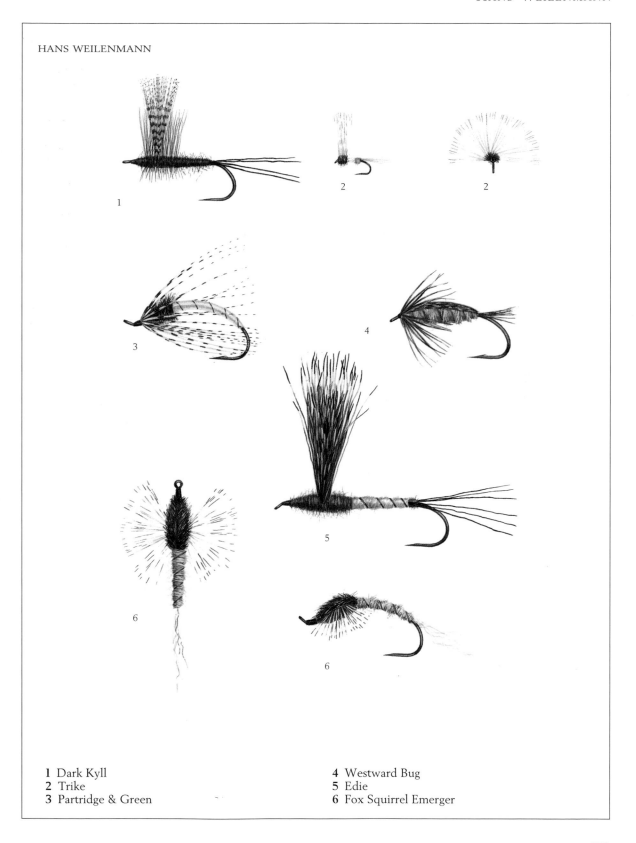

1 Dark Kyll
2 Trike
3 Partridge & Green

4 Westward Bug
5 Edie
6 Fox Squirrel Emerger

is: give it a try! I believe it lives at the same level of achievement as the Gold Ribbed Hare's Ear and Sawyer's Pheasant Tail nymph. Enough said.

The larger the fly you try to imitate, the more difficult it usually is to produce a dry fly which is both a good floater and an acceptable copy of the slender silhouette of the natural insect. As far as the mayflies go, they don't come much larger than the fly which is generally referred to as *the* mayfly, *Ephemera danica*.

The best pattern I have come up with to imitate the dun phase of this mayfly is the Edie. The name derived from the initials of the natural. The Edie is tied in Comparadun style, the technique developed by Al Caucci and Bob Nastasi. It combines key features like ease of tying and durability with good visibility and excellent floating capabilities.

Let me indicate the durability of a well-tied Comparadun. A few years ago I sent a couple to a friend, Mike Weddell, to try out. Mike wrote back to complain about the flies. He said one had come apart after just sixty-three trout . . .

The Fox Squirrel Emerger uses a subtle technique to produce a splayed hair hackle to assist an emerger pattern to float in the surface film. I refer to it as the reverse splay. I use it mostly for emerger patterns, like this one, but also for subsurface patterns which I want to sink slowly. Here the splayed hair hackle acts as an underwater parachute.

I generally use squirrel fox body hair because it has just the right texture and colour for most of my nymph patterns, and it can be used with any kind of straight, smooth hair or hackle fibres.

To explain the reverse splay I will describe it while tying the Fox Squirrel Emerger. After tying in the trailing shuck, copper ribbing and body material, finish the ribbed body, leaving just under half the hook shank empty. Next tie in the strands of peacock herl for the wingcase. So far everything is fairly straightforward, so now for the reverse splay. Cut off a bunch of hair from the back of a fox squirrel skin and remove most of the underfur. Make sure most of the tips are aligned. Tie the bunch in at the same spot where you tied in the peacock herl, tips pointing to the back of the hook. Trim the butt-ends and dub a small amount of hare's ear dubbing to form a thorax. Do not make this thorax too bulky and leave yourself sufficient room near the eye of the hook. Now for the fun part! Gently split the bunch of squirrel in two equal parts and pull the peacock herl forward. If the chemistry is right, you will be rewarded with a near 360-degree splay of hair. Tie the herl down, trim and complete the fly with a whip-finish.

Dark Kyll

HOOK: Sprite Gaelic Supreme or Partridge GRS3A (D/E, wide gape, fine wire) size 12 or Tiemco 102Y size 11

THREAD: Brown

WING: Single upright wing of wood-duck breast fibres or substitute

TAIL: 4 moose body hairs, split by a small clump of dubbing

BODY: Dark brown Partridge SLF dubbing along the whole body length

HACKLE: Brown (natural red cock), wound in open turns over the thorax area and trimmed flush with the body of the fly

Trike

HOOK: Partridge Marinaro Midge hook K1A (D/E, very fine wire, offset wide gape) size 26

THREAD: Finest white

HACKLE: Badger cock trimmed flush with the underside of the body

TAIL: Badger cock fibres

EGG SAC: Bright green rabbit fur dubbing

ABDOMEN: White moose mane, flattened

THORAX: Black ostrich herl

Partridge & Green

HOOK: Partridge sedge hook K2B (U/E, curved shank sedge hook) size 10 – 16

THREAD: Black

RIB: Fine copper wire

BODY: Bright green fluorescent waxed flat floss

THORAX: Grey ostrich herl

HACKLE: Brown partridge

Westward Bug

HOOK: Partridge GRS2A, H1A or Tiemco 900BL size 10 – 14

THREAD: Black

HACKLE: Grouse wing covert

UNDERBODY: Medium lead wire, double or triple wire (see text)

TAIL AND BACK: Hen pheasant, shell-back

RIB: Fluorescent orange waxed floss

BODY: Dubbed tan rabbit fur

Edie

HOOK: Partridge H1A (D/E, 2X long shank, wide gape) size 10

THREAD: Brown

WING: Dyed olive-grey deer hair, splayed 180 degrees

BUTT: Dubbed Partridge SLF dubbing, mixed equal parts dark brown and dark olive

TAILS: 6 moose body hairs, split by a small clump of dubbing

BODY: Dubbed cream rabbit fur

RIB: Brown sewing thread

THORAX: Dubbed Partridge SLF dubbing, mixed equal parts dark brown and dark olive

Fox Squirrel Emerger

HOOK: Partridge sedge hook K2B size 10 – 16

THREAD: Black

SHUCK: Trailing strands of untreated wool, lightly dyed tan/olive

RIB: Fine copper wire

BODY: Untreated wool, lightly dyed tan/olive, dubbed

WINGCASE: Peacock herl

LEGS: Fox squirrel body hair (see text)

THORAX: Dubbed hare's ear fur

DAVE WHITLOCK

Both professionally and personally Dave Whitlock is a man totally devoted to the world of fly fishing and conservation. Twenty years ago he resigned his position as a petroleum chemist to become a full-time professional in the arts of fly fishing. He pooled his talents in art, writing, photography, fly fishing and lecturing in his new career. He regularly contributes his art and writing to many publications. He has co-authored and illustrated many books and has written and illustrated three books of his own. He is in demand throughout the world as a lecturer on fly fishing and conservation and runs fly-fishing schools yearly in the US and abroad.

Dave is a recipient of many awards including the FFF Conservation Man of Year Award in 1981 and the Max Ander's Wild Trout Award in 1976. He also received the Buz Buzeck Flytyer's Award, the highest honour in the world of fly tying. It recognizes his innovation in new fly patterns and his national fly-tying activities. In 1987 Dave was inducted into the National Fresh Water Hall of Fame and was also presented with the FFF James E. Henshall Award for his work in warm-water fishing and conservation. He also received FFF's Ambassador Award for national and international promotion of fly fishing and conservation.

His international fishing experience is wide. In addition to extensive fishing all over North America, Dave has fished in Mexico, Venezuela, New Zealand, Cuba, Belize, Russia, Britain, Yugoslavia, Czechoslovakia and Hungary.

These six flies are my favourite six flies in the sense that they are *my* flies. They do well for a number of people here in North America as well as in Europe and even in South America. I have been tying flies since I was nine years old and over the years I have developed some of my own methods. I have always been a creative person, trying to discover things for myself and I always tried to figure out what fish were feeding on and come up with a fly that really did perform well for what fish are expecting to see in the way of food. There are of course many wonderful fly-fishing innovators who have gone before me but it has always been my forte to want to improve on nature or on other people's efforts towards nature. These six flies are some of the results of that.

The Red Fox Squirrel Nymph is probably the first fly of any consequence that I came up with

for trout and it was a result of becoming very interested in tying fur-bodied or soft-bodied nymphs. Nymph fishing in the United States has come into its own in the last twenty-five years and I think that probably I was responsible for much of that because up until maybe thirty years ago there was very little nymph fishing here for a number of reasons.

First, it wasn't profitable because it was very difficult to catch fish on nymphs, and secondly, the quality of the nymphs was such that they were unrealistic and they didn't imitate natural foods well. Fly fishers didn't have the tackle and the abilities to fish them properly.

Polly Rosborough and Ted Trueblood both interested me in tying efficient soft-bodied nymphs. In my efforts to develop a hair-bodied nymph I came across the red fox squirrel which has a beautiful belly skin colour like sand or a very

162

Dave Whitlock with a fine brown trout from the White River, Arkansas.

pretty orange and the back is more of a hare's ear with a salt-and-pepper blend of grey, brown, tan, cream, black and white with a bar on the back. The nymph was devised utilizing this hair and it turned out to be probably the best nymph I ever created because it is a totally impressionistic or suggestive nymph. It looks like so many different types of food forms – mayfly nymph, damsel nymph, scud, stonefly nymph or caddis larva or pupa. It also sometimes looks like a small crayfish. I put it in the category of the Pheasant Tail nymph or the Gold Ribbed Hare's Ear in the sense that they are suggestive of a number of food forms. I tie it from size 2 to size 18 and I vary its length and thickness to simulate one food more than another. I usually tie it on a 2X long hook and in the general proportions of the one illustrated. It has been a really good fly for me.

My second fly is Dave's Improved Damsel. I had become very active in fishing the spring creeks and western streams that were laden with vegetation and moved fairly slowly. They were very good damsel nymph streams. Many of the western lakes also had an enormous number of damsels in them. I devised a straight-bodied damsel as well as a wiggle damsel. Both of them hung hook-down and when the TMC 400T hook came out, called a swimming-nymph hook, I tied on this. I changed its centre of gravity by adding two small lead eyes to make it sink fairly rapidly but this also allowed it to move through the water with the hook up. It really did improve its effectiveness because during the damsel season when nymphs are migrating into aquatic vegetation to hatch, you must cast the nymph right into the vegetation and move it through. With the hook hanging down and without a weed guard you were constantly picking up weed. Using the up-swimming hook I was able to come up with a nymph that looked and swam realistically. I could get it in and out of the areas where trout were looking for damsels without it hanging up.

In all the flies that I tie I like to utilize the softness of the hackle in order to give an impressionistic leg. I don't believe in legs that are relatively stiff. The more flexible and more movement you can get in a nymph or underwater fly pattern, the better fish will respond to it. Almost all of the flies that I tie which are called nymphs, or are nymphal imitations, are usually tied either without legs or with very flexible soft feathers to simulate the legs.

Dave's Hopper is a universally effective hopper pattern. I remember back in the 1950s when I became so infatuated with fishing out west in the Rocky Mountains I became very interested in catching browns and rainbow trout on grasshoppers, usually through July, August and September. In those days I wasn't a particularly good caster. There was a fly at the time called a Joe's Hopper. It was a decent-looking pattern but it had a very large collar hackle and when you cast it in those mountain winds it would twist your leader. It also sat very high on the water when the grasshoppers I observed sat very low in the water, sometimes they even sank. I started by trimming just the collar but I lost floatability when I did that. At the same time a close friend and associate, Joe Brooks, suggested that I make a Muddler Minnow and grease the top of that with floatant and use it as a grasshopper. It worked pretty well but it didn't have the look of a grasshopper so I hybridized the Joe's Hopper and Muddler Minnow to produce the more realistic Dave's Hopper. A few years later I added the kicker legs.

It has been an enormously successful fly all across Canada as well as the lower forty-eight states and even into South America. It is the number-one brown-trout fly in Chile in the hopper areas down there. None of the many other patterns developed since the growth in popularity of hoppers in the last fifteen to twenty years has stayed around very long. According to the Umpqua Feather Merchants it is the top-selling hopper pattern in the world. It has to be good to have that kind of following. It is tied from about a size 14 earlier in the year to a size 6 towards the end of the year. I usually vary the underside from pale cream to a dark yellow, or a pale green or olive to orange depending on the natural's underside.

The Electric Leech is a fly I designed out of a Marabou Leech. I wanted to satisfy myself that the fly had both plenty of action and movement in the water like a real leech. It should have a nice swimming shape to it and should be attractive in water that was either dark or discoloured a little. It always bothered me whenever I was fishing a rather dark-coloured fly fairly deep that the fish may not see it very well. So I married the darkness of the marabou and the soft saddle hackle and the fur body which is a fairly standard pattern, with Flashabou, a new material at the time. I came up with a beautiful dark swimming silhouette incorporating several strips of this highly reflective and very flexible Flashabou tinsel into the tail, around the body and the head. The uniqueness of that is we have dark and action and flash all built into one fly. It certainly has proved effective for people who have used it. It works on both river and lake but particularly well on the latter.

I usually tie it about two to three inches in length and let it sink down deep and fish it very slowly, pausing for a moment, then make a slow retrieve with pauses letting the Flashabou do its work against the dark background. I also add a silver peacock herl across the back to give a little iridescence particularly in clear water.

For a number of years in the late 1960s to the mid 1970s I pursued large brown trout all over North America. Everywhere I went it was obvious that these large browns fed on a wide range of food forms. One that seemed common to many areas was the sculpin minnow and there were a number of imitations available, including the Muddler Minnow, the Troth Bullhead and Spuddler. I wasn't satisfied with any of these so I devised a more realistic fly, the Whitlock Sculpin which I think fished a little bit better. Later on I learned how to make the back and tail of the streamer marry with the body with the matuka method. I now call it a Matuka Sculpin.

If you really want to catch large trout of any type you need large hooks, and the Partridge low-water salmon hook up to size 5/0 is ideal. The appeal of the fly lies in its matuka tail and back, its cream body and its very wide shovel-shaped head made out of deer hair, stacked, trimmed and coloured. It is a fly I usually fish either early morning or late evening particularly on the larger rivers. Sometimes it's an excellent night pattern. Normally I fish it on about a two- to three-foot leader and either a Hi-D sink-tip or full sinking line so that I can keep the fly moving deeper along the bottom. It has been a terrific producer of fish including the largest brown trout I have ever caught of twenty-two-and-a-half pounds. I have probably caught between thirty and forty browns over ten pounds on this fly.

I tie it in three colour variations: the natural one illustrated, an olive colour and a dark chocolate brown colour. Sculpins adopt the colours of the river bed rather like a chameleon, so it is probably best to make a fly nearer the colour of the river bed. When night fishing the darker patterns work best, as do dressings with a very bulky head.

Just over a decade ago I was involved in putting a fly selection together for L.L. Bean. One thing I was trying to do was select an assortment of minnow imitations containing shiners, shad, black nose dace, etc. I produced a series of small fish imitations called the Dave Whitlock's Match the Minnow Series and this included the Golden Shiner as well as half a dozen others. With the series I tried to simulate the profile, colour and motion of various small fish. The fly is more of a design than a pattern and it can be varied to imitate different fish by amending the colours and shades. The pattern is even more realistic if you bend the body a little, into a half-moon shape shank. The minnow takes on an irregular fluttering action that makes it look crippled. The straight shank is illustrated but I recommend that the body should be slightly concave.

Red Fox Squirrel Nymph

HOOK: Tiemco TMC 5262 (2XL, 2X heavy, D/E) size 2 – 18

THREAD: Orange or black Danville flymaster 6/0

CEMENT: Dave's Flexament

WEIGHT: Lead wire, diameter of the hook wire, 8 – 12 wraps

TAIL: Red fox squirrel back hair

RIB: Oval gold tinsel

ABDOMEN: Red fox squirrel belly fur mixed 50:50 with sienna or fox tan Antron dubbing

THORAX: Red fox squirrel back hair mixed 50:50 with charcoal Antron dubbing

LEGS: (On sizes 10 and larger) tan and brown hen neck or back hackle or partridge, one turn

HEAD: Orange and black thread, or thorax dubbing

*A beautiful cutthroat trout caught by Dave Whitlock
from the Snake River, Wyoming.*

Dave's Improved Damsel

HOOK: Tiemco TMC 400T (1XF, upward curved
shank, S/E) size 8 – 10

THREAD: Waxed olive Danville 6/0

CEMENT: Dave's Flexament

BODY WEIGHTING AND EYES: Wapsi X small lead
eyes

TAIL: 2 small grizzly hen rump marabou dyed pale
olive with a single strip of pearl-olive Flashabou

RIB: Pearl-olive Flashabou

HEAD AND BODY: Pale olive Partridge SLF dubbing

BACK AND WINGCASE: Pale olive Swiss straw
(synthetic raffia)

LEGS: Sections from grizzly hen body feathers, dyed
pale olive, set at 45 degrees to the body

Dave's Hopper

HOOK: Tiemco TMC 5263 (3XL, 2X heavy, D/E)
size 14 – 16

THREAD: Yellow Danville 6/0 Flymaster

CEMENTS: Dave's Flexament and Tiffilm fixative

TAIL: Stiff red deer hair

BODY: Yellow polypropelene yarn

RIB: Brown (natural red) or grizzly cock hackle

UNDERWING: Deer hair dyed pale yellow or gold

WING: Brown speckled oak turkey wing quill

LEGS: 2 sections of golden pheasant tail feathers,
overhand knotted to shape hopper's thigh and calf

COLLAR AND HEAD: White tail or roe deer hair,
trimmed to shape and coloured with waterproof felt
pens

DAVE WHITLOCK

1 Red Fox Squirrel Nymph
2 Dave's Improved Damsel
3 Dave's Hopper
4 Whitlock Electric Leech
5 Whitlock Matuka Sculpin
6 Whitlock Match the Minnow Golden Shiner

Whitlock Electric Leech

HOOK: Partridge low-water salmon hook, size 1/0 – 10

THREAD: Black Danville 6/0

CEMENT: Dave's Flexament

WEIGHT: Lead wire, 19 – 15 wraps

TAIL: Black turkey marabou tip

BODY: Mixed black African goat and rabbit hair, in a 50:50 blend

PALMER HACKLE: Long, webby, soft, black saddle hackle

BODY AND TAIL BACK: 3 – 6 peacock herls

BODY AND TAIL FLASH: 2 – 4 Flashabou strands

HEAD: Black thread and wound with Flashabou

Whitlock Matuka Sculpin

HOOK: Partridge low-water salmon hook, size 5/0 – 8

THREAD: Cream or yellow Danville single strand tying floss

CEMENT: Dave's Flexament

BODY-HEAD FOUNDATION: Mason hard nylon, the size of the hook wire

WEIGHT: Lead wire, the diameter of the hook wire, 10 – 20 wraps

RIB: (Over the matuka feathers) medium brass wire

BELLY: Cream coarse dubbing

BACK AND TAIL: Cree neck hackles, natural and dyed olive, 4 of each colour

GILLS: Red Antron dubbing

HEAD: Mule or white deer hair, cream, with natural grey, black, olive and gold markings after trimming to shape

EYES: Small brown and black plastic eyes

Whitlock Match the Minnow Golden Shiner

HOOK: Mustad 9575 (very long shank, S/E) size 2 – 8

THREAD: Cream Danville 6/0

CEMENT: Dave's Flexament, Zap-a-Gap superglue

UNDERBODY: Aluminium or stainless steel tape

BODY (BELLY): Pearl mylar tubing, dyed gold

BACK AND TAIL: 4 golden olive cock neck hackles

CHEEK (optional): 2 cock pheasant feathers

EYES: A pair of small gold and black plastic eyes

GILLS: Red paint

HEAD: Tying thread with dorsal side marked black

RUTH J. ZINCK

CANADA

Ruth Zinck has been fishing for over sixty years, progressing from cane poles, bobbers and worms, spincasting and lures, to a split-cane rod and a fly. She began tying flies in 1970 – the only female in the class. Since then she has won fly-tying awards and has been among the demonstration tyers at many of the Federation of Fly Fishers' conclaves (now renamed the International Fly Fishing Show). She has also assisted at the Youth conclaves. Ruth served as an International Director of the FFF for six years and is currently Senior Vice-President for Alberta, Saskatchewan and the 'Pertinent Territories' for the Western Rocky Mountain Council of the FFF. Ruth has written for various FFF journals and books as well as for other publications.

Ruth usually fishes in Alberta and Montana and she has fished widely in Ontario, Quebec, Newfoundland, British Columbia, Oregon and New Zealand. Her favourite waters are the Bow and Crowsnest Rivers and Midnapore Lake in Alberta and the Missouri River near Craig, Montana.

Living for most of her life in Ontario, Ruth moved to Calgary, Alberta in 1981, with her husband, a Lutheran clergyman, now retired. She is unique, so far as this book is concerned, for being a grandmother three times over.

He finished the fly with a flourish. 'There it is, Moore's Muskrat!' Don Moore, co-founder of Ontario's Izaak Walton Club, had used an extremely simply nymph design and tied the rough, impressionistic creation with muskrat fur. He then did the obvious and named it after himself. Later, when I found several mahogany-coloured mink tails in a bag of sundries purchased in a weak moment at a farm auction sale, I also did the obvious. I tied up a dozen of the simple, rough, impressionistic nymphs and named them after me.

This fly is not so much a pattern as it is a style. Almost any fur can be used to tie it. In the future we may be inundated – Bob's Badger; Otto's Otter, Robert's Rabbit – though not all colours may be as effective as muskrat and mink. This is a 360-degree or all-round fly, any side is up. The buggier the thorax looks, the better it is, but there should be a distinct taper to the tail. The nymph may be weighted heavily, lightly or not at all.

It was May of 1978 when I first used the Zinck Mink and it enticed a trout to the take on my third cast. Through the years it has consistently been successful on lakes, rivers and small streams, though it seems to be more effective in spring than later in the year.

One mid-June evening on the Bow River in Calgary, I used the Zinck Mink in a size 14 on a floating line and cast it up and across an obvious seam in the current. The fly settled just under the surface. At the very end of the drift, as the fly was about to swing, a good-sized rainbow engulfed it. The Zinck Mink took another seven fish that evening and three of them broke my tippet.

I have caught brookies, rainbows, browns and Rocky Mountain white fish with this fly. I have trolled it, fished it just under the surface and close to the bottom, and it has produced with every method. Why does the Zinck Mink work so well?

Perhaps it is because its dark, reddish brown colour is similar to many nymphs and, having no top or bottom, it looks good from all angles. Also, its rough, straggled tie appears very much alive in the water. Then again, it could be that it has its own charisma and just cannot be resisted!

The K-Z Corixa was developed to overcome a perplexing problem at Midnapore Lake. This water is one of five private, man-made, stocked facilities in south-east Calgary and its rainbow trout are often frustratingly close-mouthed.

It was early September 1988 and Joan Kirkham was visiting me from Ontario. We had been rowing around the lake for two hours without a strike while fish sporadically assaulted a surface which appeared bereft of insects. We have tried a multitude of dry, wet and sinking specimens without success and, in spite of our considerable expertise, had begun to feel like novices.

We were about to head for the dock when a wind gust moved the boat and Joan's dry was pulled under and taken. The trout was sacrificed in the name of research and its stomach revealed a recent diet of grey-backed, black insects that looked like water boatmen. We consulted Schwiebert's *Nymphs* and tentatively identified them as corixa bugs.

We spent that evening developing a pattern. To give the impression of an air bubble, we wrapped the bend of the hook with metallic Astro cord and later brought it forward along the body underneath the finished fly before tying off the head. In order to create a wide body we used tightly twisted black yarn lashed to each side of the hook and then sheathed it with three layers of the same yarn fully unwrapped. After tying off the Astro cord, the covert was brought forward to the eye, tied down and brought back a short distance and cut off to resemble a head tuft, A black rubber strip threaded through the midsection completed the design. It looked good.

Back at the lake next day, the fish appeared to agree and took the K-Z Corixa readily. We fished it on a floating line with a long leader. We let the fly sink, retrieved it to the surface and then let it sink again. Often it was taken as it first hit the water.

This fly will work on still water wherever corixa are found. If necessary, the covert can be darkened with a Pantone pen and then I'm ready for the perplexing problem of the water boatmen variety. I won't leave home without it.

A year had passed since I had unsuccessfully fished Ontario's Rainbow Ranch during what was called the 'White Caddis Fall'. The flies had covered the water in a communal death wish and at that time I had nothing even close to what the trout in the three ponds were sipping off the surface.

Back in Calgary, I kept thinking about those caddis. I had some thin packing foam and white Ethafoam among my tying materials. After some experimentation, the Blatantly Blank Foam Caddis evolved. Now I was back at the ponds with what I thought would be the answer. It was early June 1990.

Number One pond was designated 'catch and release' and the trout were large and leader-shy. I tied on a 6X tippet and carefully cast the newly developed white foam caddis. It landed softly and sat close to the surface film when suddenly there was a swirl and it was gone. I struck and broke off. I increased the tippet size and the next rainbow was brought to hand . . . and the next and the next. There was no evidence of shyness with this fly on the leader.

Later, I thought of using this white fly as a blank. Many times I had been on a stream with no caddis in my kit of the colour the fish favoured that day. Perhaps a quick dye job on the foam caddis would solve the problem. I stuck a few Pantone pens in my vest and headed for a quiet backwater on the Bow. The caddis in evidence were olive-bodied. I folded the fly's foam wing back and applied a Pantone pen. A few strokes and the change was complete. I used a light tan on the underside of the wing and cast it towards a rise. The fly floated close to the surface and the colour held. On the fourth cast a fish confirmed the experiment a success.

A friend offered to field-test the fly on a Montana spring creek. He told me later that he had encountered a yellow caddis and that the doctored fly and filled the bill.

Besides the convenience of always having the correctly coloured caddis at hand, I believe the soft body and wing of this fly fools the fish into that extra second of delayed rejection that helps in successfully setting the hook. Because it depends primarily on the wing for buoyancy and

RUTH J. ZINCK

1 Zinck Mink
2 K-Z Corixa
3 Blatantly Blank Foam Caddis
4 Prince Nymph
5 Wright's Royal
6 Foam Wing Double Trouble Trico

THE WORLD'S BEST TROUT FLIES

sits so flush on the surface, I find the Blatantly Blank Foam Caddis performs best on non-turbulent water.

The Prince Nymph had been featured in the Spring 1985 issue of *Flyfisher*, the magazine of the FFF. Its unique design was so appealing that I secured the necessary biots and tied a series in several sizes. Midnapore Lake was the testing ground. Would this nymph appeal to fish as well as the fisher? I attached a size 12 to my sinking line and trolled the fly as I worked the boat to the opposite, more productive shore. The trip across took much longer than usual because of the trout I caught on the way over.

That September I fished the Sheep, a small river that borders the town Okotoks just south west of Calgary. Because of its accessibility, the water is heavily used and the fish wary. The first time the fly touched the river it was snatched by a small rainbow. As I worked upstream, the Prince lured fish after fish. I was using a floating line and the fly was unweighted. I was casting up and across, and the strikes most often occurred at the end of the drift. It was a great afternoon.

The day I used the Prince Nymph while floating the Bow River from McKinnon Flats to the Carseland Weir, was the day I sincerely blessed Doug Prince for creating this fantastic fly. I was using a size 14 on a floating line with several small split shot ahead of the fly. A strike indicator completed the rig. It was the only pattern I used the entire day. There was no need to switch. Others may have caught more or larger fish but the twenty-incher the sucked in the Prince as it swept across its lie gave me an experience I still remember. I can hear it at this moment: the scream of the reel and the throb of the rod as the power of the fish and the thrust of the river sang on the line in unbearable cadence until the tippet could sustain it no longer and the fish leaped free.

Why does this fly appeal to fish and fishers? The white biot 'delta' wings were what first attracted me. Their visibility and the added flash of mylar on the body is what likely catches the eye of the fish. Peacock iridescence does no harm and the forked tail and soft hackle make the Prince look alive and extremely edible. I think it is everything a nymph should be and the fish obviously agree.

I first heard about Phillip Wright's terrestrial adaptation of the Royal Wulff during a Calgary Hook and Hackle Club meeting in the mid 1980s. Ron Pike had just returned from fishing the Crowsnest River in south-western Alberta and was raving about the fly's prowess. He had caught and released a proliferation of rainbows, mostly large, and all on size 16 Wright's Royals. It seemed to be an extraordinary fly. The pattern was no secret as Jack Dennis had included it in Volume II of his *Western Trout Fly Tying Manual*. I decided that this was a fly I must try . . . sometime.

The year that my husband and I decided to camp on the Crowsnest I remembered the fly and finally tied up a dozen. It was autumn when Ron had bragged about them and this was spring. They might not work but I'd give them a chance.

The afternoon that I first used them, I realized that Ron had not stretched the truth. Trout of all sizes fell to the fly again and again. They took it even when it was tattered and waterlogged. The frenzy continued for over two hours and when the attacks on this fly finally ceased, no other pattern would entice a take. I left the river satiated.

The Wright's Royal has been an attractor wherever I have fished, but it appears to be especially effective on any stretch of the Crowsnest River. Whether it creates the illusion of a flying ant, a misshapen mayfly or a baffling beetle in the brain of the fish, it triggers takes more often than not. Any fly so consistently successful deserves a space in everyone's flybox. It has a special place in mine.

I had begun saving pieces of thin packing foam in the mid 1980s. I had no use for the material then but it reminded me of Pellon, an interfacing material used in dressmaking that had been utilized for wings by some enterprising tyers a few years earlier. Others also found the foam intriguing and in 1988 Elna Foust of 'Fishaus' in Hamilton, Montana gave me some tiny wings her husband had stamped out with a 'biscuit-cutter' tool he had made. I never used them but to this day I don't know if despair at seeing my highly invisible tiny Tricos sink prompted my foam-wing Trico design or if it was a residual memory of tiny wings. Whatever the source, they worked. The flies were more easily seen and they floated, like decent spinners should.

It takes a long time to bring a good fish to hand with a tiny fly and a gossamer tippet. An exhausted trout has a lesser survival rate than does one played quickly and released without excessive handling. For this reason I decided to tie several foam-wing Trico spinners on one hook . . . a larger one. On its first outing on Hebgen Lake, Montana the Double Trouble Trico took an 18¼-inch brown trout on a size 14 hook and 4X tippet – an unusual but more secure combination for Trico matching.

Zinck Mink

The fly may be weighted.

HOOK: Mustad 9671 (D/E, 2XL) size 10 – 14

THREAD: 6/0 Flymaster, black or to match the fur

TAIL: Guard hairs from a mink tail or body

ABDOMEN: Under-fluff from mink fur (no guard hair)

THORAX: Under-fluff and guard hair, allowing the guard hair to protrude

K-Z Corixa

HOOK: Mustad 3399 size 10 – 16

AIR BUBBLE: Metallic Astro cord

COVERT: Light mottled turkey wing

BODY: A half strand black polypropylene

LEGS: One strip of black rubber pulled through mid-body with a darning needle

Blatantly Blank Foam Caddis

The wing should have very shallow shaping in the top of its elongated heart-shape. Too deep a cut will hinder flotation. When the two wraps of spade hackle are tied in, the top half is brought forward, tied down and the centre hackle cut out. What is left forms the antennae. The lower hackle is trimmed to represent legs. Do not stretch the body material when wrapping as this will diminish the buoyancy.

HOOK: Mustad 94840 size 12 – 16

THREAD: 6/0 Flymaster, white

BODY: White Ethafoam, narrow strip

WING: Thin packing foam cut in an elongated heart-shape at least twice the body length

LEGS AND ANTENNAE: Two turns of white spade hackle

Prince Nymph

HOOK: Mustad 9671 (D/E, 2XL) size 10 – 14

THREAD: 6/0 Flymaster, black

TAIL: Two dark brown goose biots, tied forked

RIB: Fine flat gold tinsel or mylar

BODY: Peacock herl

HACKLE: Brown (natural red) hen, the upper fibres trimmed off

WING: Two white goose biots tied in a wide 'V' on top of the body, just behind the eye

Wright's Royal

HOOK: Mustad 94840, size 8 – 16

THREAD: 6/0 Flymaster, black

BODY: Peacock herl with a centre band of red floss. The front peacock herl is wound over the wing roots

WING: Light elk, extending just beyond the bend

HACKLE: Brown (natural red) cock, palmered over the front peacock herl

Foam Wing Double Trouble Trico

When making the wings cut two rectangles as long as the total wing span and as wide as the width of the wings. With each rectangle, bring the ends together and shape the wings but don't cut them apart. Tie each set in at the fold as each abdomen is completed. Remember you are tying two small flies on one hook. Each set of wings should have about one-third of the shank between them.

HOOK: Mustad 94840, size 14

THREAD: 8/0 Uni-Thread, black

TAILS: Micro-Fibetts, uncoloured. Twice the body length; three on the back fly, two on the front

BODIES: Black or dark brown fine mending yarn. Unwind and use only one ply or less

WINGS: White packing foam 1mm thick or less

Editor's note: Ruth Zinck included the Usual in her original list of six flies. To avoid duplication, she kindly agreed to a substitution.

HAIR-WING DRY FLIES

Al Beatty

During the last thirty-six years my fly tying has evolved from tying simple nymphs to full-dress Atlantic salmon patterns. My main forte, however, is the hair-wing dry fly.

I have heard from many good fly tyers that tying hair-wing flies is a disappointing experience and one they tend to avoid. You really need not experience this frustration if you follow two very critical principles I'll outline for you here.

As in any other construction project, you must have the right materials for the job. Tying hair wings is no different and the properties of the hair you use is the first principle I'll review with you. In this case I'll also assume we'll be tying deer hair for most of our tying material, as moose and elk hair may not be readily available in your country.

HAIR SELECTION

To construct wings and tails easily on hair-wing patterns you need hair with well-defined markings and fibres that are fairly dense in cell construction. Typically this hair is located on the animal parallel to the back bone, down over the rump, and along the shoulders. The best-quality hair is harvested in the summer or early autumn because the hair fibre is denser and you have less underfur to remove in the tying process.

At this point you're thinking, that's great if you could have the luxury of selecting hair from a complete hide. In reality, most of us purchase our hair from a fly-fishing store. It's already cut into small squares and displayed for sale. As you look at the hair displayed, focus your attention on the coloration of the hair fibre and you will be able to tell whether it's acceptable for hair-wing flies or not. First look at a single hair fibre and notice it starts with a fine black tip which is followed by a light tan band. Below the band is an area that is dark grey gradually fading into a very light grey at the base of the fibre. This is the part of the fibre where you need to focus your attention.

The method used here I call the Light & Dark Calculation. Simply stated: if more than half of the hair fibre is dark grey before it starts to fade to light grey, then this is the hair you need to tie hair-wing flies – the more dark, the better. If most of the hair fibre is light grey, you are heading for frustration because the hair will have a natural tendency to flare and spin under the hook. Just follow the simple rule of the Light & Dark Calculation, and you will be half-way to your objective – better hair-wing flies.

STATIC CLING

The second obstacle you need to overcome is natural static electricity which causes hair fibre to cling to anything and everything. I have discovered two solutions for eliminating this problem. They are products readily available in a supermarket or grocery store. In the US they are marketed under the brand names Static Guard and Bounce Pads.

Static Guard is a product that is sprayed on a woman's dress to remove the static electricity that causes the dress to cling to the body. A Bounce Pad is a small white or pink sheet of material that is placed in a tumble dryer to keep static electricity from forming. I spray either myself, my tools and my material with Static Guard or I keep a Bounce Pad in my lap while tying and periodically touch my hands to the pad. Either method is effective.

Now you know the simple rules for success – the right material that is static free. The rules may be simple but they are also critical.

HAIR-WING PROPORTIONS

The number of fibres, how long they are, and where you place them on the hook is critical to the fly's posture when it lands on the water and whether, as an imitation, it is acceptable to the fish. In the next few paragraphs I will describe several simple techniques and measurements I think you'll find helpful. Read this section carefully. The proportions described have been used to tie my selected patterns and are applicable to other hair-wing flies.

The hair tail

I do not count the number of fibres in a hair tail. Instead I refer to the parts of the hook to provide my measurements. The shank is used to provide the hair-tail length. Therefore, on a completed fly the tail should extend beyond the body a distance equal to the length of the hook.

Determining the number of fibres for a tail on a particular hook size is a little more challenging. The method I use is to make a comparison between the diameter of the clump of hair and the diameter of the hook's eye. The size of the clump of hair should be equal to the outside of the eye of the hook after giving the fibres a half twist. I accomplish the twist by holding the tips of the fibres with the fingers of one hand and the base end of the fibres with the fingers of the other hand. I then rotate my hands a half turn to twist the fibres. The point where the twist occurs is where I make the size comparison to the hook's eye. I use the same formula for all hair tails no matter what type of hair I'm using – deer, elk, moose, etc.

The hair wing

On any hair fly with wings that are upright and divided, each wing post is of equal diameter to the tail. You make this comparison in one of two ways; the twist method as described above or by making a visual comparison to the tail that's already on the hook. On any divided, upright wing the wing length is always equal to the length

of the hook shank. It is then tied on the shank one-third back from the eye. It is important to remember, on a properly tied hair-wing fly, that the three clumps of hair forming the wings and the tail are all the same length and the same diameter.

The rules for tying a Trude or down-wing style are not as clearly defined. Typically the diameter of a single Trude wing is twice the diameter of the outside of the hook's eye since the wing is tied undivided. The length of the down-wing and where it's placed on the hook is a different matter. Some down-wings are tied on the hook at the one-third point and are equal to the length of the shank, just like an up-wing version. The Royal Trude is an example of this proportion. However, other down-wing flies can have a wing that is longer than the shank and are tied on the shank just behind the hook, etc. The Elk Hair Caddis is an example.

TYING TECHNIQUES

Hair Flare Control: Even when you have the correct hair for the job, it will still have a tendency to flare. In the US a flared tail or wing is not acceptable on many western hair-wing patterns. Therefore controlling the natural tendency of hair to flare is an important technique and one easily learned. I will explain my technique using a typical Wulff pattern as an example.

After selecting your hair, cleaning out the underfur, evening the tips in a hair stacker, and determining the correct length and number of fibres, you are ready to tie the hair tail on top of the hook. It is tied on the shank at the half point with very tight wraps. As you wrap over the fibres towards the bend you gradually relax the pressure on the thread so the turns of thread are snug against the hair but not tight enough to flare it. When you wrap from the bend back to the middle of the hook, gradually tighten your wraps the closer you get to the middle. I call this technique Hair Flare Control. Trim off the excess hair fibres before you tie on the wings.

When you tie the wings on at the one-third point on the shank, you start with several snug, but not tight, wraps. As you wrap towards the middle apply more pressure thus forming tighter wraps. Gradually relax your thread turns as you return to the starting position, the one-third point. Trim off the excess hair at the wings at an angle parallel to the shank to provide a smooth taper to the body. Then wrap several turns of thread to cover the trimmed hair ends. At this point your incomplete fly should have a tail protruding to the rear and the tips of the wings pointing forward.

Standing up the wings: I use two methods to stand up the wings. Either method is effective. The first method is to wrap a cone of thread in front of and tight against the wings. The cone should taper down from the wings to the hook eye. Evenly divide the clump of hair into two wing posts and wrap about five snug, but not tight, wraps around each wing post. By taking a turn of thread back around the body after you wrap each wing post, you can pull the thread to hold the wing in any position. I call this technique Setting the Wing and usually set the wing so it is at a ninety-degree angle to the shank. I like to separate the individual wing posts by forty-five degrees.

Another technique for standing the wing is what I call Through the Clump. You start this method with your tying thread directly behind the wing at the one-third point. Pull up about a quarter of the hair fibres and wrap a tight turn of thread between them and the original bunch of hair. Pull up the next quarter of hair fibres and wrap the thread. Repeat this process until the thread is in front of the wings. Wrap a tapering cone of thread in front of the wings, as you did before. Divide the wings and wrap each wing post. When using this method you don't have to set the wing. This technique is especially effective if you are tying hair-wing flies that have a wing of fanned hair instead of divided wings. Although I did not cover this type of pattern in my selection, a Comparadun is such an example.

INDEX

(All page numbers marked in bold indicate a reference to illustrations)

A

Adams, 90, **91**, 100, 141
Ameletus sp., 121

B

Baetis Emerger, **147**, 148
Baetis rhodani, 38, 104, 157
Bakelaar, Theo, 12, 15–19
Balloon Emerger, 104, **107**
Barden, Bob, 25
Beaded Pheasant Tail Nymph, 90, **91**
Beatty, Al, 13, 20–23, 175–177
Bessel, John, 85
Big Bull Goldbead Stonefly, 16, **18**
Biot Spinner, **66**, 67
Black and Orange Beetle, **143**, 144
Black Foam Beetle, 85, **87**
Black Gnat, 13, 30, **31**
Black Spider, 112, **115**
Blades, William Fitzgerald, 126
Blae & Black Buzzer, 30, **31**
Blatantly Blank Foam Caddis, 170, **171**
Blood Leech, 35, **36**
blue-winged olive, 40
B'NL Midge Pupa, 78, **79**
Borger, Gary, 80
Brassie, **143**, 144
Brown Sedge Pupa, 113, **115**
Brown Drake Spinner, **127**, 129
Buller Caddis, 45, **47**
Butler, Glen, 34
Butler's Bug, 34, **35**

C

caddis, *see* sedges
Caenis Nymph, 25, **27**
Calf's Tail Emerger, 52, **54**
Callibaetis, 90
Cameo Lady, 30, **31**
Canning, Paul, 12, 24–28
Carnill, Bob, 13, 29–32
Carniolica Yellow Sally, 58, **59**

Carty, Peter, 48
Cased Caddis, 30
Caseless Caddis, 152, **155**
Catgut Nymph, **131**, 132
Chan, Brian, 13, 33–37
Cheumatopsyche sp., 121, **123**
Church, Bob, 158
Cinnamon Sledge, 58, **59**, 117, **119**
Cock de Leon Caddis, 100, **102**
Coffin Fly, **127**, 128
Coloburiscus, 48
corixa, 30, 170
Counterfeit Cricket, **79**, 81
Crocheted Caddis Emerger, 69, **71**
Crocheted Caddis Pupa, 68, **71**, **72**
Crocheted Gold Head Brown Stonefly Nymph, 69, **71**
Culard, 152, **155**
cul de canard patterns, 12, 25, 56–60, 64–**66**, 67, 90, **131**, 133, 153

D

damselfly, 34
Damselfly Nymph, 34, **35**, 69, **71**, 164
Dark Kyll, 158, **159**
Dark Olive Dun, **95**, 96, 157
Dave's Hopper, 164, **167**
Dave's Improved Damsel, 164, **167**
Delta Wing Emerger, 104, **107**
Dennis, Jack, 89
Dormouse Nymph, 58, **59**
Double Legs, 16, **18**
DRF Yellow & Black Spider, 30, **31**

E

Ecdyonurus torrentis, 41
Edie, **159**, 160
Edmonds, H. H. and Lee, N. N., 38
Edwards, Oliver, 12, 38–44
Electric Leech, 164, **167**
Elk Hair Caddis, 21, **23**, 80, **147**, 148
Emerging Nymph, 100, **102**

En bette Swot, 52, **54**
Entwistle, Tony, 13, 45–50
Ephemera danica, see Mayfly
Ephemera guttulata, 126
Ephemera simulans, **127**, 128
Ephemera varia, 129
Ephemera vulgata, see Mayfly
Ephemerella ignita, 40
Espersen, Mogens, 13, 51–55

F
Fantastic Caddis, 69, **71**
February Snow Flake, **75**, 76
F Fly, 57, **59**
Fiery-Brown Beetle, 134, **139**
Floating Nymph, 65, **66**
Flymphs, 52
Foam Post Emerger, 84, **87**
Foam Stillborn, 100, **102**
Foam Wing Double Trouble Trico, **171**, 172
Fox Squirrel Emerger, **159**, 160
Fratnik, Marjan, 12, 56–60
F Sedge, 57, **59**

G
Gammarus, *see* shrimps
Goldbead Hare's Ear Shaggy, 16, **18**
Goldbead Peacock Runner, 16, **18**
Goldbead Pheasant Tail, 16, **18**
Goldbead Zonker, 16, **18**
Goldheads, 13, 15–19, 69
Golden Drake, **127**, 128
Gold Ribbed Hare's Ear, 13, 25, 51
Goofus Bug, *see* Humpy
grasshoppers, 81, 164
Great Brown Spinner, **127**, 128
Great Yellow Spinner, **127**, 128
Green Caddis Worm, 112, **115**
Green Gimriver Dun, 109, **115**
Green Gimriver Nymph, 112, **115**
Grey Dun, **95**, 96, 117, **119**
Grey Wulff, 20, **23**

H
Hackle Stalk Buzzer, 25, **27**
Hair wing dry flies – tying techniques, 175–177
Halladay, Leonard, 90
Hare and Copper, 45
Hare's Ear Stonefly Nymph, 122, **123**
Harrop, René, 12, 61–67

Hatching Elk, 52, **54**
Hatchin' Something, 52, **54**
Haystack, 24, **27**
Heptagenia sulphurea, 41
Heptagenid Nymph, 40, **43**
Hexagenia limbata, 128
Hidy, Vernon S., 52
hooks, 14
Humpy, 21, **23**, 89, **91**
Hydropschidae, 90

I
Isonychia sp., 121
Isoperla grammatica, 41

J
Jysk Chillimps, 52, **54**

K
Klinkhamer Special, 12, 13, 151, **155, 156**
Kolbu, Torill, 12, 68–73
Kowalski, Jurek, 12, 74–83
Kowalski's Mayfly, **75**, 76
K-Z Corixa, 170, **171**

L
LaFontaine, Gary, 84
large brook dun, 41
large dark olive, 38, 104, 157
large green stonefly, 48
Leadhead Nymph, 152, **155**
leeches, 34, 164
Leisenring, James, 52
Leiser, Eric, 55
Leptophlebia sp., 100, **102**
Litobrancha recurvata, 128
Little Sister Sedge, 122, **123**
Little White Head Nymph, **131**, 132
Luallen, Wayne, 12, 78–83

M
Mackerel Nymph, **131**, 132
Marriner, Paul, 13, 84–88
Martin, Darrel, 12, 89–93
Match the Minnow Golden Shiner, 165, **167**
Matthews, Craig, 80
Matuka Sculpin, 165, **167**
Mayfly (*E. danica, E. vulgata*), 26, 76, 105, 126–129, 160
Mazura, Václav, 13, 94–97

midge imitations, 25, 29, 34, 69, **71**, 78–79, 90, **91**
Mikulak, Art, 34
Mikulak Sedge 34, 35
Morales, Marcelo, 12, 98–102
Mosely May, 26, **27**
Moser, Roman, 12, 103–108
Muddle May 21, **23**

N
Nelson Brown, **47**, 48
Nesameletus, **47**, 48
Netopir Fly, 57, **59**
No-Hackle Dun, **143**, 144
No.9 Nymph, 117, **119**
No.11 Nymph, 117, **119**

O
Olive and Black Woolly Bugger, 85, **87**
Olive Dun, 13
Olsson, Lars-Åke, 12, 16, 109–115
Once and Away, 152, **155**

P
Palu, Francesco, 12, 116–119
Parachute Adams, 141, **143**
Partridge and Green, **54**, 158, **159**
Partridge and Orange, 13, 40, **43**
Partridge Flymph, 52, **54**
Pawson, Tony, 74
Pearly Hare's Ear, 25, **27**
Perkins, Clive, 25
Perky, 25, **27**
Pete's Coloburiscus, **47**, 48
Pheasant Tail Nymph, 16, **75**, 76, 90
Pink Nymph, **131**, 132
Plastic Gum Beetle, 136, **139**
Plushille Trout Fry, 105, **107**
Poly-Rib Buzzer, 29, 31
Polyphemus Nymphs, 116, **119**
Potamanthus distinctus, 128
Price, Taff, 58
Prince Nymph, **171**, 173
Pritt, T.E., 38

R
Rabbit Fur Fly, 136, **139**
Red Butt Chironomid, 34, **35**
Red Fox Squirrel Nymph, 162, **167**
Red Gill, **47**, 48

Remerger, 152, **155**
Reverse Hackle, 84, **87**
RFC Scud, 90, **91**
Rhyacophila Larva, 40, **43**, 152
Rhyacophila Pupa, **147**, 148
Rindlisbacher, Jules, 57
Royal Trude, 20, **23**
Royal Wulff, 20, **23**

S
Sakaguchi, Masao, 12, 120–124
Sasula, Krzyszatof, 132
Schwiebert, Ernest, 9, 125–129
sculpins, 148, 165
sedges, 34, 40, 45, 57, 58, 68–72, 74, **95**, 96, 100, 103–104, 112–114, 117, 121, 132, 148, 151–152, 170
Shaw, Jack, 36
short nymph method, 130
shrimps, 33, **35**, 64, **75**, 94, **95**
Sikora, Adam, 12, 130–133
Silhouette Caddis, **147**, 148
Silver Sparkle Bottom Caddis Pupa, 104, **107**
Siphlonurus sp., 56, 121, **123**
Skating Spider, 98, **102**
Sloane, Robert, 13, 134–140
Small Black Stonefly Nymph, 122, **123**
Smith, Jennifer, 9, 141–145
Snipe and Purple, 40, **43**
Sparkle Dun, 80
Sparkle Parachute, **79**, 81
Spent Mayfly, 105, **107**
Spey Matuka, 100, **102**
spiders, 38
Squirrel Sedge, 113, **115**
Stenoperla prasina, 48
Stenopsyche sp., 121–122, **123**
Stick Fly, 74, **75**
stoneflies, 16, 40, 41, **47**, 48, 58, 69, 122, 146
Stuck Shuck Midge, **79**, 80
Sunset Fly, 137, **139**
Surface Polyphemus, 116
Swimming Caddis Pupa, 103, **107**
Szajnik, Franciszek, 132

T
Taeniopteryx Stillborn, 146, **147**
Tailwater Dun, **66**, 67
Tassie Spinner, 136, **139**
Thong, 85, **87**

Trichoptera sp., *see* sedges
Tricorythodes sp., 157, 172
Trike, 157, **159**
Troth, Al, 21, 80, 148
Transitional Dun, 76, **66**
Transitional Nymph, 65, **66**

U
Usual, 84, **87**

V
Vainio, Juha, 12, 146–149
van Klinken, Hans, 12, 151–156
Versatile Nymph, **75**, 76
Voljc, Bozidar, 56–60
Voljc Sedge, 58

W
Waterhen Bloa, 38, **43**
Weilenmann Hans, 13, 157–161
Western Lake Nymphs, 136, **139**
Westward Bug, 158, **159**

White Top Deer Hair Caddis, **79**, 80
Whitlock, Dave, 12, 162–168
Whopper, **79**, 81
Williams, 30, **31**
Woolly Bugger, 85, 142, **143**
World Flying Championships, 9, 15, 24, 38, 45,
    68, 74, 84, 94, 130, 146
Woven Nymph, **131**, 132
Wright, Phil, 141
Wright's Royal, 12, 141, **143, 171**, 172

Y
Yellow Caddis, **95**, 96
Yellow Drake Spinner, **127**, 128
Yellow Grouse Sculpin, **147**, 148
yellow may dun, 41
Yellow Sally, 41, **43**, 58

Z
Zinck Mink, 169, **171**
Zinck, Ruth, 13, 85, 169–173